Donovan, Frank R.
    The women in their lives; the distaff side
of the Founding Fathers.   Dodd, 1966.

    1. Statesmen, American 2. U.S. - Hist. -
Revolution - Biog. 3. Women in the U.S. -
Biog. I. T.

THE WOMEN IN THEIR LIVES

The Distaff Side of the Founding Fathers

The Women
in Their Lives

THE DISTAFF SIDE

OF THE FOUNDING FATHERS

By Frank Donovan

ILLUSTRATED

DODD, MEAD & COMPANY

NEW YORK

Contents

Contents

Illustrations

CHAPTER I

The Mothers of the Founding Fathers

"ALL THAT I AM or hope to be, I owe to my darling mother"
is a cliché that, in some form, has been put into the mouths
of many men of great accomplishment. Some said something
like this. George Washington, for instance, late in life solemnly averred: "I attribute all of my success in life to the
moral, intellectual, and physical education which I received
from my mother." This is a rather surprising statement from
one who, by all external evidence, did not particularly like
his mother. On the whole, the principal founders of the
United States did not consider their mothers as important
women in their lives. As a result, not much is known about
the mothers of the Founding Fathers.

The attitude toward motherhood in the eighteenth century
was very different from that of the twentieth. Sons were, in
the main, more dutiful than they are today. Most were affectionate or at least respectful. But reverence was reserved
for the father. Motherhood was more or less a biological fact
of life, not a sacred institution. The father was the provider,
the mentor, the guide, the decision maker. In general, by the

1

time a boy entered his teens his mother was part of a childhood background and usually had little influence on the
young man's future.

This attitude is well exemplified in Benjamin Franklin's
Autobiography, which he addressed to his son. He devotes
several pages to his male forbears. His grandfather Thomas
is discussed at length, his uncles are described in some detail,
as is his father. His sole reference to his mother, in his early
years, consists of: "My mother, the second wife, was Abiah
Folger, a daughter of Peter Folger, one of the first settlers of
New England." He then goes on to comment at some length
on his maternal grandfather. Throughout the *Autobiography*
he mentions his mother only twice again, once to say that she
was always in good health and again to say that she tried to
reconcile a quarrel between him and his brother James.

According to Benjamin it was his father who intended to
devote him "as the tithe of his sons to the service of the
Church"; it was his father who took him out of school at the
age of ten to teach him his own trade of candle-making. The
boy had "a strong inclination for the sea," but his "father
declared against it." It was his father who took him around
Boston to watch artisans of various trades at work so that he
might choose a career, and it was his father who apprenticed
him to his brother James to become a printer. All of this
happened between the ages of ten and twelve and, if the
Autobiography is to be believed, Mrs. Franklin had nothing
to say about it.

At table Benjamin's father "always took care to start some
ingenious or useful topic for discourse, which might tend to
improve the minds of his children. By this means he turned
our attention to what was good, just, and prudent in the

conduct of life." Apparently, in the household of the elder Franklin, a wife was to be seen but not heard.

During the twenty-nine years between the time that he ran away from home at the age of seventeen and his mother's death, Benjamin saw her only three times — on visits to Boston which were not made for that purpose. He wrote to her occasionally. In one instance his father wrote him that Abiah was concerned about her son's free-thinking religious convictions and his membership in the Masons. Benjamin replied — to his father, not his mother — explaining that he placed virtue higher than orthodoxy in his religious convictions and then continued: "As to the Freemasons, I know no way of giving my mother a better account of them than she seems to have at present, since it is not allowed that women should be admitted into that secret society. She has, I must confess, on that account some reason to be displeased with it; but for anything else, I must entreat her to suspend her judgment till she is better informed, unless she will believe me when I assure her that they are in general a very harmless sort of people, and have no principles or practices that are inconsistent with religion and good manners."

In his exhaustive biography of Benjamin Franklin, Carl Van Doren quotes only one letter to his mother, written shortly before she died. It starts: "We read your writing very easily — I never met with a word in your letters but what I could readily understand; for, though the hand is not always the best, the sense makes everything plain." He then went on to tell her about the servants in his home, her grandchildren, his health, and other intimate trivia. Not a word is said about the American Philosophical Society which he had already organized, the lightning rod that he had invented, or the academy that he was starting. Apparently, he did not feel that his mother would be interested in such things. In the index of Van Doren's biography, Abiah is listed six times. Seven other women in Franklin's life are listed more frequently.

It is not strange, therefore, that little is known about Abiah Folger other than that she was born in Nantucket where her father was a fairly prominent citizen who had purchased her mother for twenty pounds, as an indentured servant, and later married her. She married Josiah Franklin, a widower with seven children, and bore ten of her own, of which Benjamin was number eight. With so many mouths to feed it is understandable that she had little time for anything else. Her life is summarized in the words that her son wrote for her tombstone. "She was a discreet and virtuous woman."

Much more has been written about Mary, mother of George Washington, but it is difficult to determine what is fact and what is legendary. There is probably no other outstanding man who has been the subject of so much false history as Washington, and this also applies to everybody who was connected with him. All early biographies depict the Washingtons as a sort of holy family composed entirely of saintly individuals. Many writers have drawn a parallel between Mary and Martha Washington and the Mary and Martha of the Bible. A comparison of Martha Washington and the Martha of the New Testament has some validity. The earlier Martha is symbolic of a good housekeeper, and this the later Martha surely was. But the comparison of George's mother with the biblical Mary belies the facts. When the rosy curtain of legend is pierced, Mary Washington is disclosed as a pipe-smoking old harridan with a sharp tongue and a violent temper, most of whose surviving letters are whining complaints that her children do not take care of her; that she is "poore" and ill and without food — all of which was definitely untrue.

Like Abiah Franklin, Mary Ball was a second wife. Her husband, Augustine Washington, was a widower with two sons when she married him. She bore him six more children, of whom George was the oldest. Mary had been orphaned at the age of twelve and her guardian was a man named George Eskridge, for whom George was probably named. Unlike Abiah, Mary seems to have had something to say about her sons during their youth. It may have been on her insistence that George was not sent to England to be educated, like his older half brothers. His mother did not want him to leave home.

George's statement later in life that all his "moral, intellectual, and physical education" was due to his mother may have been something that he said because it sounded well. True, she was a strict disciplinarian with a very positive mind. She was also grasping and persistent. These qualities can be found in her son, somewhat modified. George was acquisitive and persevering; for the latter quality America has much to be grateful. But Mary did not have the qualifications to exert much intellectual influence on her son. Morally, she may have been his mentor. His reference to physical education is obscure. He was a superb specimen of a man and an expert horseman, but, except biologically, his mother could have had little to do with this.

George did not spend much time with his mother after he was about fourteen. His father had died when he was eleven, and the boy lived for an extended period with his older half brother Lawrence at Mount Vernon. While Lawrence lived, it would seem he had more influence on George's develop-

ment than the mother had. The legendary biographies are
rife with examples of what an obedient son George was. In
fact, he never obeyed his mother in anything after he was
fourteen. At that age Lawrence wanted to send him to sea.
Mary was the boy's guardian and, on the advice of her half
brother (who suggested that George be apprenticed to a
tinker), refused her consent. Short of running away, George
could not become a sailor.

His mother next appears on the scene when her to-be-
famous son was twenty-three and was about to accept a position as aide to General Braddock. Mary hurried to Mount
Vernon to dissuade him, perhaps to order him to stay home.
George listened politely — and paid no attention to her
wishes. For the rest of his life he stayed away from her as
much as he could, except for occasional, dutiful visits to her
farm. He invited his mother-in-law to live at Mount Vernon,
but never made such a suggestion to his mother.

For the most part he bore with stoic fortitude her complaints and demands. He was always polite, unless she became too unreasonable. Then, on one or two occasions, he
lashed out with sharp, critical letters. His letters to her
usually ended: "I am, Honored Madame, your most dutiful
and obedient son." She was always "Honored Madame,"
never "Dear Mother." And he was always dutiful and
obedient — never "Your loving son."

A minor indication of Mary's unreasonableness occurred
on the Braddock campaign. After George persisted in going
against her wishes she wrote asking him to send her some
butter and provide her with "a Dutch man," presumably as
a farmer. Where she expected her son to get either the butter
or the man in the wilderness of western Pennsylvania is not
explained. George replied, patiently: "I am sorry it is not in

my power to supply you with a Dutch man, or the butter as you desire, for we are quite out of that part of the country where either are to be, as there are few or no inhabitants where we now lie encamped, and butter cannot be had here to supply the wants of the camp."

When George was on the verge of his final western campaign against the French his mother again protested, and her son again politely ignored her, writing: "Honored Madame: If it is in my power to avoid going to the Ohio again, I shall, but if the command is pressed upon me by the general voice of the country, and offered on such terms as cannot be objected against, it would reflect eternal dishonor on me to refuse it; and that, I am sure, must, or ought, to give you greater cause of uneasiness than my going in an honorable command."

Mary was apparently pleased when her son married Martha, although she did not attend the wedding and there is no indication that she was invited. In her mind one good thing came of it immediately. She wrote her brother in England: "There was no end to my troubles while George was in the army, but he has now given it up."

Financially, Mary should have been able to get along reasonably well. Augustine had left the bulk of his estate to his two sons by his first marriage, but he had left the homestead, Ferry Farm, to Mary until George reached his majority, and another tract to which she presumably should have moved at that time. Actually, George did not take possession of Ferry Farm; he rented it to his mother and never collected any rent. So Mary had the income from both properties, yet she always claimed that she was in dire financial straits. One letter to another son, John Augustine, reads:

Dear John, — I am glad to hear you and all the family is well, and should be glad if I could write you the same. I am a going fast, and it, the time, is hard. I am borrowing a little corn — no corn in the corn house. I never lived so poor in my life. Was it not for Mr. French and your sister Lewis, I should be almost starved, but I am like an old almanac quite out of date. Give my love to Mrs. Washington — all the family. I am, dear John, your loving and affectionate Mother.

P.S. I should be glad to see you as I don't expect to hold out long.

Mary constantly called on George for money to supplement the income from her farms. Her son never refused her demands, although he was frequently short of cash himself. Mary had a habit of forgetting the money that he gave her and in later years George noted in his account book the name of somebody who had witnessed the transaction. He summarized his financial relationship with his mother by writing:

She has had a great deal of money from me at times, as can be made appear by my books . . . and over and above this has not only had all that was ever made from the plantation but got her provisions and everything else she thought proper from thence. In short, to the best of my recollection I have never in my life received a copper from the estate, and have paid many hundred pounds (first and last) to her in cash. However, I want no retribution; I conceived it to be a duty, whenever she asked for money, and I had it, to furnish her, notwithstanding she got all the crops, or the amount of them, and took everything she wanted from the plantation for the support of her family, horses, etc., besides.

Washington passed close to Ferry Farm on his frequent trips to and from Williamsburg, and he usually paid a dutiful call on his mother — but if he remained overnight he stayed at the home of his brother-in-law, Fielding Lewis, in nearby Fredericksburg. In 1772, when Mary was sixty-three, her financial affairs became so critical that George built her a house in Fredericksburg and took over the management of her properties himself, allowing her to take anything that she needed from the produce of the plantations. Later, the financial strain became so great that George suggested that she break up housekeeping and go to live with one of her children — but not himself. She would not be happy, he said, at Mount Vernon. Because of visitors she would always have to be dressed or remain in her room, which would not please her. "Nor, indeed," he said, "could you be retired in any room in my house; for what with the sitting up of company, the noise and bustle of servants, and many other things, you would not be able to enjoy that calmness and serenity of mind which in my opinion you ought now to prefer to every other consideration in life."

In 1781 Mary became a source of great embarrassment to George when some members of the General Assembly of Virginia proposed that she be granted a pension because they believed that she was "in great want, owing to the heavy taxes she was obliged to pay." When Washington heard of this he immediately wrote to his informant:

True it is, I am but little acquainted with her *present* situation of distresses, if she is under any. As true it is, a year or two before I left Virginia (to make her latter days comfortable and free from care) I did, at her request but at my own expense, purchase a commodious house, garden and lots (of her own choosing) in Fredericksburg, that she might be near my sister Lewis, her only daughter, and did moreover agree to take her land and Negroes at a certain yearly rent, to be fixed by Colonel Lewis and others (of her own nomination) which has been an annual expense to me ever since as the estate never raised one half the rent I was to pay. Before I left Virginia I answered all her calls for money; and since that period have directed my steward to do the same.

Whence her distresses can arise, therefore, I know not, never having received any complaint of his inattention or neglect on that head; . . . confident I am that she has not a child that would not divide the last sixpence to relieve her from *real* distress. This she has been repeatedly assured of by me; and all of us, I am certain, would feel much hurt at having our mother a pensioner while we had the means of supporting her; but in fact she has an ample income of her own.

Shortly before he left for New York to become President, George rode to Fredericksburg for what he said was "the last act of personal duty I may (from her age) ever have it in my power to pay her." Mary had cancer of the breast and died a few months later. She was buried at Fredericksburg, presumably at her own wish, but the grave was never marked and, shortly after, could not be identified. George wrote to a brother:

Awful and affecting as the death of a parent is, there is consolation in knowing that Heaven has spared ours to an age beyond which few attain, and favored her with the full enjoyment of her mental faculties and as much bodily strength as usually falls to the lot of fourscore. Under these considerations and a hope that she is translated to a happier place, it is the duty of her relatives to yield due submission to the decrees of the Creator. When I was last at Fredericksburg, I took a final leave of my mother, never expecting to see her more.

In his exhaustive biography of George Washington, Douglas Southall Freeman summarized Mary and her relationship with her famous son as follows:

From her renowned son in his manhood, she never had elicited the warm love a man usually has for his mother. She had seemed to him grasping, unreasonable in her demands and untidy in her person. Doubtless, too, he had been irked by her poor management, and when he had been close enough for her to know what he was doing, he must have been irritated by her ceaseless concern for him. She had unstinted care at the hands of her daughter, Betty Lewis, but if she was beloved in the community where she lived, no echo of affection for her has survived in the writings of travelers or in the four extant letters of her townsfolk. In old age she may have been unlovely and unlovable, yet, when she bore her son George, she must have possessed qualities that reappeared in him, some of them softened, perhaps, and some of them disciplined. There is no valid reason for doubting the tradition that she had fine physique and figure and that she was a skillful horsewoman. At least a measure of her acquisitiveness was possessed by George, especially during his early manhood, and this similarity was perhaps the chief reason for misunderstanding between the two. Persistence in the mother was perseverance in the son. It was from her, also, that he probably received his love of trees, of rivers, of beautiful prospects and of fruitful nature.

The relationship between John Adams and his mother was more conventional than those of Benjamin Franklin or George Washington. Both of John's parents were strict, pious Puritans, and no one in the Adams family ever did anything that was not proper. John had all the proper respect and affection for his mother that is to be expected from a loving son. In this way, at least, the Adamses were a perfectly normal family.

Still, the superior position of the father in the life of a boy in the eighteenth century is again evident from John Adams' autobiography. Of his mother he merely says: "My mother was Suzanna Boylston, a daughter of Peter Boylston of Brookline, the oldest son of Thomas Boylston, a surgeon and apothecary who came from London in 1656." And later: "My father married Suzanna Boylston in October, 1734, and on the nineteenth of October, 1735, I was born." Nothing is said of her character, her temperament, her virtues. At the same place John describes his father as "the honestest man I ever

knew. In wisdom, piety, benevolence, and charity in proportion to his education and sphere of life, I have never seen his
superior."

Suzanna Adams, who was twenty years younger than her
husband, is scarcely mentioned again in the autobiography
until her death; and here, too, she takes second billing to her
husband. The younger John wrote:

On the twenty-fifth of May in this year 1761, my venerable
father died in his seventy-first year, beloved, esteemed, and revered by all who knew him. Nothing that I can say or do can sufficiently express my gratitude for his parental kindness to me, or
the exalted opinion I have of his wisdom and virtue. It was a
melancholy House. My father and mother were seized at the same
time with the violent fever, a kind of influenza, or an epidemic
which carried off seventeen aged people in our neighborhood. My
mother remained ill in bed at my father's funeral, but being
younger than my father and possessed of a stronger constitution,
she happily recovered and lived, to my inexpressible comfort, till
the year 1797, when she died at almost ninety years of age.

As with the Franklins, it was the father who seemed to
make the decisions about a son's life in the Adams family.
John wrote: "My father had destined his first born, long
before his birth, to a public education." And again: "My
enthusiasm for sports and inattention to books, alarmed my
father, and he frequently entered into conversation with me
upon the subject. I told him [I did not?] love books and
wished he would lay aside the thoughts of sending me to
college." The older John replied: "You know . . . I have set
my heart upon your education at college and why will you
not comply with my desire?" When the boy explained that
he could not get along with his schoolmaster, his father arranged for him to change schools and John reported: "My
father soon observed the relaxation of my zeal for my fowling

piece, and my daily increasing attention to my books. In a little more than a year, Mr. Marsh pronounced me fitted for college." Apparently his mother had little to say about where or how John was educated. Had there been a P.T.A. in those days there surely would have been more fathers at the meetings than there are today.

Although John has, quite naturally, much more to say about the Adamses than the Boylstons, his father's marriage to Suzanna Boylston was something of a step up for an Adams of Braintree. Both families were old Puritan stock and the younger John's paternal grandfather had gone to Harvard. But the Boylstons of Brookline, with Boston connections, were somewhat more sophisticated than the farmer from Braintree. One of Suzanna's uncles, "Zabdiel the Physician," had "first introduced into the British Empire the practice of inoculation for the smallpox." In later years John intimated that his father's marriage lifted the Adams family of Braintree out of the obscurity of small-town life.

After graduating from Harvard and teaching school in Worcester while he studied law, John returned home to live with his parents and to practice in Braintree. He continued to live with his mother after his father's death in 1761 until his own marriage in 1764. Then he moved virtually next door to a smaller farm which his father had left him. Three years after she became a widow, Suzanna married Lieutenant John Hall. Somewhat later, she and her second husband occupied John's farm when he moved to Boston.

There is no record of the home life or activities of Suzanna Adams. Her first husband was a New England farmer and she obviously led the life of a New England farm wife, with much work and little relaxation. Her husband "by his industry and enterprize soon became a person of more property and consideration in the town. . . . He became a selectman, a militia officer, and a deacon in the church." Since the elder John had three farms and was well established by the time he married, it may be assumed that Suzanna had one or more bond servants to help with the housework. She probably had as much education as was common for girls of good family in those times, which was not much. Perhaps she was above the average in this respect; her family had a penchant for learning. But there are no letters to indicate how she wrote or thought. Her son mentions her "moral precepts" which had an early influence on him, but he dilates at greater length on the moral philosophy of his maternal grandmother who was "a person possessed of more literature than was common in persons of her sex and station, a diligent reader and a most exemplary woman in all the relations of life. She died of a consumption and had leisure to draw up advice to her children, which I have read in her handwriting in my infancy, but which is now lost. I know not that I have seen it for sixty years, and the judgment of a boy of seven years old is not [worth much] to be recollected, but it appeared to me then wonderfully fine." This is more than he had to say about his mother in his entire autobiography.

The farm house over which Suzanna presided was a rectangular two-story clapboard structure, close to the coast road. Like most such houses in New England, it was severe, unadorned, and purely functional. It was built around a central chimney whose fireplaces provided heat for its four rooms — two upstairs and two down — and for cooking. In back was a lean-to which contained a narrow kitchen and another, probably a servant's, room. There were two cramped cubbyholes under the eaves where the three sons whom Suzanna bore slept in cozily constricted quarters.

Because John was never physically far from his mother until ten years after she remarried there was no occasion for correspondence between them; and, for the next ten years, John's wife, Abigail, kept in constant touch with Suzanna and occasionally mentioned her in letters to John in Europe. Since both John and Abigail were indefatigable letter writers it seems somewhat surprising that there is no correspondence between either of them and Suzanna while the younger Adamses were both in Europe.

From a few references to his mother in John's diary it is obvious that she was more outspoken than the seemingly meek Abiah Franklin, although probably less sharp-tongued than Mary Washington. One lengthy entry described a quarrel between his parents. Apparently the elder John, as a town selectman, sometimes brought indigent girls home, for whom the town would pay board. Suzanna did not seem to approve of this practice and was quite outspoken about it. In John's description of the scene, **P.** and **M.** stand for *pater* and *mater*.

How a whole family is put into a broil sometimes by a trifle. My P. and M. disagreed in opinion about boarding Judah, that difference occasioned passionate expressions, those expressions made Dolly and Judah snivel. . . . My P. continued cool and pleasant a good while, but had his temper roused at last, though he uttered not a rash word, but resolutely asserted his right to govern. My Mamma was determined to know what my P. charged a week for the girls' board. P. said he had not determined what to charge but would have her say what it was worth. She absolutely refused to say. "But I will know if I live and breathe. I can read yet. Why don't you tell me what you charge? You do it on purpose to tease me. You are mighty arch this morning. I won't have all the town's poor brought here, stark naked, for me to clothe for nothing. I won't be a slave to other folks' folk for nothing." And after the girls cried: "I must not speak a word [to] your girls, wenches, drabs. I'll kick both their fathers, presently.

[You] want to put your girls over me, to make me a slave to your wenches." Thus when the passions of anger and resentment are roused one word will inflame them into rage. . . .

M. seems to have no scheme and design in her mind to persuade P. to resign his trust of selectman. But when she feels the trouble and difficulties that attend it she frets, squibs, scolds, rages, raves. None of her speeches seem the effect of any design to get rid of the trouble, but only natural expressions of the pain and uneasiness which that trouble occasions. Cool reasoning upon the point with my father would soon bring her to his mind or him to hers.

On another occasion John refers to the "cruel reproaches" of his mother which induced him to undertake a law case for which he did not consider himself prepared. And, at a later date when John's brother Elihu wanted to join the Continental Army, Abigail wrote: "Your good mother is really violent against it, I cannot persuade nor reason her into a consent. Neither he nor I dare let her know that he is trying for a place." Apparently the old lady always knew her own mind and did not hesitate to express herself.

John's wife, Abigail, was a dutiful and presumably an affectionate daughter-in-law. When she left to join her husband in Europe in 1784 she had this to say about her leave-taking:

And then another scene still more afflictive, an aged parent from whom I had kept the day of my departure a secret knowing the agony she would be in. I called at her door. As soon as the good old lady beheld me, the tears rolled down her aged cheek, and she cried out, "O! why did you not tell me you was going so soon? Fatal day! I take my last leave; I shall never see you again. Carry my last blessing to my son." — And I was obliged to leave her in an agony of distress, myself in no less.

Suzanna's last illness may have been a factor in keeping Abigail from her husband's side when he was inaugurated as

President of the United States. When he left Quincy his mother was very ill, as was Abigail's twenty-one-year-old niece who was living with them. Abigail attended both women, the old and the young, in their final hours and then wrote her husband:

This, I hope, is the last letter which you will receive from me at Quincy. The funeral rites performed, I prepare to set out on the morrow. . . . Our aged parent is gone to rest. My mind is relieved from any anxiety on her account. I have no fears lest she should be left alone, and receive an injury. I have no apprehensions, that she should feel any want of aid or assistance, or fear of becoming burdensome. She fell asleep, and is happy. . . .

I want no courting to come. I am ready and willing to follow my husband wherever he chooses; but the hand of Heaven has arrested me. Adieu, my dear friend. Excuse the melancholy strain of my letter. From the abundance of the heart the stream flows.

John wrote that his mother was "a fruit fully ripe" who had gone to "a country where there will be no war or rumor of war, no envy, jealousy, rivalry, or party," and added, "My mother's countenance and conversation was a source of enjoyment to me but is now dried up forever at Quincy."

Thomas Jefferson gave three pieces of information about his mother in his autobiography — the dates of her birth, her marriage, and her death. That is all. Not a word about her character, her influence on her son, her temperament, or whether she was a good, bad, or indifferent parent. Little more is known about her after her marriage except that she bore ten children over a period of fifteen years. Of his forebears, Jefferson wrote:

The first particular information I have of any ancestor was my grandfather, who lived at the place in Chesterfield called Ozborne's, and owned the lands afterwards the glebe of the parish.

He had three sons: Thomas who died young, Field who settled on the waters of Roanoke and left numerous descendants, and Peter, my father, who settled on the lands I still own, called Shadwell, and joining my present residence. He was born February 29, 1707–8 and intermarried 1739 with Jane Randolph, of the age of nineteen, daughter of Isham Randolph, one of the seven sons of that name and family, settled at Dungeoness in Goochland. They trace their pedigree far back in England and Scotland, to which let every one ascribe the faith and merit he chooses.

My father's education had been quite neglected; but being of a strong mind, sound judgment, and eager after information, he read much and improved himself, insomuch that he was chosen, with Joshua Fry, Professor of Mathematics in William and Mary College, to continue the boundary line between Virginia and North Carolina which had been begun by Colonel Byrd; and was afterwards employed with the same Professor Fry, to make the first map of Virginia which had ever been made, that of Captain Smith being merely a conjectural sketch. . . . He was the third or fourth settler, about the year 1737, of the part of the country in which I live. He died, August 17, 1757, leaving my mother a widow, who lived till 1776, with six daughters and two sons, myself the elder.

As with Adams and Franklin it seems to have been the boy's father who was responsible for his education and early development. Jefferson wrote: "He placed me at the English school at five years of age; and at the Latin at nine, where I continued until his death." Thomas was fourteen when his father died. Later in life he expressed a considerable veneration for the memory of his father, who, despite his sketchy education, was an avid reader of Addison, Pope, Swift, and Shakespeare. Thomas was apparently referring to his father when he wrote: "I thank on my knees him who directed my early education for having put into my possession this rich source of delight; and I would not exchange it for anything which I could then have acquired."

But of his mother, not a word. Although they were separated for much of the nineteen years between his father's death and her own, there does not exist a single letter that passed between them. In his account books there are records of money that he paid to her when he rented her farm and some of her slaves, and mention of provisions that he sent from Monticello to her home, for which he charged her. When she passed away he made a note in his diary: "My mother died about eight o'clock this morning — in the fifty-seventh year of her age." Her only epitaph is an entry in the records of the court house at Chancellorsville, an appraisal of her personal possessions at the time of her death:

One large halfworn portmanteau trunk	£10	- -
One small trunk	3	- -
One smelling-bottle seal and ring for keys	2 6	-

One of Jefferson's recent biographers, John Dos Passos, says: "There is something strangely frigid about the scanty references to his mother that may well betoken real dislike." His earliest capable biographer, Henry Randall, wrote: "His mother was every way worthy of his highest respect and deepest love, and she received them." These opposing expressions of opinion were formed on very flimsy evidence. The fact is that nothing is known about Jefferson's relationship with or attitude toward his mother. His failure to mention her in any of his thousands of letters cannot be automatically construed as dislike or lack of interest. Jefferson had an almost pathological aversion to writing about his personal life, and particularly about the females in the family. Unlike Washington and Adams he kept no daily diary other than his meticulous farm journal and commonplace book. These told much about the weather and agricultural, building, and land

transactions, but little about people. It is possible that
Thomas rode regularly from Monticello to Shadwell to see
his mother. But if he did, it seems incredible that somebody
did not make a record of it or that it never became part of
the tradition of the family.

Jane Randolph was a granddaughter of the first of that
name to emigrate to Virginia, in about 1660. The first Randolph, William, prospered mightily, as did all of his seven
sons. At one time or another they held most of the important
posts in the colony and all had large estates and vast tracts
of land. Isham, Jane's father, was Colonial Agent in London
when Jane was born and became Adjutant General of the
colony when he returned. His estate at Goochland has been
described as an "abode of refinement and elegant hospitality."

Peter Jefferson, Thomas' father, has been described as a
frontiersman who was a cut below the Virginia gentleman.
This is not quite correct. He spent much time in the wilderness as a surveyor, but at the time of his son's birth he owned
some five thousand acres above tidewater Virginia, had an
interest in 50,000 acres farther west, and employed a steward
and five overseers. Peter was in business, in a land company,
with Jane's cousin William Randolph. When he wanted a
homesite at the time he married Jane, William Randolph
traded him two hundred acres on the Rivanna River "for
and in consideration of Henry Wetherburn's biggest bowl of
arrack punch to him delivered at and before the sealing and
delivery of these presents the receipt whereof the said W.R.
doth hereby acknowledge." After Peter and William drank
the punch — and recovered from the effects — the former
built Shadwell, naming it after his wife's birthplace in England. Jane brought her husband a dowry of £200, but no
land — land was inherited by sons.

The actual frontier of forts and stockades was some one hundred miles west of Shadwell, but the area was quite remote from tidewater civilization. Indians occasionally visited his home when Thomas was young, but they were friendly Indians. Although Shadwell was not the frontier it was surely a great change for the tenderly nurtured girl whom Peter took from the "elegant" abode at Goochland.

William Randolph, Jane's cousin, died when Thomas was two years old and his will requested Peter to move to his estate, Tuckahoe, and look after his two motherless daughters. William's affluence is indicated by the legacy of three slaves as personal maids for each of his girls. Jane was undoubtedly much happier at the more substantial estate at Tuckahoe, where she had frequently visited as a girl.

What with bearing ten children and taking care of her own and cousin William's, Jane was probably kept quite busy during the fifteen years of her marriage. When her husband died he named four friends as executors of his estate. Jane had life rights in Shadwell, which passed to Thomas on her death. The boy was left in a household that was virtually all female; six of the eight children who survived infancy were girls and the only other boy was a baby when Thomas was in his teens. He was apparently very bored at Shadwell after his father's death. In one of his earliest surviving letters he told a friend: "To tell the plain truth I have not a syllable to write you about. For I do not conceive that any thing can happen in my world which you would give a curse to know or I either. All things here appear to me to trudge on in one and the same round: we rise in the morning that we may eat breakfast, dinner, and supper and go to bed again that we may get up the next morning and do the same: so that you never saw two peas more alike than our yesterday and today."

The slight evidence that exists indicates that Thomas never consulted his mother nor regarded her opinion, even as a youth. In fact, Jefferson never had much regard for any woman's opinion. Later in life he would write:

When I recollect that at fourteen years of age, the whole care and direction of myself was thrown on myself entirely, without a relation or friend qualified to advise or guide me, and recollect the various sorts of bad company with which I associated from time to time, I am astonished I did not turn off with some of them and become as worthless to society as they were.

When Thomas was sixteen he wrote to one of the executors of his father's estate:

Sir, I was at Colonel Peter Randolph's about a fortnight ago and my schooling falling into discourse, he said he thought it would be to my advantage to go to the college, and was desirous I should go as indeed I am myself for several reasons. In the first place as long as I stay at the mountains the loss of one fourth of my time is inevitable, by company's coming here and detaining me from school. And likewise my absence will in a great measure put a stop to so much company and by that means lessen the expenses of the estate in housekeeping. And on the other hand by going to the college I shall get more universal acquaintance, which may hereafter be serviceable to me; and I suppose I can pursue my studies in the Greek and Latin as well there as here, and likewise learn something of the mathematics. I shall be glad of your opinion.

From this letter it would seem that his mother had no voice in this sixteen-year-old decision.

Jefferson seems to have ignored his mother; Washington was certainly annoyed by his. John Adams had proper respect and affection for his maternal parent. Nothing is known, other than legend, of the relation between Alexander Hamilton and his mother. She died when he was thirteen and he seldom mentioned her thereafter. The outstanding and widely known fact of his parentage is that he was a bastard. He was also a near genius. The enigma is: Where did the genius come from? His father was a failure at everything he attempted. If there is anything in heredity, it would seem that Alexander's great intellect must have come from the distaff side.

Alexander's mother was born Rachel Faucett on the island of Nevins, one of the present-day Virgin Islands. There is conflicting evidence as to the date but 1729 is the most probable. Her parents separated when she was young and she was brought up, in comfort if not in affluence, by a strong-willed mother who, legend has it, virtually forced her to marry at the age of sixteen a wealthy Danish Jew named John Lavien. Rachel had a son by Lavien in 1746, but the marriage was far from a happy one.

There is no question that Rachel was Alexander's mother, although some of his descendants and adulatory biographers have sought to cushion his illegitimacy; and scandal-happy reporters have had fine fun with far-reaching surmises as to his father. Alexander's son recorded that Rachel's marriage to Lavien "proving unhappy, she applied for and obtained a divorce, and removing to St. Christopher's, there married James Hamilton and had by him several sons." Other male parents to whom Alexander has been imputed include Lavien, a planter named Thomas Stevens, Dr. William Hamilton (no relation to James), Governor Waltershoff of St. Croix, and — the most fascinating fantasy — George Washington. This latter stems from the preference that George showed Alexander when he was the General's aide during the Revolution and, later, in the President's cabinet; and is physically explained by Washington's visit to Barbados in

1751. It is assumed that Rachael might have sailed over to
Barbados long enough to have conceived a child. This legend
is entirely without foundation, as is the one that Hamilton
had Negro blood.

Those of the early biographers who admit the facts of
life as to Alexander's illegitimacy present Lavien as a cruel
monster and Rachel as a much wronged young lady. Such
records as exist indicate that Lavien thought that he was the
one who was wronged. Some time about 1750 he had his wife
locked up in the fort at Christiansted on St. Croix, where
they lived, because she had committed certain unspecified
"errors." To accomplish this under the Danish law of the
day, which applied on St. Croix, Lavien must have alleged
that his wife had "twice been guilty of adultery" and that he
was no longer living with her. When Rachel was let out she
returned home to her mother on Nevins, leaving her son
with the father.

Sometime during the next two years Rachel met an attractive thirty-three-year-old James Hamilton, the fourth son of
Alexander Hamilton, Lord of Grange in Stevenston Parish,
Ayrshire, Scotland. One forgiving biographer wrote: "As
soon as she saw him her restlessness was gone, her passion
appeased, her adventuring at an end. From now on, she
would be true to James." A divorce was difficult in the islands
and in this case was complicated by the fact that Nevins was
British and St. Croix Danish. Lavien was an influential Dane
and it is unlikely that the Danish courts would have given
serious consideration to a petition from Rachel. In any event,
the wife made no effort to get a divorce. She lived openly
with Hamilton, first on Nevins and then on the nearby island
of St. Kitts. In 1753 she bore a son, James, and in 1755
another, Alexander. Hamilton always said that he was born

in 1757 and most of his biographers give this date; as does his tombstone. But records in the islands, and other evidence, make the earlier date almost certain.

In 1759 Lavien divorced his wife. The petition, which has only recently come to light, says that "John Michael Lavien, burgher and free resident of this place, finds himself greatly impelled to seek divorce from his wife, Rachel Lavien, for the reason that she, while she lived with him some years ago, committed such errors which as between husband and wife were indecent and very suspicious, notwithstanding his instituting her arrest and action against her, in the belief that everything would be better and that she like a true wife would have changed her ungodly mode of life and would live with him as was meet and fitting." Instead, claimed Lavien, Rachel has now "absented herself from him for nine years and gone elsewhere, where she has begotten several illegitimate children." (A more literal translation from the Danish would make it "obscene children.") The petition further claimed that Rachel had "shown herself to be shameless, rude, and ungodly," had "completely forgotten her duty and let husband and child alone, and instead gave herself up to whoring with everyone," which things were "so well known that her own family and friends must hate her for it." Because Rachel was the guilty party, local law forbade her to remarry.

James Hamilton was a merchant. (This fact later led John Adams to call Alexander "the bastard son of a Scots peddler.") When his business failed on St. Kitts he moved his family to St. Croix to take a job. When he again failed at this he deserted Rachel and the boys and went back to St. Kitts. Rachel, with some help from a brother-in-law named Lytton, opened a store. Her elder son was apprenticed to a carpenter and Alexander, aged eleven, went to work for a merchant named Cruger. Rachel died in 1768, when Alexander was thirteen, and the boy went to live with Cruger, a bachelor. The court awarded the mother's scanty estate to her legitimate son, Peter Lavien. The Hamilton boys received nothing.

There is not one scrap of authentic information as to the influence of Rachel on her son, but there are stories of her teaching him morality and opening his eyes to the wonders of books. She also is supposed to have placed him at a tender age in a Jewish school, from which his father quickly removed him when the child came home chanting the Decalogue in Hebrew. These things may or may not be true. There is no question that, as a child, he was extremely precocious. By the time he reached his teens he was keeping Cruger's books and, at fourteen, was managing a branch store.

In later years Hamilton, surprisingly, evidenced a good deal of affection for the father who had deserted his sons and their mother. In 1783 he wrote to his brother James sending him fifty pounds and asking:

But what has become of our dear father? It is an age since I have heard from him, or of him though I have written him several letters. Perhaps, alas! he is no more, and I shall not have the pleasing opportunity of contributing to render the close of his life more happy than the progress of it. My heart bleeds at the recollection of his misfortunes and embarrassments. . . . I entreat you, if you can, to relieve me from my doubts, and let me know how or where he is, if alive; if dead, how and where he died. Should he be alive inform him of my inquiries, beg him to write to me, and tell him how ready I shall be to devote myself and all I have to his accommodation and happiness.

Alexander's forgiveness for his father's unpaternal attitude may be due to James Hamilton's link with the aristocratic world, which his son considered as a passport to good society.

He later wrote that: "My blood is as good as that of those who plume themselves upon their ancestry." James Hamilton's connection with nobility was rather tenuous, but Alexander's grandson made the most of it in his biography of his grandfather:

The Hamiltons of Grange belonged to the Cambuskeith branch of the house of Hamilton, and the founder of this branch, in the fourteenth century was Walter de Hamilton, who was the common ancestor of the Dukes of Abercorn, Earls of Haddington, Viscounts Boyne, Barons Belhaven, several extinct peerages, and of all the Scotch and Irish Hamilton families. He was fifth in descent from Robert, Earl of Mellent, created by Henry I of France and His Queen, who was a daughter of Jeroslaus, Czar of Russia.

Of the mother who misbehaved there was only silence.

The longest lived but the least known of the mothers of the Founding Fathers was Nelly Conway Madison. In his exhaustive six-volume biography of James Madison, Irving Brant mentions her marriage and family in the first volume, her death in the sixth, and refers to her but three times in the remaining four volumes. After marrying James Madison, Sr. in 1749, at the age of eighteen, Nelly Conway apparently never left home until she died eighty years later at the age of ninety-eight. Of course home — the Madison mansion, Montpelier — was a good place to be. Here she bore twelve children over a term of twenty-two years, of whom James Jr. was the first.

Like Washington and Jefferson, Madison was a Virginia gentleman but he did not make much fuss about it. In fact, he always underplayed his family position. He described his background by writing: "In both the paternal and maternal line of ancestry they were planters and among the respectable though not the most opulent class." *The William and Mary Quarterly* took a somewhat different view: "As shown by their offices and family connections, the Madisons from the earliest date held place with the ruling class of Virginia." Of his mother, Madison wrote that she was "Nelly Conway, descended from some of the early settlers. Her father Francis lived near Port Royal in the county of Caroline, whose father Edwin Conway married Elizabeth Thompson." James did not mention — in fact, he probably did not know — that his mother was descended from Sir Edward Conway, Baron of Ragley, who was knighted by the first Queen Elizabeth for supervising the sack of Cadiz.

Nor was Nelly Conway interested in the noble pirate Sir Edward when she married Virginia planter James Madison and went to live in his modest wooden house beyond the Rappahannock. It was a few years later that the older James started to build the nucleus of Montpelier. The younger James was born at the home of his mother's parents during the first year of her marriage. Late in life he recalled that Montpelier was built "when he was a mere lad, capable of carrying in his hands some of the lighter furniture from the old house to the new."

James Jr. was a bookworm from his early childhood. He went away to school when he was eleven and, since there is no record of any tutor, his education prior to that time was undoubtedly in the hands of his mother, or, more probably, his widowed paternal grandmother, who lived with her son and had both the ability and the time to supervise the children's education. Young James was sent away to school immediately after she died.

As with other families of the day, the father was the leading figure in the Madison household until his death. James apparently never wrote to his mother and there is but fleeting reference to her in his frequent letters to his father. On one occasion he wrote: "I am exceedingly rejoiced to hear of the happy deliverance of my Mother and would fain hope your rheumatic pains will not continue much longer." This referred to the birth of his brother Reuben, an event that he seemed to consider on a par with his father's attack of rheumatism. In another instance when he was staying with a relative in Williamsburg he wrote his father: "It would be very agreeable to me if I were enabled by such rarities as our part of the country furnishes, particularly dried fruit, etc., which Mr. Madison is very fond of, to make some little returns for the culinary favors I receive." It seems unusual to write to a father, rather than a mother, to get goodies from home. Nowhere does James refer to the influence of his mother although there is ample evidence that he was dutiful and affectionate. Presumably such influence as Nelly had on her famous son was in terms of manners and breeding rather than direct action.

James Jr. inherited Montpelier and his mother lived there until her death, only eight years before his own. During much of her life, James was away from home; first at Princeton, then after a short interval at Richmond, Philadelphia, and Washington in the service of the state and the nation. Madison is the only one of the principal Founding Fathers who never had any business other than government service — plus, of course, farming; which was the basic business of every Virginia gentleman.

After his father's death in 1880 James became the head of the family, but during his sixteen years in Jefferson's cabinet and the White House his brothers, who had married and lived in the neighborhood, were more active in managing the estate. Nelly had a separate apartment at Montpelier, to the right of the central hall, and lived there independently for twenty-eight years after her husband's death.

There is evidence of the concern of Nelly's children for at least her material welfare. Jame's wife, Dolley, recorded: "I recollect that soon after the death of Father Madison a bag of gold said to have been left in his desk was a subject of frequent conversation in the family, all of which left me under the impression that it was presented as a gift by common consent of his children to their mother. I remember also hearing Mrs. Rose mention her brother William Madison's having placed the bag in the hands of his mother." During the last decade of Nelly's life, after James and Dolley returned to Montpelier to live, they were both attentive to her in a formal way. One visitor noted that: "The old lady seldom joined the family circle but took her meals by herself," and added that she was visited daily by Mr. and Mrs. Madison at her two o'clock "audience hour." Another visitor to the "old wing" at Montpelier described Nelly thus:

"She was sitting, or rather reclining, on a couch; beside her was a small table filled with large, dark, and worn folios and quartos, of most venerable appearance. She closed one as we entered and took up her knitting which lay beside her. Among other inquiries, I asked her how she passed her time. "I am never at a loss," she replied; "This and these," touching her knitting and her books, "keep me always busy; look at my fingers and you will perceive I have not been idle." In truth her delicate fingers were polished by her knitting needles. "And my eyes, thanks be to God, have not failed me yet, and I read most part of the day. But in other respects I am feeble and helpless, and owe everything to *her*," pointing to Mrs. [Dolley] Madison who sat near us. "She is *my* mother *now*, and tenderly cares for all my wants."

Perhaps the only moral of this montage of the mothers of

the Founding Fathers is that motherhood — or rather the attitude toward motherhood — has changed mightily in two centuries. There is a tendency these days to look to the mothers of great men for the key to their greatness. Woodrow Wilson bragged of being a "Mamma's boy." Sara Delano Roosevelt is certainly more widely known than the father of F.D.R. Old Joe Kennedy is an exception; but all reports on this family emphasize how unusual is such a patriarch, and many of the more human qualities of the late President are generally attributed to his mother.

Surely the six women who bore the men who led in establishing the United States must have had something to do with the qualities that made their offspring great. But the offspring, and their contemporaries, either did not appreciate this influence or did not give it recognition. Despite George Washington's sanctimonious remark on the subject (which is belied by everything else he ever wrote about his mother), the Founding Fathers did not credit their mothers as being among the important women in their lives.

The Mothers of the Founding Fathers   31

CHAPTER II

Several Women and Benjamin Franklin

THE FIRST WOMAN in the life of the first of the Founding
Fathers was a fictional one — if we believe Benjamin Franklin's
Autobiography. The seventeen-year-old apprentice printer
had decided to run away from his master in Boston, his
brother James. Since this was a criminal offense it must be
done secretly. So he had a friend book his passage on a New
York bound sloop, "Under the notion of my being a young
acquaintance of his that had got a naughty girl with child
whose friends would compel me to marry her, and therefore
I could not appear or come away publicly." There were
surely naughty girls in Boston in 1723, but there is no reason
to doubt Franklin's statement that this particular delinquent
female was a figment of his imagination; particularly since
he freely admitted later involvement with prostitutes in
Philadelphia and the attempted seduction of a little milliner
in London.

Franklin was quite frank about his sexual relationships. It
is difficult to visualize the sage and philosopher, the older
Franklin, frolicking with prostitutes; but in the section of

his *Autobiography* which he addressed to his son he told the lad: "Through this dangerous time of youth, and the hazardous situations I was sometimes in among strangers, remote from the eye and advice of my father, . . . that hard-to-be-governed passion of youth hurried me frequently into intrigues with low women that fell in my way, which were attended with some expense and great inconvenience, besides a continual risk to my health by a distemper which of all things I dreaded, though by great good luck I escaped it."

These intrigues which satisfied his youthful lust took place after he had broken off his first engagement to the girl who, for forty-four years, would be known as Mrs. Franklin, although her right to bear this name was based only on the somewhat vague legal status of a common-law wife. Benjamin and Deborah Franklin were never formally married.

Benjamin's initial introduction to Deborah Read is a story made familiar by every "Boy's Life of Benjamin Franklin." Unable to find work in New York he had walked across New Jersey and pulled an oar all night in a large rowboat going down the Delaware. He arrived in Philadelphia on a Sunday morning, almost penniless and tired, dirty, disheveled, and hungry. A passing boy directed him to a bakery where he ordered "three-penny worth" of bread. This staple was a good deal cheaper in Philadelphia than in Boston and he received "three great puffy rolls," which would now be called loaves of bread. His pockets were bulging with stockings and shirts so he walked down High Street with a loaf of bread under each arm while he munched on the third. At the corner of Fourth Street fifteen year old Deborah Read was sweeping the steps of her parents' home. The dirty apparition with his bread and the bulging pockets of his strange Boston-cut clothes amused Deborah. She laughed at her future husband.

A few days later fate threw the fifteen-year-old girl and the seventeen-year-old boy together. The printer whom Franklin had come to Philadelphia to see could not give him regular work, but offered board and lodging in return for occasional labor. Then a new printer, Keimer by name, hired him. As he did not want his journeyman living with a competitor he boarded him with the Reads.

Little is known about the Reads except that Deborah's father was a carpenter and she had a younger brother and sister. She was sweeping the stoop on Sunday morning because housework rather than schoolwork filled her life. In those days formal education for the daughter of a carpenter was not considered essential, or even desirable, although Deborah had somewhere learned to read and write — after a fashion — and do simple arithmetic.

A portrait of Deborah in later life indicates that she was no beauty — and, like most portraits of the day, it was probably flattering. Franklin described her as "sturdy, handsome, and high colored." Handsome is a rather polite way of saying that a woman is neither beautiful nor pretty; but sturdy she surely was. In the Pennsylvania Dutch idiom it might be said that she was not "very much good for pretty" but she was "pretty much good for strong."

Franklin lived with the Reads for about a year and the proximity of an eighteen-year-old boy must have been an exciting experience for the girl of sixteen who made his bed, tidied his room, and helped to prepare his meals. This was probably her first close relationship with a member of the opposite sex of her own generation. In the Philadelphia of that day there was little organized social activity for young people of her class. It was the custom, when the day's work was done, for young ladies to sit with their mothers on the stoops of the rows of small, plain, brick houses which made up most of the town and watch the boys go by — the opposite of today's girl-watching. Although the Reads were not Quakers they were of the same type of solid, materialistic citizens to whom gaiety and elegance were far removed. The austere garb of Quaker principles still permeated the City of Brotherly Love. There was little time for young people to play and no place, except at church, for a "nice girl" of Deborah's social status to meet boys.

Benjamin was surely Deborah's first love. He was an interesting boy with a virility that belied his somewhat pudgy appearance. At the age of eighteen there is no evidence that he had any experience with the opposite sex, but by his own admission he was interested. Intellectually he was already far ahead of Deborah. Then and later she neither shared nor understood his intellectual pursuits; but they surely impressed her.

What Benjamin thought of Deborah during this first year of living under the same roof, and the details of their relationship, are not quite clear from his autobiography, the only source of information on the subject. Apparently the basis of the double life which they would later live together was established at this time. Benjamin had interests outside the home in which Deborah never shared. Of this year he wrote: "I began now to have some acquaintance among the young people of the town, that were lovers of reading, with whom I spent my evenings very pleasantly; and gaining money by my industry and frugality I lived very agreeably." But all of his evenings were not spent with his erudite companions for he also recorded: "I had made some courtship during this time to Miss Read. I had a great respect and affection for her, and had some reason to believe she had the same for me."

At the age of eighteen Benjamin's career took a giddy turn when Pennsylvania's Governor, Sir William Keith, offered to finance him in his own print shop. On Sir William's advice Benjamin took ship for London to purchase equipment, supposedly with a letter of credit from the Governor in the ship's mail pouch. Actually, no such letter existed. The Governor was a man "who wished to please everybody; and having little to give, he gave expectations." As to his affair or engagement with Deborah, Franklin wrote: "As I was about to take a long voyage, and we were both very young . . . it was thought most prudent by her mother to prevent our going too far at present, as a marriage, if it was to take place, would be more convenient after my return, when I should be, as I expected, set up in my business. Perhaps, too, she thought my expectations not so well founded as I imagined them to be." Before the vessel sailed he "interchanged some promises with Miss Read."

These promises were soon forgotten by Benjamin in the excitement of the English metropolis, where his skill promptly procured him a job with one of London's leading printers. He shared his room with a weakling named James Ralph who had accompanied him from Philadelphia and who now sponged on Franklin while he sought work as an actor. Ralph did not find a place in the theater but he quickly found a mistress in the person of a widowed milliner. When he was forced to take work outside of London he left the milliner in Franklin's care. The little widow, said Franklin, "was often in distresses, and used to send for me and borrow what I could spare to help her out of them." Not unnaturally,

Benjamin felt that this entitled him to some special privilege. "I grew fond of her company, and . . . presuming upon my importance to her, I attempted familiarities which she repulsed with a proper resentment."

What with Ralph and the widow and "going to plays and other places of amusement," Benjamin made no progress in saving toward his fare back to Philadelphia. He "quite forgot," by degrees his, "engagements with Miss Read." In fact, he wrote her only once during the two years that he spent in London to rather callously "let her know that I was not soon likely to return."

Meanwhile, back in Philadelphia, things were not going well for Deborah and her family. Her father had died shortly before Benjamin left. The widow Read and her three children were in difficult straits. Then a man named Rogers came on the scene — possibly, like Franklin, as a lodger. And, like Franklin, he courted the jilted Deborah, who was now approaching the very marriageable age of eighteen. Her mother and family friends pressed her to accept Rogers. He was a good workman, a potter. His prospects were as good or better than Franklin's — and Franklin seemed to be gone for good. At a time when newspaper announcements of betrothals and marriages prominently mentioned the fortune which the bride brought to her husband, Deborah's prospects, without a dowry, for winning a husband were slim except for Rogers. She married him.

Within weeks after the marriage Deborah came home to Mother, to stay. Rogers proved to be a "worthless fellow" and Deborah was not happy with him and refused to "cohabit with him or bear his name." Then, as now, a husband's worthlessness or a wife's unhappiness were not considered valid reasons for a divorce. There was no divorce — Deborah merely left. At times she displayed a fiery temper, and this may have had something to do with it. And there was a rumor, which arose after the marriage, that Rogers already had a wife elsewhere. But the underlying reason for the failure of her match with Rogers was undoubtedly that Deborah was still in love with Benjamin.

When Franklin returned to Philadelphia, Deborah was living in depressed seclusion. There was no assurance that her marriage to Rogers was bigamous, and she was ashamed of the stigma that attached to a woman who left her husband for any lesser cause. For another year or more Rogers was still around town running into debt. Then he left for the West Indies, to be heard of no more.

Franklin makes but fleeting reference to any relationship with Deborah during the first four years after his return to Philadelphia, although for the latter half of this period he was living and working only two blocks away from the Read home. This was the era of his "intrigues with low women," with whom he surely did not class Deborah. She still had a husband, albeit a discarded one, and anything more than a casual relationship with Benjamin would have had to be clandestine. Also, the young printer was far too busy to think of a renewal of a serious alliance with his ex-fiancée.

After his return from London in 1726 Franklin worked for a year in the store of a Quaker who had paid his fare home. Then he worked as shop foreman for Keimer for a year. In 1728 he went into business for himself as a printer with a hard-drinking partner named Meredith, whose father put up £100 to finance the venture, hoping that Franklin would be a good influence on his son. That same year he organized the Junto — a club whose members were mostly young artisans like himself who were anxious to improve themselves economically and intellectually. From this club stemmed America's first public library and, ultimately, the American Philosophical Society. In 1729 Franklin started a newspaper, *The Pennsylvania Gazette.* In 1730 he borrowed money to buy out the partner, who was still hitting the bottle, and, at the age of twenty-four, was a printer and newspaper publisher on his own.

When Franklin and Meredith started up they had rented a house for £24 a year. The press was on one side of the lower floor; the partners slept above. They arranged with a glazier named Godfrey and his wife to occupy the other side of the house and board the partners. Sometime in 1730, as Franklin later recalled it:

Mrs. Godfrey projected a match for me with a relation's daughter, took opportunities of bringing us often together, till a serious courtship on my part ensued, the girl being in herself very deserving. The old folks encouraged me by continual invitations to supper, and by leaving us together, till at length it was time to explain. Mrs. Godfrey managed our little treaty. I let her know that I expected as much money with their daughter as would pay off my remaining debt for the printing house, which I believe was not then above a hundred pounds. She brought me word they had no such sum to spare. I said they might mortgage their house in the loan office. The answer to this, after some days, was that they did not approve the match . . . and therefore I was forbidden the house, and the daughter shut up.

Whether this was a real change of sentiment or only artifice, on a supposition of our being too far engaged in affection to retract, and therefore that we should steal a marriage which would leave them at liberty to give or withhold what they pleased, I know not. But I suspected the latter, resented it, and went no more. Mrs. Godfrey brought me afterwards some more favorable accounts of their dispositions, and would have drawn me on again; but I declared absolutely my resolution to have nothing more to do with that family. This was resented by the Godfreys;

we differed, and they removed, leaving me the whole house, and I resolved to take no more inmates.

Franklin's description of his financial demands on the relatives of the Godfreys may sound callously commercial, but it should be borne in mind that it was a widespread viewpoint of the day that monetary considerations were more important than romantic affection in arranging a marriage. Franklin's expectation of money with a bride as part of the proposed "treaty" was by no means unusual.

Franklin was undoubtedly lonely rattling around in the house by himself — and with nobody to feed him. This, and perhaps the Godfrey affair, turned his thoughts toward marriage and he actively started to seek a wife. "I looked round me, and made overtures of acquaintance in other places; but soon found that the business of a printer being generally thought a poor one, I was not to expect money with a wife unless with such a one as I should not otherwise think agreeable."

According to Franklin, when all else failed his thoughts turned again to Deborah; at least that is the impression given by this unromantic account of their union which he included in his *Autobiography*.

A friendly correspondence as neighbors and old acquaintances had continued between me and Mrs. Read's family, who all had a regard for me from the time of my first lodging in their house. I was often invited there and consulted in their affairs, wherein I sometimes was of service. I pitied poor Miss Read's unfortunate situation, who was generally dejected, seldom cheerful, and avoided company. I considered my giddiness and inconstancy when in London as in a great degree the cause of her unhappiness; though the mother was good enough to think the fault more her own than mine, as she had prevented our marrying before I went thither and persuaded the other match in my absence. Our mu-

tual affection was revived, but there were now great objections to
our union. That match [with Rogers] was indeed looked upon as
invalid, a preceding wife being said to be living in England; but
this could not easily be proved, because of the distance. And
though there was a report of his death, it was not certain. Then,
though it should be true, he had left many debts which his successor might be called on to pay. We ventured however over all
these difficulties and I [took] her to wife Sept. 1, 1730.

Franklin's *Autobiography* — which it must be remembered,
was addressed to his son William — may leave much untold.
It indicates that he ignored Debby, his first love, for four
years, though they were practically next door neighbors.
Then, when he found that he could do no better and needed
a substitute for his "intrigues with low women" he snapped
his fingers and Deborah came running. There is no reference
to love or romance other than the comment "our mutual
affection was revived" and this Franklin mentions more or
less as an aside, as though of minor consequence. It would
seem more likely that what Franklin termed "affection" had
been revived at some time during the previous four years.

Regardless of Franklin's reasons for taking a mate — and
for choosing Deborah — there is little doubt that she was
sincerely in love with the genius with whom she would spend
the rest of her days; the love that had bloomed when she was
sixteen had never faded. Her marriage with Rogers had been
an expediency born of resignation to the loss of her love and
the pressure of family and friends. Now she willingly entered
into an unholy alliance with the man whom she truly loved.

For it was an unholy alliance. When Franklin wrote "I
took her to wife" it was merely a euphemism which would
sound well to his son. There was no wedding, no recording
of nuptials at Christ Church, which Deborah attended, nor
with the civil authorities. Deborah and her mother merely

moved two blocks up High Street into Franklin's home. There was nothing else that the couple could do if they were to be together. Rogers had fled to the West Indies to escape his creditors and it was rumored that he had died there. But there was no proof, and if he later turned up alive any man who married Deborah might have shared with her the penalty for bigamy — thirty-nine lashes on the bare back and imprisonment at hard labor. Deborah might have risked this for the man she loved. Franklin surely would not.

Thus to begin with they were "living in sin." After a couple live together for a certain length of time their union is recognized as a common-law marriage — and forty-four years obviously qualifies as a "certain length of time." In any event the irregularity bothered neither Benjamin nor Deborah, and her mother and their mutual friends seemed to accept this common-law liaison as adequate. In fact, society in general accepted it, and the two children whom she is known to have borne him after their union were always regarded as legitimate. There was a third child — who may have been a factor in the seemingly sudden decision to take Deborah "to wife."

When Deborah and Mrs. Read moved in with Benjamin they may have been accompanied by a little stranger, either in Deborah's arms or her womb. Or the little stranger may have arrived from elsewhere. His name was William Franklin. There is no doubt that Franklin was his father. Historians have been fascinated for almost two centuries by the question, Who was William's mother? There may have been another — an unknown — woman in Franklin's life.

All Franklin experts endorse the opinion that William was illegitimate, but the evidence is quite circumstantial. The strongest point is that the charge of bastardy was made frequently by political opponents during Franklin's lifetime and he never denied it. This is somewhat weakened as conclusive evidence by the fact that Franklin did not deny other, more damning, political allegations. On one occasion he stood before the British Privy Council for an entire day and listened to a tirade that accused him of every crime in the book without saying a word in his own defense. He later justified this by remarking: "Splashes of dirt thrown upon my character I suffered while fresh to remain. I did not choose to spread by endeavoring to remove them, but relied on that vulgar adage that they would rub off when they were dry."

Another point which is quoted to prove that William was born out of wedlock — or what passed for wedlock in the Franklin menage — is that Benjamin makes no reference to his son's birth in his *Autobiography*. It seems strange that at some point in the story of his life which he wrote for his son he did not say, "and then you were born." However, while this may indicate that there was some irregularity about William's birth, it throws no light on the identity of William's mother. It would be equally embarrassing to say to one's son, "I married your mother because I had gotten her pregnant" or to say, "Son, you are a bastard."

There is one piece of evidence that would seem to place William's birth prior to 1731 — the earliest he could have arrived if he had been conceived after Deborah and Benjamin started to live as man and wife. In 1746 the boy was commissioned as an ensign in Pennsylvania armed forces for an expedition against the French in Canada. While fifteen-year-old officers were not unknown in England, they were invariably young noblemen. There is no record of a fifteen-year-old son of a provincial printer being so honored. To be so commissioned William should have been at least eighteen

— which would mean that when Deborah and Benjamin started to live together the boy was a two-year-old toddler.

Opposed to this is a letter from Franklin to his mother dated April 12, 1750, in which he wrote: "As to your grandchildren, William is now nineteen years of age, a tall proper youth and much of a beau." This would place William's birth late in 1730 or early in 1731. It is possible of course, that Benjamin was protecting his old mother from the facts of life, not wishing to admit that he had fathered a child prior to his marriage. Shortly before his death in 1813 William himself wrote: "My health, considering I am in my eighty-second year, is generally good." This would place his birth in 1730 or 1731 — but it is possible that William, too, had been misled as to his true age.

One expert school of thought has it that Deborah was William's mother but that he was either conceived or born before she and Benjamin lived together. The reasoning for this is based on the last sentence in Franklin's description of his union with Deborah: "Thus I corrected that great *erratum* as well as I could." Franklin used the words *erratum* or *errata* frequently in his *Autobiography* when referring to willful misdeeds that he had committed. The terms came from his trade in which *erratum* is a technical term meaning a printer's or writer's error. The *erratum* in this case may have referred to the repudiation of his "understanding" with Deborah when he was in London. Or it may refer to the fact that Deborah was or had been pregnant by Benjamin before he took her as his common-law wife.

The charge of bastardy was first publicly hurled against Franklin in the 1760s when there was much political discord in Pennsylvania. Franklin was then the leader of a group which sought to have the province changed from a proprietorship held by William Penn's absentee sons to a crown colony. Advocates of the proprietorship were bitter and vindictive against him. One of them wrote and printed a pamphlet titled *An Epitaph on a Certain Great Man* in which he alleged that William's mother was a servant, "his handmaid Barbara," to whom Franklin gave "the pitiful stipend of ten pounds per annum on which he had cruelly suffered her to starve; then stole her to the grave in silence, without a pall." Barbara is almost certainly a product of the imagination of the political hack who wrote the pamphlet. There is ample evidence that Franklin had no servant, male or female, before his union with Deborah or for a short time after. And nowhere else in all the literature on Franklin is there a reference to Barbara.

Another writer attributed William to the unnamed relation of Godfreys by commenting:

At the age of twenty-four he sought to negotiate a matrimonial engagement with a very deserving young woman. He demanded with her a portion of one hundred pounds, and required her father to mortgage his house to raise the money. The bargain was broken off, though the woman in question soon became the mother of his only son.

None of Franklin's other early detractors named names. One said that William's mother "was probably one of the 'low women' with whom he tells us that he had intrigued in those days, and who died in obscurity and was forgotten before anybody took any interest in the question." Another allowed that "The name of the mother most happily is not known; but as the law against bastardy was then rigidly enforced against the woman and not against the man, she was, in all likelihood, one of that throng who received their lashes in the market-place and filled the records of the council with prayers for the remission of fines." A third alleged: "He had this son by an oyster wench in Philadelphia, whom he left to die in the streets of disease and hunger."

None who charged that Deborah was not William's mother offered any proof and all who drooled over low women, oyster wenches, and serving maids whom Franklin cruelly wronged and then discarded either opposed Franklin politically or were merely scandalmongers.

There is no real evidence that Deborah was not William's mother but it is a reasonable supposition that, if she was, the child was conceived and possibly born before September, 1730. Franklin wrote that before their union "Miss Read . . . was generally dejected, seldom cheerful, and avoided company." This would surely be a fitting description of a woman who became pregnant some time after her husband went to the West Indies. Franklin admits his sex hunger prior to his marriage in his reference to "low women." In writing to his son he obviously would not refer to intimate relations with his mother. Deborah loved the man and if she gave in to his importunities she was not the first nor the last young woman to be guilty of a similar weakness.

Perhaps the best indication that Deborah was William's mother was their relationship for forty-four years. She reared him as her son with loving and tender care. She called him her son and he called her Mother. While it is probable that Deborah would have forgiven Benjamin for an affair with another woman before their union, it seems unlikely that she would have raised that other woman's child as her own and given him love and affection equal to that which she lavished on her own children.

From Franklin's many essays on the subject of women and marriage may be drawn a conception of the home life of

Benjamin and Deborah. He extolled marriage as the only proper state for man but stressed the role of a wife as a helpmate and friend. He said nothing of romance or passion or married love. His letters to her did not start with "Darling" or "My Dearest Wife." Almost invariably the salutation was "My Dear Child," although, on at least one occasion, it was a mere brusque "Dame." In a power of attorney which he issued to her shortly after their union he first wrote: "I . . . make and appoint my trusty and loving friend Deborah Franklin my true and lawful attorney." As an afterthought he crossed out "friend" and substituted "wife."

Perhaps the best description of Deborah as a wife is contained in a poem that he wrote about her. Legend has it that, at a meeting of the Junto, someone took exception to married men singing songs that poets had written in praise of their mistresses. A few days later Franklin gave another member a poem which he had written about his wife, asking him to recite it at the next meeting. Entitled *I Sing My Plain Country Joan,* the poem extolled Deborah's homely virtues in nine stanzas such as these.

> Not a word of her face, her shape, or her eyes,
>   Of flames or of darts shall you hear;
> Tho' I beauty admire 'tis virtue I prize,
>   That fades not in seventy years.
>
> In health a companion delightful and dear,
>   Still easy, engaging, and free,
> In sickness no less than the faithfullest nurse
>   As tender as tender can be,
>
> In peace and good order, my household she keeps
>   Right careful to save what I gain
> Yet cheerfully spends, and smiles on the friends
>   I've the pleasure to entertain.

Elsewhere in the poem he mentioned his wife's "compassionate breast" and her "cool sense." He admitted that Deborah had faults but added that "they're exceedingly small." He concluded by saying:

> Were the fairest young Princess, with million in purse
>   To be had in exchange for my Joan,
>   She could not be a better wife, mought be a worse,
>   So I'd stick to my Joggy alone.

The word "Joggy" applied to Deborah is interesting. It was a pet name for Joan, but it was also used as a familiar name for a homely woman or the sweetheart of a peasant.

Elsewhere Franklin wrote that "The married state is, after all our jokes, the happiest, because conformable to our natures. Man and woman have each of them qualities and tempers in which the other is deficient, and which in union contribute to the common felicity. Single and separate, they are not the complete human beings; they are like the odd halves of scissors: they cannot answer the end of their formation." This scissors analogy is a good description of the Franklin union. Deborah and Benjamin were joined together, but they were not one. Franklin became the most universal individual in the age of the "compleat man" with interests and accomplishments as diverse as the imagination could conceive. Deborah shared none of these interests. She never was, nor aspired to be, anything but a housewife and in the early years a business helpmate.

Franklin described the first years of their union by writing:

> We have an English proverb that says,
>   He that would thrive
>   Must ask his wife;
> It was lucky for me that I had one as much disposed to industry and frugality as myself. She assisted me cheerfully in my business,

folding and stitching pamphlets, tending shop, purchasing old linen rags for the paper makers, etc., etc. We kept no idle servants, our table was plain and simple, our furniture of the cheapest.

There is evidence that Franklin's frugality exceeded Deborah's, for he continued:

> For instance my breakfast was a long time bread and milk (no tea) and I ate it out of a twopenny earthen porringer with a pewter spoon. But mark how luxury will enter families, and make a progress, in spite of principle. Being called one morning to breakfast, I found it in a china bowl with a spoon of silver. They had been bought for me without my knowledge by my wife, and had cost her the enormous sum of three and twenty shillings, for which she had no other excuse or apology to make, but that she thought *her* husband deserved a silver spoon and china bowl as well as any of his neighbors.

The Franklins did not start life as typical newlyweds. In addition to her mother and probably the baby William, the household included Franklin's apprentice and his journeyman. Others came and went from time to time, but the work involved in taking care of the initial six would have appalled a modern home maker. Labor-saving devices for the home did not exist. Cooking was done in an open fireplace, which had to be constantly fed with wood — there was no stove. To get water, which was heated in the fireplace, Deborah did not turn a tap; she went out to a well and carried in buckets. Cleaning a floor did not mean pushing a vacuum. There were no carpets or rugs in the Franklin household until later years. The bare floors must be scrubbed on hands and knees. Deborah probably did not sand them and make interesting patterns in the sand — a custom that prevailed in households which did have idle servants.

And Deborah had housekeeping chores unknown to modern wives. When she became a bride in September one of her first jobs was probably making the winter's supply of candles. These were bought from a candle maker by rich folks, but not by the frugal Franklins. Providing the house with light involved lugging an immense kettle into the fireplace, filling it with smelly tallow and suet, keeping the fire going for hours, and then pouring the hot liquid into molds. Later, Franklin's shop sold a soap made by one of his brothers, but at first Deborah was probably concerned with saving wood ashes, fat, and grease to combine with lye in this same kettle to make soap.

Although the house did not have a sink or a refrigerator or a kitchen stove it did have two pieces of equipment which are uncommon today except as decorations. Somewhere there was a spinning wheel and a loom. Shortly before the Revolution, when nonimportation from Britain was tried as a coercive measure against the mother country, Franklin would rail against those who wore garments of factory-made cloth. He had once dressed, he bragged, in clothing made from fabrics spun and woven by his wife, and he would be proud to do so again.

Cooking for the six or more people who were part of the Franklin menage would seem to be a day's work in itself. There were no frozen foods nor canned goods nor mixes. Serving a simple lunch of soup and a sandwich involved making the bread and preparing the soup, from scratch, over an open fire.

In his *Autobiography* Franklin made much of his simple tastes in food — witness the reference to breakfasts of bread and milk. But there is other evidence that he liked to eat well, and Deborah was at least a fairly good cook. When Franklin was later in England she took delight in sending "goodies for my Pappy." When her husband was heading an expedition to build forts near Bethlehem to protect the Moravian settlers against Indian attack, Deborah, in Philadelphia, was the unofficial commissary for the officers. Writing from an outpost with the unpronounceable name of Gnadenhathen, he told her:

> We have enjoyed your roast beef, and this day began on the roast veal; all agree that they are both the best that ever were of the kind. Your citizens, that have their dinners hot and hot, know nothing of good eating; we find it in much greater perfection when the kitchen is four score miles from the dining room.
>
> The apples are extremely welcome, and do bravely to eat after our salt pork; the minced pies are not yet come to hand, but suppose we shall find them among the things expected up from Bethlehem, on Tuesday; the capillaire is excellent, but none of us having taken cold as yet, we have only tasted it.

The "capillaire" to which he refers was a syrup made from maidenhair fern to be taken as a cold cure. Another of Deborah's many housekeeping activities was the concoction of such simple remedies.

At about the same time as Franklin took Deborah "to wife" he started a store in the half of his house that had formerly been occupied by the Godfreys. The need for somebody to "mind the store" may have been a factor in his decision to take a wife. In addition to all else, Deborah somehow found time to help her husband tend the store. At first they sold only stationery and legal forms printed in the shop next door, but their mercantile activities soon branched out to embrace anything on which they could make a dollar. Through the years advertisements in Franklin's *Gazette* indicated the scope of merchandise which the couple stocked from time to time in a lively confusion of sights and smells. Included were "soap, ballads, slates and pencils, ink and ink powders, pounce and pounce boxes, sealing wax, wafers, lead

pencils, fountain pens [what they then were is not known],
quills for pens, ink horns, sand glasses, mezzotints, maps,
sack [Spanish wine], lampblack, chocolate, linseed oil, coffee,
powdered mustard, compasses and scales, patent medicines,
dividers and protractors, a secondhand chaise, another with
four wheels, Rhode Island cheese and cod fish, quadrants,
fore-staffs, nocturnals, mariners' compasses, lumber, edgings,
scarlet cloth, black broadcloth, white stockings, duck, iron
stoves, a horse for riding or driving, tea, saffron, lottery
tickets, mackerel by the barrel, a copper still, spermaceti,
palm oil, spectacles, a fishing net, bottles, Spanish pistoles,
and a fishing boat."

A staple of the establishment was a line of proprietary
medicines which Deborah's mother concocted in the kitchen
of the Franklin home and which were advertised in the
Gazette shortly after the Reads moved in:

The widow Read, removed from the upper end of High Street
to the new printing-office near the market, continues to make and
sell her well-known ointment for the itch, with which she has
cured abundance of people in and about this city for many years
past. It is always effectual for that purpose, and never fails to
perform the cure speedily. It also kills or drives away all sorts of
lice in once or twice using. It has no offensive smell, but rather
a pleasant one; and may be used without the least apprehension
of danger, even to a sucking infant, being perfectly innocent and
safe. Price 2s a gally-pot containing an ounce; which is sufficient
to remove the most inveterate itch, and render the skin clear and
smooth.

She also continues to make and sell her excellent *Family Salve*
or ointment for burns or scalds (price 1s an ounce) and several
other sorts of ointments and salves as usual.

At the same place may be had Lockyer's Pills, at 3d a pill.

The Franklins also traded in the unexpired time of in-

dentured servants and in slaves. In the latter case they usually
acted as brokers, but they sometimes bought slaves for their
own account and then hired them out until they were sold.
In her later years Deborah kept a little Negro boy of whom
she was very fond. Advertisements in the *Gazette* for this
aspect of the business offered:

A servant man's time for near three years, to be disposed of. He
is a joiner by trade and a very good workman.

A likely servant maid's time for four years to be disposed of.
She works well with her needle.

A very good tailor, having one year and ten months to run; fit
for either town or country business. And a servant lad for six
years, fit for country business.

To be sold for her passage. A likely young woman, well clothed,
can sew and do household work. Term of time as you can agree
with her. N.B. Her passage is £8. Also a breeding Negro woman
about twenty years of age. Can do any household work.

. . . A likely Negro wench about fifteen years old, has had the
smallpox, been in the country above a year and talks English. Inquire of the printer hereof.

A likely young Negro fellow about nineteen or twenty years of
age, to be disposed of. He is very fit for labor, being used to plantation work, and has had the smallpox.

Two likely young Negroes, one a lad about nineteen, the other
a girl of fifteen.

Husband and wife jointly kept the shop's books, a chore
at which Deborah was more capable than her spouse. Her
bookkeeping was meticulous, including even a sixpence "lent
the stranger from Boston." Her spelling left something to be
desired. She sold an ounce of ink to "the seck stone of the
church," an almanac to "Cristefer the Fishman," and some
paper to "Mary the Papist that is at Cozen Wilkinsons."

In 1732 Deborah's housekeeping, shop tending, and bookkeeping were interrupted by the birth of a son, Francis. The

child lived but four years before he succumbed to smallpox. On his gravestone the bereaved parents engraved: "The DELIGHT of all that knew him." The doting attitude of the Franklins toward this baby is evidenced — as is their growing affluence — by the portrait that they had painted of him at the age of two; the first portrait in the Franklin family and an unusual extravagance for a tradesman.

By 1735 the Franklins were well out of the woods financially. Everything to which they had turned their hand was showing a profit. Both the print shop and the store were thriving. Benjamin was public printer for Pennsylvania, New Jersey, and Delaware and printed the paper money for the first two colonies. The *Gazette* was rapidly overtaking the other, older Philadelphia paper in circulation and advertising. Franklin had started *Poor Richard's Almanac* in 1732 and it was now a national best seller. In her account books Deborah irreverently recorded sales of thousands of almanacs under the title "Poor Dicks."

During the period of their lives when Franklin was primarily a printer, he and Deborah were seldom separated. Like other tradesmen of the day he operated his business from his home; going to work meant coming downstairs. But though they were physically together in the same building there was little intellectual or romantic companionship. There was none of the modern "togetherness" in the Franklin family. They worked side by side as a team, each performing functions essential to their joint success. But, except at work, they were together mainly at table or in bed. Benjamin's union with Deborah had made unnecessary the "inconvenience and expense" of his previous "intrigues with low women." She catered solicitously to his creature comforts, and did it economically. Franklin was satisfied and frequently recorded his happiness in their life together. If Deborah wanted something more there is no record of her longing.

Perhaps some dissatisfaction was evidenced by her occasional outbursts of fiery temper in which she gave vent to her rage with a coarseness and vulgarity that would have done credit to an accomplished fishwife. Deborah's temper was one of the "exceedingly small faults" that Franklin mentioned in the poem about his wife. It did not seem to bother him — he learned to roll with the punches. He never mentioned her outbursts, specifically, but he undoubtedly had Debby in mind when he wrote what was supposed to be a letter from a reader of the *Gazette* in which he said, in part:

the inconveniency (as 'tis commonly thought) of a scolding wife, which has conveniencies enough in it to make it (when rightly considered) esteemed a happiness. For I speak from experience (as well as a long course of observation): women of that character have generally sound and healthy constitutions, produce a vigorous offspring, are active in the business of the family, special good housewives, and very careful of their husbands' interest. As to the noise attending all this, 'tis but a trifle when a man is used to it, and observes that it is only a mere habit, an exercise, in which all is well meant, and ought to be well taken.

Benjamin had some social life outside the home. There were the weekly sessions of the Junto and occasional meetings with his Junto cronies in taverns. In these early years he seldom entertained friends at home. During their first year of marriage he joined the Masons. Deborah had no part in these male activities. As a couple, Deborah and Franklin seem to have had little to do with tradesmen of their own social class, except on business. And while the budding aristocracy of Philadelphia looked approvingly on the industrious and ambitious tradesman, they did not at that time consider Franklin as a social equal. Shakespeare's words "The gentry think scorn of leather aprons" applied to Philadelphia's elite. Franklin's accomplishments later made him more than acceptable to both the social and intellectual upper class, but they never accepted Deborah nor included her in invitations to their homes. Perhaps the common-law marriage had something to do with this, but it is more likely that Deborah herself rebuffed such intercourse. She was contemptuous of simpering social graces and had no interest in the profound discourses of the intellectuals. Deborah's whole life was her husband, her children, her home, and the shop.

The era of working together for Deborah and Benjamin lasted until 1748 when Franklin, who had taken a partner, retired from business but continued to receive one half the profits. He had also financed half a dozen young men in establishing print shops and newspapers in other colonies and in the West Indies, from each of which he received one third of the profits. The Franklins were wealthy by contemporary Pennsylvania standards with an income of about £100 a year, equal to that of the Governor of the province.

During this period Benjamin had started to become a public figure and his great mind was reaching out in several directions. He had organized the first public library in the colonies, the American Philosophical Society, the Pennsylvania militia, and Philadelphia's first fire department. He was clerk of the Pennsylvania General Assembly, Postmaster of Philadelphia, and Grand Master of Pennsylvania's Masons. He had perfected his first invention, the Franklin stove. To gather the famed "Sayings of Poor Richard" from the "wit and wisdom of the ages" he had taught himself to read French, Spanish, Italian, German, and Latin.

Deborah had no part in any of this. She continued to keep house, mind the store and read only in English. As an added chore she was Philadelphia's unofficial postmistress when her husband was otherwise engaged. She now had one or more servants to help in the home and there were carpets on the floor and china and silver on the table, but affluence changed neither her manner nor her habits. She was essentially a housewife who seldom left her home. In 1744 she gave birth to another child, a daughter Sarah, who became Benjamin's adored Sally.

When Benjamin retired the Franklins moved from busy High Street — now renamed Market Street — to quieter, outlying Arch Street. Here Franklin hoped to devote himself entirely to his new-found interest in electricity. Friends from the Junto thronged his study to make experiments with electrical tubes and Leyden jars. Franklin invented the lightning rod and raised one over his own home. Further, he brought a wire from the rod into the hall and rigged up a contraption which rang bells when lightning struck the rod.

Deborah's only connection with the activities through which her husband would establish the basis for electricity as a science was to object to the bells. A strong bolt of lightning not only set them jangling but sent blue flashes bouncing around the hall. She thought this was dangerous — and she was right. But her husband paid no heed to her fears. He kept the bells and years later wrote to her from London: "If the ringing of the bells frightens you, tie a piece of wire from one bell to the other, and that will conduct the lightning without ringing or snapping, but silently. Tho' I think it best the bells should be at liberty to ring, that you may know when the wire is electrified, and, if you are afraid, may keep at a distance."

Since colonial Philadelphia did not consider playing with electricity a proper business for a grown man, Franklin was

frequently called away from his experiments to perform public services. He was sent to Carlisle to make a treaty with the
Indians; to Maryland to collect transport for General Braddock; to Bethlehem to supervise the erection of forts. He was
appointed Deputy Postmaster General of the colonies and
rode far afield to inspect post offices and roads. Deborah
loudly complained that all the world claimed the privilege of
troubling her Pappy with their calamities and distresses.

While on his frequent trips Franklin wrote regularly to
his wife. The best description of his letters is that they were
friendly and mildly affectionate. Usually he first told her
what he was doing and then devoted more space to business
and financial affairs. The following excerpt is typical:

> Among the Government orders I left with you, are two written
> ones drawn on Mr. Charles Norris for considerable sums; you did
> not tell me when I asked you, what money you had in hand; if
> you want before my return, present one of those orders to Mr.
> Norris, and he will pay the whole or a part, as you have occasion.
> . . . Be careful of your accounts, particularly about the lottery af-
> fairs. My duty to mother, Love to Sally, . . . I am, my dear child,
> Your loving husband, B. Franklin.

Another letter in its entirety, read:

> Dame. Send 50 reams largest demi to Mr. Daniel, printer at
> Jamaica. Send 30 reams ditto to Peter Timothy. Send the ream
> of thick blue paper to Parker. Send half the brown paper in the
> house to Parker, t'other half to brother John in Boston; No, send
> it *all* to Boston. Nota Bene. [in margin]. Don't forget to enter it.

Deborah was no longer required to mind the store but she
was very much involved in running the post office during
Benjamin's absences. When he appointed a man named Dun-
lap as postmaster of Philadelphia he told him:

I would not have the office removed on any account from my house during my absence, without my leave first obtained. And as Mrs. Franklin has had a great deal of experience in the management of the Post Office, I depend on your paying considerable attention to her advice in that matter.

As I leave but little money with Mrs. Franklin for the support of the family, and have left all the receipts of the Post Office for the payment of her expenses during my absence I expect and require that you account with her, and pay her, every Monday morning, the postage of the preceding week, taking her receipt for the same.

Deborah's household accounting was not as careful or complete as her bookkeeping for the store. A typical page from her account book read:

paid the woman that Irons for us	£1	-	-
paid the poor tax 15 and fier compoiney 1-6		16	6
Laid ought fullishley		10	-
and generousley		10	-
paid for a pair of purpill shoes for Salley		7	6
a pound of anchovise		3	6
my Cash did not quite hold ought this month			
Salleys french master		10	-
a bras dogs and fier Shoefil fier and tong	7	15	-
for splittin sume large wood and			
Clering the Seller		9	-
a lim of veel		7	-
paid our tacks	8	8	-

She finally gave the whole thing up and closed the book with the plaintive entry: "September the 1st took for famely expenses in Cash £6-0-0 as I am not abell to set down every penney. I think to doe this way."

During the era of the debunking biographies of famous Americans which started in the 1920s the impression was created — and still persists — that Franklin was something of a lecher; that he had affairs with many women on both sides of the Atlantic. Scandal-hunting biographers twisted letters and quoted out of context to prove that the eminent Doctor (his work in electricity had brought him several honorary degrees) liked the ladies much too much; and that he liked them young.

It is a fact that Franklin's letters to several other women were much different from those addressed to his wife. Most of his female correspondents were women of wit and intellect, with whom Franklin delighted to banter. His letters ooze charm and are replete with risqué compliments and *double-entendres*. It is also true that, from the time he was about fifty years old, he seemed to have great fascination for young women, several of whom adored him. But this adoration was for his character rather than his person. His manners, his charm, and his wit all appealed to the opposite sex; but he had a quality in his relationship with women that went beyond this. At a time when they were emerging from chattel-hood, Franklin treated women with a twentieth-century concept of equality — but he tempered this with a gallantry which is virtually unknown in today's war of the sexes. The combination made him irresistible to many intelligent females. But there is not one iota of real evidence that while Deborah lived Franklin had anything other than platonic relations with the several other women in his life.

The first young lady to titillate the scandalmongers was Catharine Ray. So far as is known Franklin had no close friendships with women during the first fifteen years of his union with Deborah; his letters to Catharine Ray, starting in 1755, are the first addressed to a woman outside his family. Catharine was twenty-three when forty-eight-year-old Franklin, on a Post Office trip, met her in Boston at the home of his brother John. They left Boston together and traveled, alone in a carriage, on a two-day trip to Newport. The intervening night together in a tavern has caused raised eyebrows; but Franklin is the authority that their sojourn was innocent. A statement in a letter that he wrote her, which is probably facetious, would indicate that he tried but was rebuffed. In some fatherly advice he tells her to get a good husband: "You must practice *addition* to your husband's estate, by industry and frugality; *subtraction* of all unnecessary expenses; multiplication (I would gladly have taught you that myself, but you thought it was time enough, and wouldn't learn) he will soon make you a mistress of it." In another letter he compared Catharine to the snow that was falling as he wrote: "pure as your virgin innocence, white as your lovely bosom — and as cold."

On the Rhode Island shore Franklin put Catharine in a small boat and anxiously watched her out of sight on her journey to her home on Block Island. From here she promptly wrote Franklin three letters that have subsequently disappeared. Then, because she received no answer, she wrote him a rather panicky note:

Excuse my writing when I tell you it is the great regard I have for you will not let me be silent, for absence rather increases than lessens my affections; then my not receiving one line from you in answer to three of my last letters . . . gives me a vast deal of uneasiness and occasioned many tears, for surely I have wrote too much and you are affronted with me or have not received my letters in which I have said a thousand things that nothing should have tempted me to [have] said to anybody else for I knew they would be safe with you—I'll only beg the favor of one line what is become of my letters tell me you are well and forgive me and love me one thousandth part so well as I do you and then I will be contented.

The fact that Catharine's three indiscreet letters are missing has led those who would see evil in Franklin's relations with the young lady to assume that the indiscretions were too fervent expressions of affection. This may be so, for in replying to her note Franklin wrote:

You may write freely everything you think fit, without the least apprehension of any person's seeing your letters but myself. You have complimented me so much in those I have already received, that I could not show them without being justly thought a vain coxcomb for so doing. . . . I know very well that the most innocent expressions of warm friendship, and even those of mere civility and complaisance, between persons of different sexes, are liable to be misinterpreted by suspicious minds; and therefore though you say more, I say less than I think and end this letter coolly in the plain common form, with only Dear Miss, Your humble servant, B. Franklin.

It is probable that Catharine had a girlish crush on Franklin. He was the first distinguished man whom she had ever met and a charming one to boot. He treated her as an intellectual equal and was taken by her wit and gaiety. He also admired her person and his somewhat daring personal compliments were exciting. It is not surprising that Catharine was impressed, and for a time may have fancied herself in love with the older man. Franklin's early letters to her seem to indicate that he was trying deliberately to put a prudent distance between them. In his first letter he wrote:

I left New England slowly, and with great reluctance. . . . I almost forgot I had a *home*, till I was more than half way towards it; till I had, one by one, parted with all my New England friends. . . . Then, like an old man, who, having buried all he loved in this world, begins to think of heaven, I began to think of and wish for home; and, as I drew nearer, I found the attraction stronger and stronger. My diligence and speed increased with my impatience. I drove on violently, and made such long stretches, that a very few days brought me to my own house, and to the arms of my good old wife and children, where I remain, thanks to God, at present well and happy.

In other letters he continued to remind Catharine that he had a wife and a twelve-year-old daughter. Catharine sent him a cheese and in acknowledging the gift he wrote:

Mrs. Franklin was very proud that a young lady should have so much regard for her old husband as to send him such a present. We talk of you every time it comes to table; she is sure you are a sensible girl, and a notable housewife; and talks of bequeathing me to you as a legacy; but I ought to wish you a better, and hope she will live these 100 years; for we are grown old together, and if she has any faults, I am so used to 'em that I don't perceive 'em, as the song says,

Some faults we have all, and so may my Joan,
But then they're exceedingly small;
And now I'm use'd to 'em, they're just like my own,
I scarcely can see 'em at all. . . .

Indeed I begin to think she has none, as I think of you. And since she is willing I should love you as much as you are willing to be lov'd by me; let us join in wishing the old lady a long life and a happy.

With her respectful compliments to your good mother and sisters, present mine. . . . Sally says, Papa, my love to Miss Katy.

And he had some "fatherly advice" for his young admirer which was surely not that of a lover:

Kill no more pigeons than you can eat. — Be a good girl, and don't forget your catechise. — Go constantly to meeting — or church — till you get a good husband; — then stay at home, and nurse the children, and live like a Christian. — Spend your spare hours, in sober whist, prayers, or learning to cypher.

He then continued with his advice of addition, subtraction, and multiplication and concluded:

I hope you will become as expert in the *Rule of Three;* that when I have again the pleasure of seeing you, I may find you like my grapevine, surrounded with clusters, plump, juicy, blushing, pretty little rogues, like their Mama. Adieu. The bell rings, and I must go among the grave ones, and talk politics. Your affectionate friend, B. Franklin.

Catharine Ray did get a husband in 1758; William Greene, who would be Rhode Island's Governor after the Revolution. When Benjamin next saw Catharine, at her farm in Warwick where he visited with his daughter Sally, she had already borne two of her six children. The couple saw each other only twice after this. In 1775 Franklin stopped off on returning from a trip to Washington's camp outside Boston. He took her eldest son Ray back to Philadelphia with him to attend the Academy which Franklin had founded and treated him as a grandson. The next year Catharine and her husband visited Franklin in Philadelphia.

Though they met only four times the friendship between Benjamin and Catharine continued until his death. For over thirty years they carried on a warm and intimate correspondence which was not affected by distance or time. For much of this period Franklin was in Europe and there was sometimes a lapse of years between letters. Great events transpired during this era but they were seldom mentioned in the letters that passed between Catharine and Benjamin. They wrote about themselves, their thoughts, and their families. Catharine addressed him as "My dearly beloved friend," sent him "as much love as you wish," and signed herself "Your friend that loves you dearly." After many years Catharine told him:

"I impute a great part of the happiness of my life to the pleasing lessons you gave me in that journey."

By 1757 Franklin was the most prominent man, politically, in Pennsylvania; the only one who was respected and trusted by the wealthy merchants of Philadelphia, the small trades-men, the German farmers, and the Quakers — groups that were usually at odds. There had been a long-standing dispute between the Pennsylvania Assembly and the distant propri-etors as to the tax right of the Assembly to tax the Penns' land. In 1757 it came to a head and Franklin was sent to England to reason with the proprietors and, if necessary, to appeal to the king. Benjamin would spend fifteen of the remaining seventeen years of Deborah's life in England. He returned home in 1762 and went back in 1764 to stay until the eve of the Revolution.

Deborah did not accompany her husband to England. He expected to be gone only a few months and someone had to handle their business affairs at home. Before his ship left Benjamin wrote his wife: "I leave home, and undertake this long voyage more cheerfully, as I can rely on your prudence in the management of my affairs, and education of my dear child; and yet I cannot forbear once more recommending her to you with a father's tenderest concern." As his stay lengthened, ultimately to five years on this visit, Deborah gave as an excuse for not joining him a dread of the ocean voyage. For many years Franklin had been corresponding with a London printer named William Strahan, from whom he ordered books for the library company. When Franklin's daughter Sally was but seven and Strahan's son William twelve, the fathers had jokingly proposed a match between them. When the two printers finally met in London they quickly became close friends and the idea of a union between their children was taken more seriously — at least by Strahan, who wrote Deborah coaxing her to come to England. After praising Benjamin effusively the Londoner continued:

Now, Madam, as I know the ladies here consider him in exactly the same light I do, upon my word I think you should come over, with all convenient speed to look after your interest; not but that I think him as faithful to his Joan as any man breathing; but who knows what repeated and strong temptation may, in time, and while he is at so great a distance from you, accomplish. Besides, what a delightful expedition would this be to Miss Franklin, and how much must it amuse and improve her, to see and live a while in this great city. I know you will object to the length of the voyage and the danger of the seas, but truly this is more terrible in apprehension than in reality; of all the ways of traveling it is the easiest and most expeditious; and as for the danger, there has not a soul been lost between Philadelphia and this, in my memory. . . .

I cannot take my leave of you without informing you that Mr. F. has the good fortune to lodge with a very discreet good gentlewoman, who is particularly careful of him, who attended him during a very severe cold he was some time ago seized with, with an assiduity, concern, and tenderness which, perhaps, only yourself could equal; so that I don't think you could have a better substitute till you come over, to take him under your own protection.

Franklin was sure that his wife would not come and wrote her that Strahan "has offered to lay me a considerable wager, that a letter he has wrote to you will bring you immediately over hither; but I tell him I will not pick his pocket; for I am sure there is no inducement strong enough to prevail with you to cross the seas." Deborah's answer to Strahan is lost but her husband told her: "Your answer to Mr. Strahan was just what it should be; I was much pleased with it. He fancied his rhetoric and art would certainly bring you over."

An unreasonable dread of an ocean voyage may have been
Deborah's real reason for not joining her husband in London — or she may have preferred the security of her home in
Philadelphia, without her husband, to living among strangers
in the distant English capital where Benjamin moved in
advanced social, political, and scientific circles. According to
her husband she was his best correspondent, but few of her
letters have come to light. His letters were frequent and full
and somewhat more affectionate than previous missives. He
did not say, in so many words, that he missed her but he let
her know that he was thinking of her. He was no longer the
frugal Franklin of earlier years and sent numerous shipments
of gifts for Deborah, Sally, and their home. The following is
typical of several letters.

I send you by Captain Budden, a large case marked D.F. No. 1.
and a small box D.F. No. 2. In the large case is another small box,
containing some English china; viz. melons and leaves for a dessert
of fruit and cream, or the like; a bowl remarkable for the neatness
of the figures, made at Bow, near this city; some coffee cups of the
same; a Worcester bowl, ordinary. To show the difference of workmanship there is something from all the china works in England;
and one old true china bason mended, of an odd color. The same
box contains 4 silver salt ladles, newest, but ugliest, fashion; a
little instrument to core apples; another to make little turnips
out of great ones; six coarse diaper breakfast cloths; they are to
spread on the tea table, for nobody breakfasts here on the naked
table, but on the cloth set a large tea board with the cups; there
is also a little basket, a present from Mrs. Stevenson to Sally, and
a pair of garters for you which were knit by the yound lady her
daughter, who favored me with a pair of the same kind, the only
ones I have been able to wear; as they need not be bound tight,
the ridges in them preventing their slipping. . . .
    In the great case, besides the little box, is contained some car-
peting for a best room floor. There is enough for one large or two

small ones; it is to be sewed together, the edges being felled down, and care taken to make the figures meet exactly; there is bordering for the same. This was my fancy. Also two large fine flanders bed ticks, and two pair large superfine blankets, 2 fine damask table cloths and napkins, and 43 ells of Ghentish sheeting holland; these you ordered. There is also 56 yards of cotton printed curiously from copper plates, a new invention, to make bed and window curtains; and 7 yards chair bottoms printed in the same way, very neat; these were my fancy; but Mrs. Stevenson tells me I did wrong not to buy both of the same color. Also 7 yards of printed cotton, blue ground, to make you a gown; I bought it by candlelight, and liked it then, but not so well afterwards: if you do not fancy it, send it as a present from me to sister Jenny. There is a better gown for you of flowered tissue, 16 yards, of Mrs. Stevenson's fancy, cost 9 guineas; and I think it a great beauty; there was no more of the sort, or you should have had enough for a negligee or suit. . . . There are also two sets of books a present from me to Sally, the *World* and the *Connoisseur;* my love to her. I forgot to mention another of my fancyings, viz. a pair of silk blankets, very fine. . . . I also forgot, among the china, to mention a large fine jug for beer, to stand in the cooler. I fell in love with it at first sight; for I thought it looked like a fat jolly dame, clean and tidy, with a neat blue and white calico gown on, good-natured and lovely and put me in mind of — somebody.

The Mrs. Stevenson referred to in this letter and in Strahan's was a widow with whom Franklin lodged during his years in London. He and William, who accompanied him on the first trip, lived handsomely in a four-room suite in Margaret Stevenson's home on Craven Street, waited on hand and foot by the widow and her daughter Mary, whom Franklin called Polly. It is surprising that the scandalmongers have never hinted at immoral relations between Franklin and Margaret Stevenson, with whom he lived for fifteen years. Her daughter was eighteen at the time that Franklin came to live with them, which would indicate that Margaret was perhaps a few years younger than fifty-one-year-old Benjamin. She fulfilled all of the other functions of a wife, nursed him when he was ill, washed and ironed his shirts herself, and in every way made the house on Craven Street as much of a home as the house on Arch Street.

Franklin quickly became the head of the English household rather than a lodger. One of his most amusing pieces of writing indicates his affection for his overseas family. It is a parody on the *Court Gazette* of the day, entitled the *Craven Street Gazette*. Franklin had been living with the Stevensons for many years by this time. Mary Stevenson was married to a Dr. Hewson and a young English relative of Franklin's, another Sally Franklin, had joined the household. When Margaret went away on a visit, leaving her daughter in charge of the household, Franklin wrote her daily bulletins of events at home in which Polly was variously the new minister, lady chamberlain, and lady of the bed chamber. Franklin was the Great Person and Old Fatsides.

This morning Queen Margaret, accompanied by her first maid of honor, Miss Franklin, set out for Rochester. . . . It is whispered that the new family administration, which took place on Her Majesty's departure, promises, like all other new administrations, to govern much better than the old one.

We hear that a certain Great Person (so called from his enormous size) of a certain family in a certain street is grievously affected at the late changes, and could hardly be comforted this morning, though the new ministry promised him a roasted shoulder of mutton and potatoes for his dinner.

It is said that the same Great Person intended to pay his respects to another great personage this day, at St. James's, it being coronation day; hoping thereby a little to amuse his grief; but was prevented by an accident, Queen Margaret, or her maid of honor, having carried off the key of the drawers so that the lady of the bedchamber could not come at a laced shirt for His Highness.

Great clamors were made on this occasion against Her Majesty.

Other accounts say that the shirts were afterwards found, though too late, in another place. And some suspect that the wanting shirts from those drawers was only a ministerial pretence to excuse picking the locks, that the new administration might have everything at command.

We hear that the lady chamberlain of the household went to market this morning by her own self, gave the butcher whatever he asked for the mutton and had no dispute with the potato woman, to their great amazement at the change of times. . . .

We have good authority to assure our readers that a cabinet council was held this afternoon at tea; the subject of which was a proposal for the reformation of manners and a more strict observation of the Lord's day. The result was a unanimous resolution that no meat should be dressed tomorrow; whereby the cook and the first minister [Polly and her husband] will both be at liberty to go to church, the one having nothing to do and the other no roast to rule. It seems the cold shoulder of mutton and the apple pie were thought sufficient for Sunday's dinner. All pious people applaud this measure, and it is thought the new ministry will soon become popular. . . .

It is now found by sad experience that good resolutions are easier made than executed. Notwithstanding yesterday's solemn order of council, nobody went to church today. It seems the Great Person's broad-built bulk lay so long abed that the breakfast was not over till it was too late to dress. At least this is the excuse. In fine, it seems a vain thing to hope reformation from the example of our great folks. . . .

Lord and Lady Hewson walked after dinner to Kensington to pay their duty to the Dowager [Hewson's mother]; and Dr. Fatsides made four hundred and sixty-nine turns in his dining room, as the exact distance of a visit to the lovely Lady Barwell, whom he did not find at home; so there was no struggle for and against a kiss, and he sat down to dream in the easy chair that he had it without any trouble. . . .

We are credibly informed that the Great Person dined this day with the Club at the Cat-and-Bagpipes in the City on cold round of beef. This, it seems, he was under some necessity of doing (though he rather dislikes beef) because truly the ministers were to be all abroad somewhere to dine on hot roast venison. It is thought that if the Queen had been at home he would not have been so slighted. And though he shows outwardly no marks of dissatisfaction it is suspected that he begins to wish for Her Majesty's return. . . .

This evening there was high play at Craven Street House. The Great Person lost money. It is supposed the ministers, as is usually supposed of all ministers, shared the emoluments among them. . . .

This morning my good Lord Hutton [James Hutton the bookseller] called at Craven Street House and . . . imparted to the Big Man a piece of intelligence important to them both . . . viz, that the amiable and delectable companion Miss Dorothea Blount [a friend of Polly's] had made a vow to marry absolutely him of the two whose wife should first depart this life. It is impossible to express the various agitations of mind appearing in both their faces on this occasion. Vanity at the preference given them over the rest of mankind; affection to their present wives, fear of losing them, hope, if they must lose them, to obtain the proposed comfort; jealousy of each other in case both wives should die together, etc., etc., all working at the same time jumbled their features into inexplicable confusion. They parted at length with professions and outward appearances indeed of ever-during friendship, but it was shrewdly suspected that each of them sincerely wished health and long life to the other's wife; and that, however long either of these friends might to live himself, the other would be very well pleased to survive him.

During his first years in London Polly Stevenson and her young friends petted and fussed over and spoiled the charming doctor. The Dorothea Blount and Miss Barwell mentioned in the *Craven Street Gazette* were among those who pampered him, and he apparently called them his daughters. He so referred to one girl, Judith Osgood, in a letter and this gave rise to later tales about Franklin's illegitimate daughter. Judith, who was about Polly's age, was married in 1770. To be Franklin's daughter, born in England, she would have been under thirteen or over forty-four in that year — or have been conceived over three thousand miles of ocean. Certainly Franklin's relation with all these young women was innocent. There was talk of love, but Franklin described what this meant in a letter to Polly: "I cannot conceive that any inconvenience can arise from my loving young ladies, and their believing that I love them. Therefore, you may assure your friend Dolly that she judges right. I love all good girls, because they are good, and her for one reason more; because you love her."

Polly Stevenson, like Catharine Ray, became a life-long friend of Franklin. He tried to arrange a match between Polly and William, but Polly was not interested. She moved to an aunt's house in 1759 — possibly to get away from William; who promptly fathered an illegitimate son, Temple Franklin, by an unknown English woman. In passing, it may be remarked that Temple later fathered an illegitimate son when he was with his grandfather in France making the third generation in the Franklin line of international illegitimacy: Benjamin's son born in Philadelphia, William's in London, and Temple's in Paris.

Polly Stevenson had an unusual mind for a female of the day. Among other things she was fascinated by all aspects of science and, when she moved away temporarily from Craven Street, asked Franklin to make natural philosophy the subject of their correspondence. The older man agreed but added: "But why will you, by the cultivation of your mind, make yourself still more amiable and a more desirable companion for a man of understanding when you are determined, as I hear, to live single? If we enter, as you propose, into moral as well as natural philosophy, I fancy when I have fully established my authority as a tutor I shall take upon me to lecture you a little on that chapter of duty." Franklin wrote to his young pupil on the workings of the barometer, the effect of color in light absorption and reflection and about tides in rivers — and a very long letter which ended: "After writing six folio pages of philosophy to a young girl, is it necessary to finish such a letter with a compliment? Is not such a letter of itself a compliment?" In one letter on the usefulness of insects he put in a sly sentence on aphrodisiacs which he assumed the young lady would be too innocent to catch. After commenting on the contributions of the silkworm, the bee, and an insect from which scarlet dye was procured, he added: "The usefulness of the cantharides, or Spanish flies, in medicine is known to all, and thousands owe their lives to that knowledge."

Years later, in 1769, Polly changed her vow to remain single and wrote Franklin that she had met a young doctor whom she might marry, although the doctor did not know it yet. Franklin, just back from a trip to Paris, replied: "Possibly if the truth were known I have reason to be jealous of this same insinuating, handsome young physician, but, as it flatters more my vanity, and therefore gives me more pleasure, to suppose you were in spirits on account of my safe return, I shall turn a deaf ear to reason in this case, as I have done with success in twenty others." When they were married and she wrote him about her new in-laws he answered: "I am apt to love everybody that loves you, and therefore I suppose I shall in time love your new mother and new sister and new Dolly. . . . But your old Dolly [Dorothea Blount] and I have agreed to love each other better than ever we did to make up as much as we can our supposed loss."

Polly continued to write Benjamin throughout the Revolution, risking trouble by sending her letters secretly into enemy territory. As with Catharine Ray there was nothing political about their correspondence; it switched from the scientific to the purely personal. Franklin was the godfather of the Hewsons' first son and, years later, proposed a match between one of his grandsons, Sally's boy, and a daughter of Polly's. After the war, and her husband's death, Polly and her children spent one winter with Benjamin at Passy, a suburb of Paris. He wanted her to return to America with him when he finally left France. She could not, but in 1787 she did come to settle in Philadelphia to be near the old philosopher. She was with him, reading aloud, shortly before his death.

If Deborah, back in Philadelphia, was jealous of the widow with whom her husband was living in London, she never disclosed it. The Stevensons chose many of the gifts which Franklin sent back to his American family and Deborah sent them corn meal, buckwheat flour, apples, dried peaches, cranberries and nuts.

When Franklin's first sojourn in England was drawing to a close he wrote Strahan that he might return to England to live there permanently: "Nothing will prevent it if I can, as I hope, prevail with Mrs. F. to accompany me." And from America he wrote the London printer: "In two years at farthest, I hope to settle all my affairs in such a manner as that I *may* then conveniently remove to England — provided we can persuade the good woman to cross the seas." But when Franklin returned to London in 1764 as colonial agent for Pennsylvania — this time expecting a long stay — Deborah still would not cross the seas, nor would she let Sally accompany her father. On this trip he could take his grandson Temple, but the ladies would stay at home.

When Benjamin returned to London he walked into a hornet's nest which had repercussions at home. The Stamp Act was about to be passed and Franklin did nothing to oppose it. He campaigned vigorously against the principle involved — the right of the British Parliament to levy internal taxes in the colonies — but he did not consider the Stamp Act in itself as a heinous thing. The sentiment back home was much different and, when it was said by his political enemies that Franklin had taken money for recommending stamp officers, a Philadelphia mob threatened to burn his home. William Franklin rode hurriedly from New Jersey and urged his mother to take refuge with him. Deborah let Sally go, but she would not budge. Instead she sent for one of her brothers and one of her husband's nephews, telling them to bring guns. She wrote to London: "We turned one room into a magazine. I ordered some sort of defense upstairs, such as I could manage myself."

When Franklin was instrumental in having the Stamp Act repealed the mood back home changed and he was lauded as a national hero. He wrote to Deborah:

As the Stamp Act is at length repealed I am willing you should have a new gown, which you may suppose I did not send sooner as I knew you would not like to be finer than your neighbors unless in a gown of your own spinning. Had the trade between the two countries totally ceased, it was a comfort to me to recollect that I had once been clothed from head to foot in woolen and linen of my wife's manufacture, that I never was prouder of any dress in my life, and that she and her daughter might do it again if it was necessary. I told the Parliament that it was my opinion, before the old clothes of the Americans were worn out they might have new ones of their own making. And indeed if they had all as many clothes as your old man has, that would not be very unlikely, for I think you and George reckoned when I was last at home at least twenty pair of old breeches. Joking apart, I have sent you a fine piece of Pompadour satin, fourteen yards, cost eleven shillings a yard; a silk negligee and petticoat of brocaded lutestring for my dear Sally, with two dozen gloves, four bottles of lavender water.

In 1776 Franklin's partnership with David Hall ended, and with it the £500 which he had been receiving annually from the print shop. Although Franklin was now agent in England for Georgia, Massachusetts, and New Jersey as well as Pennsylvania — positions which paid £1,500 a year, although sometimes tardily — his thoughts returned to frugality as he wrote Deborah:

A great source of our income is cut off, and if I should lose the post office, which among the many changes here is far from being unlikely, we should be reduced to our rents and interests of money for a subsistence, which will by no means afford the chargeable housekeeping and entertainments we have been used to. For my own part I live here as frugally as possible not to be destitute of the comforts of life, making no dinners for anybody and contenting myself with a single dish when I dine at home; and yet such is the dearness of living here in every article that my expenses amaze me. I see too by the sums you have received in my absence that yours are very great, and I am very sensible that your situation naturally brings you a great many visitors, which occasion an expense not easily to be avoided, especially when one has been long in the practice and habit of it. But when people's incomes are lessened, if they cannot proportionably lessen their outgoings they must come to poverty. If we were young enough to begin business again it might be another matter; but I doubt we are past it; and business not well managed ruins one faster than no business.

Richard Bache asked Deborah for Sally's hand and Benjamin perforce accepted his wife's endorsement of a son-in-law who was a stranger to him. He wrote: "I can only say that if he proves a good husband to her, and a good son to me, he shall find me as good a father as I can be. . . . For the rest, they must depend as you and I did, on their own industry and care." Mindful of their "reduced circumstances" — although he was still a wealthy man by Pennsylvania standards — he added that they could do no more than to fit their daughter, "handsomely out in clothes and furniture, not exceeding in the whole five hundred pounds of value."

A captivating group of females who brightened the life of Franklin during his mid-sixties were the five daughters of Bishop Jonathan Shipley who ranged in age, when he first met them, from eleven to twenty-three. In 1771 Benjamin escaped smoky London to take one of his rare vacations at the Bishop's country home and started to write his *Autobiography* in what the girls forever after called "Franklin's room." When he left he took the youngest daughter, eleven-year-old Kitty, back to London with him in the chaise to go to school. Not many sixty-five-year-old men would find it easy to talk to an eleven-year-old school girl for several hours, but Franklin seemed to enjoy drawing the young lady out and listening to her ideas.

He wrote her mother a memorable thank-you note of his visit and recounted his conversation with Kitty and her opinions as to husbands for her sisters. Georgina should have a country gentleman; Betty a rich city merchant; Emily, Kitty's favorite, deserved an earl; Anna Marie should have a rich man with many possessions because she was fond of managing. Franklin suggested a duke. Kitty then decided to let Emily have the duke and Anna Marie the earl. Franklin suggested that Kitty herself might choose a soldier, perhaps a general.

"Not unless he were very old," Kitty insisted. "I like an old man, indeed I do, and somehow or other all the old men take to me; all that come to our house like me better than my other sisters. I go to 'em and ask 'em how they do, and they like it mightily; and the maids take notice of it, and say, when they see an old man come: 'There's a friend of yours, Miss Kitty.' " "But then," asked Benjamin, "as you like an old general, hadn't you better take him while he's a young officer, and let him grow old upon your hands, because then you'll like him better and better every year as he grows older and older?" "No, that won't do. He must be an old man of seventy or eighty, and take me when I am about thirty. And then, you know, I may be a rich young widow."

Fifteen years later when Franklin was finally leaving Europe Kitty came to Southampton to see him off and promised to make him a purse if he would write something for her. Franklin kept his part of the bargain by writing for Kitty, at the age of eighty, a delightful bagatelle entitled "The Art of Procuring Pleasant Dreams." After emphasizing the importance of fresh air in the bedroom, Franklin continued:

It is recorded of Methusalem, who, being the longest liver, may be supposed to have best preserved his health, that he slept always in the open air; for when he had lived five hundred years, an angel said to him: "Arise, Methusalem, and build thee a house, for thou shalt live yet five hundred years longer." But Methusalem answered and said, "If I am to live but five hundred years longer, it is not worth while to build me a house; I will sleep in the air, as I have been used to do."

Kitty took this seriously and after a fruitless search for the source plaintively wrote him: "Where do you read that Methusalem slept in the open air? I have searched the Bible in vain to find it."

Franklin's favorite among the Shipley girls was probably Georgina, rather than Kitty, because of her lively intellect;

although both girls continued to adore him throughout the rest of his life. It was Georgina who asked him to write an epitaph for a squirrel. After his first visit to the Shipleys Benjamin asked Deborah to send the girls a squirrel, which became a family pet. It was named Mungo but usually called Skugg — a pet name for squirrels in England as Puss is for cats. Mungo got out of his cage and was killed by a dog. When Georgina advised Franklin of this and asked for an epitaph, the old philosopher gravely complied by writing:

I lament with you most sincerely the unfortunate end of poor Mungo. Few squirrels were better accomplished; for he had had a good education, traveled far, and seen much of the world. As he had the honor of being, for his virtues, your favorite, he should not go, like common Skuggs, without an elegy or an epitaph. Let us give him one in the monumental style and measure, which, being neither prose nor verse, is perhaps the properest for grief; since to use common language would look as if we were not affected, and to make rhymes would seem trifling in sorrow.

Franklin then composed a parody on an epitaph in the pompous style of the times and concluded with:

You see, my dear miss, how much more decent and proper this broken style is than if we were to say, by way of epitaph:

Here Skugg
Lies snug
As a bug
In a rug.

And yet there are people in the world of so little feeling as to think that this would be a good enough epitaph for poor Mungo.

Like Polly Stevenson, Georgina smuggled letters to Franklin in France during the war. In her first, at the age of eighteen, she told him: "You are the first man who ever received a private letter from me." Her father thought that, in view of the war, it would not be prudent to write; but,

said Georgina: "I am not at an age to be so very prudent."
And added: "I could not support the idea of your believing
that I love and esteem you less than I did some years ago."
The rest of the letter was about books. Had Franklin read
Adam Smith's *Wealth of Nations* which she considered the
only good recent book worth reading except the recently
published first volume of Gibbon's *Decline and Fall?* She
was reading everything she could about Socrates "for I fancy
I can discover in each trait of that admirable man's character
a strong resemblance between him and my much-loved
friend."

Shortly before the Revolution a woman entered Franklin's
life for a brief interlude that had a touch of cloak and dagger.
At the time it was believed in England that Franklin wielded
such influence in the colonies that any proposal which he
made for the settlement of their differences with the mother
country would be almost automatically accepted back home.
This was not true, except possibly in Pennsylvania, but those
in England who sought conciliation thought that Franklin
might bring it about.

In November 1774, at a meeting of the Royal Society, one
of the members approached Franklin and told him that,
"there was a certain lady who had a desire of playing with
me at chess, fancying she could beat me, and had requested
him to bring me to her; it was, he said, a lady with whose
acquaintance he was sure I should be pleased. . . . I had not
the least apprehension that any political business could have
any connection with this new acquaintance." The lady
proved to be Miss Howe, attractive and intelligent sister of
Admiral Lord Howe and General Sir William Howe. Franklin "played a few games with the lady whom I found of very
sensible conversation and pleasing behavior, which induced

me to agree most readily to an appointment for another meeting for a few days after."

Before the second meeting two English Quakers called on Franklin. They told him that there were certain members of the ministry who favored a policy of trying to placate the colonies, and asked him to write down a list of the conditions under which the colonies would return to a friendly footing with Great Britain. Franklin somewhat reluctantly did so but suggested that his authorship of the paper be kept secret because he was in such bad repute with the rabid majority of the ministry.

On his second meeting with Miss Howe she turned the postgame conversation to politics. She asked, according to Franklin:

"And what is to be done with this dispute between Great Britain and the colonies? I hope we are not to have a civil war." "They should kiss and be friends," says I, "what can they do better? Quarrelling can be of service to neither, but is ruin to both." "I have often said," says she, "that I wished government would employ you to settle the dispute for 'em; I am sure nobody could do it so well. Don't you think that the thing is practicable?" "Undoubtedly, Madam, if the parties are disposed to reconciliation; for the two countries have really no clashing interests to differ about. It is rather a matter of punctilio, which two or three reasonable people might settle in half an hour, I thank you for the good opinion you are pleased to express of me; but the ministers will never think of employing me in that good work; they choose rather to abuse me." "Aye," says she, "they have behaved shamefully to you. And indeed some of them are now ashamed of it themselves."

When Franklin again called on Miss Howe, on Christmas Day, the chess men were not set up. Instead:

She told me as soon as I came in, that her brother, Lord Howe, wished to be acquainted with me; that he was a very good man, and she was sure we should like each other. I said I had always heard a good character of Lord Howe and should be proud of the honor of being known to him. "He is just by," says she; "will you give me leave to send for him?" "By all means, Madam, if you think proper." She rang for a servant, wrote a note, and Lord H. came in a few minutes.

Howe assured Franklin that "that there was a sincere disposition on the part of Lord North and Lord Dartmouth to accommodate the differences with America," and asked him what he thought of sending some person to America to try to bring about an understanding. Franklin thought that "a person of rank and dignity, who had a character of candor, integrity, and wisdom, might accomplish some good." Where at Miss Howe proposed "I wish, brother, you were to be sent thither on such a service; I should like that much better than General Howe's going to command the army there."

Lord Howe then brought out a copy of the supposedly secret list of conditions that Franklin had given the Quakers and asked the American if he was the author of it. When Franklin admitted this, Lord Howe expressed his disappointment because "he had reason to think that there is no likelihood of the admission of those propositions." He suggested that, in the interests of peace, Franklin modify the terms, adding "that he should not think of influencing me by any selfish motive, but certainly I might with reason expect any reward in the power of government to bestow." Franklin wrote that this offer of a bribe was "what the French call 'spitting in the soup.' " He agreed to revise his list and then revised only the wording, still making essentially the same demands. He sent this list to Miss Howe and there were a few other meetings with the lady, acting as intermediary for her brother, but naught came of this behind-the-scenes attempt to prevent the American Revolution; Franklin was adamant on conditions which Lord Howe could not induce the ministry to meet.

While Benjamin was playing chess with Miss Howe in London, Deborah died in Philadelphia; without his presence or even his knowledge. Her son-in-law sent his clerk galloping to Trenton and William arrived only a half hour before her body left the house for the churchyard. Her son and son-in-law were chief mourners and several other friends of Franklin's were "carriers," one of whom wrote that "a very respectable number of the inhabitants were at the funeral."

Although Deborah died suddenly from a stroke, she had apparently been in poor health for a year — at least she did not write to her husband during the last year of her life, so far as is known, and this may have been the reason. In one of his last letters to her Benjamin wrote: "It seems but t'other day, since you and I were ranked among the boys and girls, so swiftly does time fly. We have, however, great reason to be thankful that so much of our lives has passed so happily."

Franklin was on the Atlantic en route for Philadelphia when "the shot heard 'round the world" was fired at Concord. Eighteen months later he was back in Europe as one of three American Commissioners to the court of Louis XVI of France. The French idolized the American sage. French intellectuals had long honored him as a scientist. The French bourgeoisie revered him as the wise author of *Bonhomme Richard*. Now French society made a pet of the rustic philosopher, as they insisted on considering Franklin, who played up to his image by wearing no wig, a fur hat, and plain clothes. He moved through the French salons like a somber pigeon in a roomful of peacocks.

The women of France, particularly, adored the old doctor.
A companion of Marie Antoinette's described a fete at which
the most beautiful of three hundred women placed a laurel
wreath on his head and kissed him on both cheeks. When
John Adams came to France he remarked, possibly with envy,
"at seventy-odd he has neither lost his love for beauty nor his
taste for it." There is an anecdote that Louis XVI became so
fed up with hearing the Comtesse de Polignac sing the praises
of the great American, he presented her with a chamber pot
decorated with Franklin's picture.

Of the women of France, Franklin wrote to a niece:

You mention the kindness of the French ladies to me. I must
explain that matter. This is the civilest nation upon earth. Your
first acquaintance endeavors to find out what you like, and then
tell others. If 'tis understood that you like mutton, dine where
you will you will find mutton. Somebody, it seems, gave out that I
loved ladies; and then everybody presented me their ladies (or
ladies presented themselves) to be embraced; that is, have their
necks kissed. For as to the kissing of lips or cheeks it is not the
mode here; the first is reckoned rude, and the other may rub off
the paint. The French ladies have, however, a thousand other
ways of rendering themselves agreeable; by their various attentions and civilities and their sensible conversation.

The legend of Franklin the lecher is strongest for his
French period, despite the fact that he was seventy years old
when he reached Paris. Provincial America had a low opinion
of the morality of French women and saw evil in some French
customs that were innocent, albeit different, than those of
America.

Even during Franklin's lifetime there were anecdotes of
the gay old dog in Paris. One is found in the diary of a Boston
Tory named Dr. Jeffries, the first American aeronaut. The
balloon was invented in 1783. Franklin witnessed one of the

first ascensions and when a bystander queried, "What good is it?" is supposed to have replied, "Of what use is a new born baby?" A French balloonist named Blanchard made the first crossing of the English Channel in 1785 with the American Dr. Jeffries as a passenger.

According to Jeffries' diary he was received in Paris with a hero's welcome. He recorded:

February 3: Evening, at nine, Mr. Franklin called on me and carried me and introduced me to Madame Morell, where I was most kindly received indeed and met there the most charming Madame de Villars. . . . Many compliments passed between us on his talents and my late enterprise. . . . I cannot describe the lovely ease and elegance, yet delicate decency with which Mme. Morell and Mme. de Villars undressed themselves in my presence, and dressed again in lovely dishabille, previous to our going to the masqued ball at the opera. . . . Met at the ball many ladies who knew me but I could not know them all, so covered with dominos and masques. . . . After a long time I found out my lovely Mme. Morell and Mme. Villars, with whom Mr. Franklin and I left the ball at four o'clock.

This is an interesting story, although almost certainly untrue. At the age of seventy-nine Franklin may still have been interested in watching ladies change into "lovely dishabille" but it taxes credulity to believe that the octogenarian danced from nine until four. Long before this he had become almost incapacitated with gout.

Franklin settled comfortably in Passy, a Paris suburb, in an all-male household except for the winter that Polly Hewson spent with him. His grandson Temple was his secretary. His other younger grandson, Benny Bache, lived with him and went to school in Paris. But Franklin had female neighbors, two of whose names were linked intimately with his. One, Madame Brillon, was apparently in her early thirties,

gay, beautiful, and married to an older, philandering husband. Their correspondence, with frequent allusions to sex,
gave rise to much of the later lecher image, particularly a
reference of Franklin's to a chess game which they played
while she was in her bath. The custom of some French ladies
of fashion to receive intimate friends while in a covered
bathtub was unknown in this country.

In one letter to her Franklin said: "When I was a young
man and enjoyed more favors from the sex than at present, I
never had the gout. If the ladies of Passy had more of the
Christian charity which I have so often recommended to you,
in vain, I would not have the gout now." After she had offered to be his confessor, he wrote:

I lay fast hold on your promise to absolve me of all sins, past,
present and future, on the easy and pleasing condition of loving
God, America, and my guide above all things. I am in rapture
when I think of being absolved of the future. . . . And now I am
consulting you upon a case of conscience, I will mention the
opinion of a certain father of the Church which I find myself
willing to adopt, though I am not sure it is orthodox. It is this:
that the most effectual way to get rid of a certain temptation is,
as often as it returns, to comply with and satisfy it. Pray instruct
me how far I may venture to practice upon this principle?

Madame Brillon's letters describe the two aspects of their
relationship. In one she said:

I had a father, the kindest of men, he was my first, and my best
friend; I lost him untimely! you have often said to me: *"Could I
not take the place of those whom you regret?"* and you told me
the custom of certain savages who adopt the prisoners that they
capture in war, and make them take the place of the relatives
whom they lose; you took in my heart the place of the father
whom I so loved, and respected.

In another letter she complained:

My good Papa, your visits never cause me any inconvenience, all those around me respect you, love you, and think themselves honored in the friendship you have granted us; I told you that the world criticized the sort of familiarity which existed among us, because I was warned of it; I despise slanderers and am at peace with myself, but that is not enough, one must submit to what is called *propriety* (that word varies in each century, in each country!): to sit less often on your knees. I shall certainly love you none the less, nor will our hearts be more or less pure, but we shall close the mouth of the malicious, and it is no slight thing even for the sage, to make them silent.

Throughout their correspondence they played a word game of love but to all except the most narrow-minded it was obviously a stimulating mental exercise. When winter residence in Paris separated them, Madame Brillon wrote that perhaps Paradise would be better where "we shall be reunited, never to leave each other again. We shall live on roast apples only . . . all parties will be given over to chess . . . every day we shall love one another in order that we may love one another still more the day after; in a word, we shall be completely happy." Franklin picked this up by pointing out that, because of the difference in their ages, he would be in Paradise forty years before her. "However, the idea of an eternity in which I shall be favored with no more than permission to kiss your hands, or sometimes your cheeks . . . is frightful. If you reject me perhaps I shall address myself to Madame d'Hardancourt [her mother] and she will be willing to live with me."

This aroused Madame Brillon's mock jealousy. She wrote, "I give you my word of honor that I will become your wife in Paradise, on condition, however, that you do not make too many conquests among the heavenly maidens while you are waiting for me. I want a faithful husband when I take one for eternity."

Franklin replied with an amusing treatise on jealousy and infidelity, and a proposal for a personal peace pact between them, paralleling the more important treaty with France which was then the subject of his serious attention:

What a difference, my dear friend, between you and me: you find in me innumerable faults, while I see only one in you (and perhaps that is the fault of my spectacles). I can sense a kind of greediness in you which causes you to monopolize all my affection; and leaves none for the other lovely ladies of your country. You fancy that it is not possible for my affection (or my love) to be divided without being thereby diminished. You are mistaken; and you forget the trifling manner in which you have treated me. You deny me, and completely disregard, all that might be sensual in our love, permitting me only a few polite and modest kisses such as you might bestow upon some little cousin. All this astonishes me, for why shouldn't I be able to give to others without subtracting from what belongs to you? The sentiments of esteem, admiration, respect, and even affection itself can multiply themselves as often as the objects that merit that affection present themselves; and still there remain the same sentiments for the original object of affection, who, consequently, should have no cause to complain of injury. . . .

You see, then, how unjust you are in your demands and in the open war which you declare against me, if I do not comply with them; in fact, it is I who have the greatest reason to complain! My poor little cupid, whom, indeed, you should have cherished, instead of being plump and playful (like those in your elegant pictures), is thin and ready to die of hunger for want of the goodly nourishment which his mother inhumanly refuses him and, moreover, now wants to clip his little wings so that he may not go searching elsewhere! I fancy that neither of us will gain anything in this war; and consequently feeling myself the weakest, I shall make overtures for peace (a thing which, indeed, should be done by the wisest).

For a peace to be durable it is necessary that the terms of the treaty be subject to the strictest principles of justice and reciprocity: in which spirit I have drawn up the following articles:

Article I. There must be peace, friendship, and eternal love between Madame B. and Mr. Franklin.

Article II. In order to keep this peace inviolate, Madame B., for her part, stipulates and agrees that Mr. F. shall visit her whenever she asks him.

Article III. That he shall remain as long as she wishes.

Article IV. That when he is with her, he shall be obliged to take tea, play chess, listen to music, or do anything that she might ask of him.

Article V. And that he shall love no other woman but her.

Article VI. The said Mr. Franklin on his part, stipulates and agrees that he will visit Madame B. whenever he pleases.

Article VII. That he will stay as long as he pleases.

Article VIII. That whenever he is with her he will do anything he pleases.

Article IX. And that he will not love any other woman as long as he finds her amiable.

Tell me what you think of these preliminaries? They seem to me to express the point of view and real intention of each party more clearly than most treaties.

I shall insist strongly on the eighth article although without much hope of your consent to carry it out; and on the ninth also, although I despair of ever finding another woman whom I could love with the same tenderness, remaining forever, my dear, dear, friend.

Franklin's other neighbor, Madame Helvetius, was the sixtyish widow of a prominent French philosopher. In Auteuil, adjacent to Passy, her salon was patronized by a group of liberal intellectuals. Franklin was first brought there by Turgot, powerful minister of finance. She had been beautiful. To her, one gallant who lived to be a hundred paid the famous compliment, "Ah Madame, if I were only eighty again." Franklin equaled this by replying, when she chided him for a delayed visit, "Madame, I am waiting till the nights are longer."

Many men admired Madame Helvetius and respected her wit and intellect. Some women held a different view. Abigail, wife of John Adams, left this catty description of the older woman:

She entered the room with a careless, jaunty air; upon seeing the ladies who were strangers to her, she bawled out, "Ah! mon Dieu, where is Franklin? Why did you not tell me there were ladies here?" You must suppose her speaking all this in French. "How I look!" said she, taking hold of a chemise made of tiffany, which she had on over a blue lutestring, and which looked as much upon the decay as her beauty, for she was once a handsome woman; her hair was frizzled; over it she had a small straw hat, with a dirty gauze scarf thrown over her shoulders. She ran out of the room; when she returned, the Doctor entered at one door, she at the other; upon which she ran forward to him, caught him by the hand, "Helas! Franklin!" — then gave him a double kiss, one upon each cheek, and another upon his forehead. When we went into the room to dine, she was placed between the Doctor and Mr. Adams. She carried on the chief of the conversation at dinner, frequently locking her hands into the Doctor's, and sometimes spreading her arms upon the backs of both of the gentlemen's chairs; then throwing her arm carelessly upon the Doctor's neck.

I should have been greatly astonished at this conduct, if the good Doctor had not told me that in this lady I should see a genuine Frenchwoman, wholly free from affectation, or stiffness of behavior, and one of the best women in the world. For this I must take the Doctor's word; but I should have set her down for a very bad one, although sixty years of age, and a widow. I own I was highly disgusted, and never wish for an acquaintance with any ladies of this cast.

The old Doctor apparently proposed marriage to Madame Helvetius, but whether seriously or as part of a mock romance with which they amused themselves is not clear. Madame Brillon thought it was serious — although the two women were never jealous of each other. When Franklin left for America they wept together and Madame Brillon blamed Madame Helvetius for letting him go.

The Frenchwoman turned Franklin's proposal down because of her memory of her late husband to whom she kept "upon the table, under a glass" in her bedroom, "a monument . . . over which hung his picture, which was very handsome." Franklin was not broken-hearted. He immediately wrote her a short, gay bagatelle:

Mortified at the barbarous resolution pronounced by you so positively yesterday evening, that you would remain single the rest of your life as a compliment due to the memory of your husband, I retired to my chamber. Throwing myself upon my bed, I dreamt that I was dead, and was transported to the Elysian Fields.

I was asked whether I wished to see any persons in particular; to which I replied that I wished to see the philosophers. "There are two who live here at hand in this garden; they are good neighbors, and very friendly toward one another." "Who are they?" "Socrates and Helvetius." "I esteem them both highly; but let me see Helvetius first, because I understand a little French, but not a word of Greek." I was conducted to him; he received me with much courtesy, having known me, he said, by character, sometime past. He asked me a thousand questions relative to the war, the present state of religion, of liberty, of the government in France, "You do not inquire then," said I, "after your dear friend, Madame Helvetius; yet she loves you exceedingly. I was in her company not more than an hour ago." "Ah," said he, "you make me recur to my past happiness, which ought to be forgotten in order to be happy here. For many years I could think of nothing but her, though at length I am consoled. I have taken another wife, the most like her that I could find; she is not indeed altogether so handsome, but she has a great fund of wit and good sense, and her whole study is to please me. She is at this moment gone to fetch the best nectar and ambrosia to regale me; stay here awhile and you will see her." "I perceive," said I, "that your former friend is more faithful to you than you are to her; she has had several good offers, but has refused them all. I will confess to you that I loved her extremely; but she was cruel to me, and rejected me peremptorily for your sake." "I pity you sincerely," said he, "for she is an excellent woman, handsome and amiable . . ." As he finished these words the new Madame Helvetius entered with the nectar, and I recognized her immediately as my former American friend, Mrs. Franklin! I reclaimed her, but she answered me coldly; "I was a good wife to you for forty-nine years, nearly half a century; let that content you. I have formed a new connection here, which will last to eternity."

Indignant at this refusal of my Eurydice, I immediately resolved to quit those ungrateful shades, and return to this good world again, to behold the sun and you! Here I am; let us *avenge ourselves!*

History has left no picture of a lecher at Passy. The two women and, to a lesser extent others, were charming companions to an old man whom they admired and adored. There were chess, and music, and poetry, and scintillating conversation and, when he left, unhappiness at the loss of a great and good friend. Madame Helvetius wrote:

I see you in your litter, every step taking you farther from us, lost to me and all my friends who love you so much and to whom you leave such long regrets. I am afraid that you are suffering and the journey is tiring you and making your ailment worse. If that is so, come back, dear friend, to us. You will adorn my little retreat. . . . You will increase our happiness and we shall contribute to yours. You cannot doubt this. You could read it in my heart and in the hearts of all my good friends, who are also yours.

And Madame Brillon said:

I had so full a heart yesterday in leaving you that I feared for you and myself a grief-stricken moment which could only add to the pain which our separation causes me, without proving to you further the tender and unalterable affection that I have vowed to you for always; every day of my life I shall recall that a great man, a sage, was willing to be my friend, my wishes will follow him everywhere, my heart will regret him incessantly, incessantly I shall say, I passed eight years with Doctor Franklin, they have flown and I shall see him no more! Nothing in the world could console me for this loss, except the thought of the peace and happiness that you are about to find in the bosom of your family.

Franklin lived for four years after his return from France in 1786. For most of the last year he was bedridden, nursed principally by his daughter Sally. Polly Hewson came to read to him, as did his Sally's nine-year-old daughter Deborah. Shortly before his death Sally sought to cheer him by saying that he would recover and live for years longer. Franklin calmly replied: "I hope not." When she suggested that he change his position in bed so that he could breathe more easily, he replied: "A dying man can do nothing easy." Sally was resting when her father quietly died at eleven P.M. with his two oldest grandsons, Temple Franklin and Benny Bache at his bedside.

CHAPTER III

The Unlucky Loves of George Washington

Benjamin Franklin sought a bride with £100 to pay off the debt on his print shop before settling on Deborah. George Washington's sights were aimed far above £100. Martha Custis, to whom he seems to have proposed at their second private meeting, was the richest young widow in Virginia. Since he was, by his own admission, in love with another woman at the time it seems reasonable to assume that Martha's wealth had something to do with the choice. Of course it may have been love at first sight — but, if so, it is difficult to explain the letter that he wrote to Sally Fairfax, avowing his love for her, while he was engaged to Martha.

There is ample evidence that the Father of His Country, who fathered no human offspring, liked girls. And there is equal evidence that, until he met Martha, he was repeatedly unlucky in love. All of the flames of his youth — to at least one of whom he proposed — married someone else. His lack of success with the ladies seems strange because George was a handsome young man. But he seems to have lacked self-confidence in pursuing his amatory affairs with the belles of

94

tidewater Virginia; perhaps social insecurity made him less aggressive than other young Virginia gentlemen.

George Washington was a gentleman; but compared with the scions of the first families of the eastern part of the state — the Lees, Randolphs, Byrds, etc. — he was on the lower rung of the upper class. He could ride to hounds with the best of them, he shot a good game of billiards, was a fine dancer, and handled cards well. These were full-time occupations for most young Virginia gentlemen. To them George added another — he worked for a living. Unlike many of his peers, he had not been sent to England to be educated — had not even gone to the local institution of higher learning, William and Mary. After four or five years of formal schooling — part of it under a convict servant whom his father bought for a schoolmaster — George dusted off his dead father's surveying instruments and went to work.

Before that he had briefly attended a school run by a minister in Fredericksburg. Here one legend introduces the first woman in his life by recording that while other boys played games, George "romped with one of the largest girls. This was so unusual that it excited no little astonishment among the other lads."

Washington's first known love was a girl named Frances Alexander to whom he composed an atrocious, unfinished, acrostic.

> *F*rom your bright sparkling Eyes I was undone;
> *R*ays, you have; more transparent than the Sun,
> *A*midst its glory in the rising day
> *N*one can you equal in your bright array;
> *C*onstant in your calm and unspotted Mind;
> *E*qual to all, but will to none Prove kind,
> *S*o knowing, seldom one so Young, you'll Find.
> *A*h! woe's me, that I should Love and conceal

Long have I wish'd, but never dare reveal,
Even though severely Loves Pains I feel;
Xerxes that great, was't free from Cupids Dart,
And all the greatest Heroes, felt the smart.

This was apparently written when George was sixteen; it is found in a notebook in which he made his first entry of a survey in 1748. The subject of the acrostic is certainly Frances Alexander, daughter of a neighboring family. Although George hurdled the difficult *x* in "Alexa" he did not or could not finish the *nder*. Perhaps the sixteen-year-old realized that he would never be a Byron — or he lost interest in Frances.

In the same notebook is another sample of George's love-sick sonnet making. The young lady who inspired this is unknown and may have been the same Frances, although there is no assurance of this, for some of George's early crushes seem to have overlapped.

Oh Ye Gods why should my Poor Resistless Heart
  Stand to oppose thy might and Power
At Last surrender to cupids feather'd Dart
  And now lays Bleeding every Hour
For her that's Pityless of my grief and Woes,
  And will not on me Pity take.
I'll sleep amongst my most inveterate Foes
  And with gladness never wish to wake,
In deluding sleepings let my Eyelids close
  That in enraptured Dream I may
In a soft lulling sleep and gentle repose
  Possess those joys denied by Day.

After this, for the rest of his life, Washington gave up writing poetry.

Somewhat later, but while he was still in his teens, there was a mystery woman in Washington's young love life who is known only as the "Lowland Beauty." Evidence of her exists in copies of three very similar letters that he wrote. One of them, to Robin Washington, contains an expression of his juvenile ardor and incipient fickleness in this meandering sentence — surely one of the longest in the literature of love:

> My place of residence is at present at His Lordships [Lord Fairfax's estate, Belvoir] where I might was my heart disengag'd pass my time very pleasantly as theres a very agreeable Young Lady Lives in the same house (Colo George Fairfax's Wife's Sister) but as thats only adding Fuel to fire it makes me the more uneasy for by often and unavoidably being in Company with her revives my former Passion for your Low Land Beauty whereas was I to live more retired from young Women I might in some measure eliviate my sorrows by burying that chast and troublesome Passion in the grave of oblivion or etarnall forgetfulness for as I am very well assured thats the only antidote or remedy that I shall be relievd by or only recess that can administer any cure or help to me as I am well convinced was I ever to attempt any thing I should only get a denial which would be only adding grief to uneasiness.

For much of the nineteenth century, several First Families of Virginia claimed the Lowland Beauty as an ancestor, although nobody knows her true identity. One intriguing possibility is that she was Lucy Grymes, who later married Henry Lee and became the mother of Lighthorse Harry Lee, one of Washington's generals, and the grandmother of Robert E. Lee, who married the daughter of Washington's adopted son. The girl who beguiled and, possibly, later consoled young Washington was Mary Cary who at the age of fourteen was visiting her sister Sally Fairfax, mistress of Belvoir, the neighboring plantation to Mount Vernon. Today, fourteen is considered too young for a girl to be "going steady," but customs were different in colonial Virginia, where twelve-

year-old girls thought and seriously wrote of matrimony. One
little lass confided to a friend in London: "I am little more
than twelve years old. . . . And yet I pretend not to ridicule
the holy sacred institution . . . you can't forbear a fling at
femalities; believe me Curiosity is as imputable to the sons
as the Daughters of Eve. . . . [Yet I am] not so eager to tye a
Knot which Death alone can Dissolve."

The extent to which Mary Cary consoled George for the
loss of the Lowland Beauty is unknown, although there is a
legend that he later asked her father for her hand. The tale
has it that, as soon as he made his business known to haughty
Colonel Cary, the father growled at him: "If this is your
business here, sir, I wish you to leave the house, for my
daughter has been accustomed to ride in her own coach."

Whether or not George asked for Mary Cary's hand, it is
certain that he proposed to another girl, Betsy Fauntleroy.
Betsy may have been the Lowland Beauty (she certainly was *a*
lowland beauty), although Washington's involvement with
her was three or four years later, when he was twenty, and
the romances of George's youth usually did not last this long.
He apparently proposed to Betsy at some indeterminate time
and was refused. Then, in May, 1752, he renewed his suit in
a letter to her which he enclosed in one to her father, saying:
"I should have been down long before this, but my business
in Frederick detained me somewhat longer than I expected,
and immediately on my return from thence I was taken with
a violent pleurisy, which has reduced me very low; but purpose, as soon as I recover my strength, to wait on Miss Betsy,
in hopes of a revocation of the former cruel sentence, and
see if I can meet with any alteration in my favor. I have
enclosed a letter to her, which should be much obliged to
you for the delivery of it." Perhaps father Fauntleroy never

gave Betsy the letter; if he did her answer must have been another resounding "no" for Washington never mentioned her again.

There were two other women whose lives briefly touched that of the most revered Founding Father in his youth; although not amorously. In the summer of 1752 George went swimming. While he disported himself in the waves two women "robbed" his clothes. Whether this means that they stole the clothes or only any valuables that they contained is not clear. A record in the Order Book of the Spotsylvania County Court House tells all that is known of the case:

3 Dec. 1751. Ann Carrol and Mary McDaniel Senr. of Fredericksburgh, being Committed to the Gaol of this County by William Hunter Gent, on Suspicion of Felony & Charged with Robing the Cloaths of Mr. George Washington when he was washing in the River some time last Summer, the Court having heard Several Evidences Are of Oppinion that the said Ann Carrol be discharged & Admitted an Evidence for our Lord the King against the said Mary McDaniel.

And Upon Considering the whole Evidences & the prisoners defence, The Court are of Oppinion that the said Mary McDaniel is guilty of petty Larceny, whereupon the said Mary desired immediate punishment for the sd Crime & relied on the Mercy of the Court, therefore it is ordered that the Sheriff carry her to the Whipping post & inflict fifteen lashes on her bare back, And then she be discharged.

Although he would later become no stranger to floggings, which he ordered for the slightest infraction of discipline when he commanded troops, it is fortunate for Washington's sensibilities that he was not there to witness the punishment. He had sailed for Barbados to care for his ailing halfbrother Lawrence before the trial.

It is strange that none of the belles who engaged the heart

of the young surveyor gave him any encouragement; none would even become engaged to him or promise to wait until he achieved a better place in the world. Apparently all had their eyes on the main immediate chance and none had second sight that would permit them to envision the clouds of glory that would later surround their suitor. There is a story that, when Washington returned to Williamsburg with Martha after he had achieved his great fame, one or more aging dames fainted at the thought that they might have been the First Lady.

One early commentator reasons that Washington's repeated failures in his young affairs of the heart were because: "He may have been too modest and diffident a young man to interest the ladies, or he was too poor at that time, or he had not received a college or university education in England or Virginia, or, as is most probable, God had reserved him for greater things . . . an early marriage might have been injurious to his future usefulness."

The great love of Washington's young life was his neighbor's wife, Sally Fairfax, nee Cary. To understand their relationship a few words of the connection between the Washingtons and the Fairfaxes are in order. George's older half-brother Lawrence built a home on the Potomac, which he called Mount Vernon in honor of Admiral Vernon, under whom he had served as a Captain at the siege of Cartagena. George spent much of his adolescence here after their father died and Lawrence had become a second father to him. Lawrence married Anne Fairfax, the girl next door at Belvoir.

Belvoir was originally owned by eccentric and irrascible Lord Thomas Fairfax, who also owned millions of acres in the western part of the state. When Lord Thomas was thwarted in a love affair he became a misogynist and a recluse in a castle that he built in the Shenandoah Valley. Belvoir was managed by his cousin and agent, Colonel William Fairfax, father of Anne and of a son, George William Fairfax, seven years older than George Washington. In his late teens Washington was a frequent visitor at Belvoir. He made his first long survey trip with George William to measure some of Lord Fairfax's western lands. In 1748, when George Washington was sixteen, George William Fairfax married Sarah (Sally) Cary and brought her to Belvoir.

To complete the story of the real estate on the banks of the Potomac, Lawrence Washington died in 1752, leaving a life interest in Mount Vernon to his wife, after which it was to go to his daughter Sarah. If Sarah died without issue it was to go to George. Sarah died in infancy, Anne remarried and moved away, George bought out her life interest and became master of Mount Vernon.

When George first met Sally Fairfax, his neighbor's bride was a charming eighteen-year-old, five years younger than her husband and two years older than George. Although she has never been described as an outstanding beauty she was charming, intelligent, graceful and humorous. George later wrote of her "mirth, good humor, ease of mind — and what else?" Sally was certainly the most fascinating and tantalizing girl that George had ever met. It is impossible to determine when he realized that he was in love with her.

There is no indication that there was anything improper in the relationship between George and Sally. The national historian of the Colonial Dames of America, Mrs. Sally Nelson Robins, devoted years of research to the subject and summed it up as follows:

After Sally married Fairfax, Washington was frequently at Belvoir and Mrs. Fairfax became his patron and instructress in the fine arts of courtesy and good breeding, while her brain, in its strength and flowering, matched his. She rounded the angles of this sturdy, remarkable young man, and gave him the rare opportunity of mingling with the essence of refinement and culture.

She enmeshed him with her charm and beauty, and while his affection for her, as he has it, was chaste, it was, probably, no less troublesome. Again his congenital and marvelous restraint kept him absolutely from the semblance of mischief. I consider his early romances but zephyrs to this one crimson whirlwind passion of his life.

The ten years between George's first meeting with Sally and his engagement to Martha were, in general, years of discouragement to George. True, he was getting ahead financially. Washington always had an eye for the dollar, and when his surveys disclosed good land he bought choice parcels for himself before the price went up. By the time he was twenty he owned some 5,000 acres; some bought, some inherited. His job as county surveyor paid £100 per year and he made as much more from private surveys. He was becoming a man of some substance.

But his military career, which started when he became Major Washington as a militia adjutant shortly before he was twenty-one (a post that also paid £100 per year), did not thrive so well. He first led troops against the French and was soundly defeated at Fort Necessity. He was with General Braddock when the English were disastrously ambushed before Fort DuQuesne. Although American history has made Washington the hero of this debacle, this was not apparent at the time. He quarreled constantly with the Governor about the amount of his pay and with other officers about rank, and several times threatened to resign.

Upon his return from the field Sally undoubtedly consoled him for his misfortunes and his real or fancied grievances.

She may have flirted with him to cheer him up. Once his diffidence was penetrated, Washington was an interesting subject for any woman, particularly such a tantalizing one as Sally. There is no record of what she felt for George; but many little things seem to indicate that she was quite possibly a tease. She openly competed with other married ladies for the attentions of General Braddock; a man who had many attentions for pretty females. This competition was, on Sally's part, undoubtedly social rather than sexual, but Washington wrote her one letter explaining the reason why "Mrs. Wardrope is a greater favorie of Gen. Braddock than Mrs. F __ x." The reason was a gift from the former of "delicious cake and potted woodcocks." George did not send this letter; by this time he may have developed enough social tact to realize that it is dangerous to comment on a lady's social affairs.

If George was involved with any other woman after he met Sally and before he married Martha, history has no record of it — with one slight exception. During one of his quarrels about rank he journeyed to Boston, in 1756, to lay the situation before Governor Shirley who was in top command of colonial forces. On the way he stayed in New York at the home of Beverly Robinson, son of the speaker of the Virginia House of Burgesses. Robinson had married Susanna Philipse. Susanna had a younger sister, Mary — called Polly. And Mary had — or would have — 51,102 acres of land from Philipse Manor which spread along the banks of the Hudson.

Washington lingered in New York for ten days on his way north. He attended "Mr. Baron's rout"; possibly without Miss Philipse for he spent only six shillings. But he probably took her twice to see the Microcosm of the World in Miniature. On one occasion his account book shows an expenditure "for treating Ladies to ye Mm. one pound eight shillings," and at another time "one pound four shillings" for the same purpose.

There is nothing to indicate that George had more than a couple of dates with the New York heiress, other than the presumption that his passion for land would not have let him ignore an attractive single woman, albeit two years his senior, who would own so much of it. Also, he wrote to a friend in Connecticut, Joseph Chew, about a year later asking him how the land lay in New York; or so it would seem from Chew's answer to this missing letter. His friend wrote:

> As to the latter part of your letter what shall I say. I often had the pleasure of breakfasting with the charming Polly; Roger Morris was there (don't be startled) but not always, you know him he is a lady's man, always something to say, the town talked of it as a sure and settled affair. I can't say I think so and that I much doubt it . . . but how can you be excused to continue so long at Philadelphia?
>
> I think I should have made a kind of flying march of it if it had been only to have seen whether the works were sufficient to withstand a vigorous attack, you a soldier and a lover . . . I intend to set out tomorrow for New York where I will not be wanting to let Miss Polly know the sincere regard a friend of mine has for her. And I am sure if she had my eyes to see through she would prefer him to all others.

The Roger Morris referred to was a British officer who had been with Washington on the Braddock campaign. Polly Philipse married him and they built a large house on Harlem Heights which, now known as the Jumel Mansion, is still a New York historical landmark. English descendants of the Morrises claim that Washington did make a flying dash from Philadelphia to propose to Polly and was turned down. This is almost surely one of the many Washington legends; his time in mid-1757 is so well accounted for that it does not seem likely he could have made a five- or six-day trip to New York.

Another story that is almost certainly part legendary had to do with Washington's first meeting with the widow Custis, who would become Martha Washington. The supposed meeting was immortalized by George Washington Parke Custis, Martha's grandson. In the florid manner of the day, George Custis wrote:

It was in 1758, that an officer, attired in a military undress, and attended by a body-servant, tall and *militaire* as his chief, crossed the ferry called William's, over the Pamunkey a branch of the York River. On the boat touching the southern or New Kent side, the soldier's progress was arrested by one of those personages who give the beau ideal of the Virginia Gentleman of the old *regime,* the very soul of kindliness and hospitality. It was in vain the soldier urged his business at Williamsburg, important communications to the governor, etc. Mr. Chamberlayne, on whose domain the *militaire* had just landed, would hear of no excuse. Colonel Washington (for the soldier was he) was a name and character so dear to all the Virginians, that his passing by one of the old castles of the commonwealth, without calling and partaking of the hospitalities of the host, was entirely out of the question. The colonel, however, did not surrender at discretion, but stoutly maintained his ground, till Chamberlayne bringing up his reserve, in the intimation that he would introduce his friend to a young and charming widow, then beneath his roof, the soldier capitulated, on condition that he should dine, "only dine," and then by pressing his charger and borrowing of the night, he would reach Williamsburg before his excellency could shake off his morning slumbers. Orders were accordingly issued to Bishop, the colonel's body-servant and faithful follower, who, together with the fine English charger, had been bequeathed by the dying Braddock to Major Washington, on the famed and fatal field of the Monongahela. Bishop, bred in the school of European discipline, raised his hand to his cap, as much as to say, "Your honor's orders shall be obeyed."

The colonel now proceeded to the mansion, and was introduced to various guests (for when was a Virginia domicile of the olden time without guests?), and above all, to the charming widow. Tradition relates that they were mutually pleased on this their first interview, nor is it remarkable; they were of an age when impressions are strongest. The lady was fair to behold, of fascinating manners, and splendidly endowed with worldly benefits. The hero, fresh from his early fields, redolent of fame, and with a form on which "every god did seem to set his seal, to give the world assurance of a man."

The morning passed pleasantly away. Evening came, with Bishop, true to his orders and firm at his post, holding his favorite charger with one hand, while the other was waiting to offer the ready stirrup. The sun sank in the horizon, and yet the colonel appeared not. And then the old soldier marveled at his chief's delay. " 'Twas strange, 'twas passing strange" — surely he was not wont to be a single moment behind his appointments, for he was the most punctual of all men. Meantime, the host enjoyed the scene of the veteran on duty at the gate, while the colonel was so agreeably employed in the parlor; and proclaiming that no guest ever left his house after sunset, his military visitor was, without much difficulty, persuaded to order Bishop to put up the horses for the night. The sun rode high in the heaven in the ensuing day, when the enamored soldier pressed with his spur his charger's side, and speeded on his way to the seat of government, where, having despatched his public business, he retraced his steps, and, at the White House, the engagement took place, with preparations for the marriage.

George Custis was not yet born when this was supposed to have happened. He may have heard some such story from his grandmother when he was a child but he did not write it down for some seventy-five years after the event. It may have some elements of truth. A Chamberlayne who was a cousin of Martha's first husband did have a home at William's Ferry on the Pamunkey. It is entirely possible that George met

Martha here on one of his many visits to Williamsburg; but
the meeting probably took place before the death of her first
husband, Daniel Parke Custis. What makes the story unlikely
is the date — 1758. Washington made only one visit to Williamsburg in that year prior to the time he is known to have
been betrothed to Martha. He was not carrying dispatches to
the Governor. He had been ill, believed he had tuberculosis,
and was going to see a doctor from whom he expected to
receive a death sentence. His route is known as far as the
home of Beverly Robinson's father. From here he would have
to ride fifteen miles out of the way to cross the Pamunkey
at William's Ferry. Considering the state of his health, the
purpose of his journey, and the fact that he was not supposed
to have known Martha, or that she was at Chamberlayne's,
this is not believable.

Also, it stretches credulity to believe that George did not
know Martha before Custis's death in 1757. Washington was
frequently in Williamsburg, where Daniel Custis had inherited a town house — the main Custis home was the White
House on the York River, thirty-five miles away. Society in
Williamsburg was small and during the meetings of the Assembly there was continual entertaining. George and Martha
moved in the same circles and it is unbelievable that they
would not have met in this way before the spring of 1758.

The only other information on George's courtship of
Martha is in two entries in his account book which show that
he visited the widow at the White House in March 16th,
1758, stayed for a day or a day and a half, and returned for
another visit the next week. Something probably happened during these visits. After the second one George immediately ordered from London "by the first ship bound to
any part of Virginia . . . as much of the best superfine blue

cotton velvet as will make a coat, waistcoat, and breeches for a tall man, with a fine silk button to suit it . . . six pairs of the very neatest shoes . . . [and] six pair gloves." At about the same time Martha ordered, also from London: "One genteel suite of clothes for myself to be grave but not extravagant and not mourning. . . . I have sent a nightgown to be dide of a fashionable couler fitt for me to ware and beg you won't [will] have it dide better than that I sent you last year but was very badly done. This gown is of a good length for me." George's blue velvet and Martha's "genteel suite" that was not mourning suggest that the couple had reached an "understanding."

Long before he dreamed of being another in the long line of Presidents from Virginia, Woodrow Wilson wrote a biography of Washington in which he summarized the love life of the first President to this time:

This was not his first adventure in love. . . . No young Virginian could live twenty-six years amidst fair women in that hale and sociable colony without being touched again and again by the quick passion; and this man had the blood of a lover beyond his fellows. Despite the shyness of a raw lad who lived much in the open, he had relished the company of lively women from the first, meeting their gay sallies sometimes with a look from his frank blue eyes that revealed more than he knew. Love had first found him out in earnest six years ago, when he was but just turned of twenty; and it had taken all the long while since to forget his repulse at the hands of a fair young beauty in that day of passion. Mary Philipse had but taken his fancy for a moment, because he could not pass such a woman by and deem himself still a true Virginian. It was more serious that he had been much in the company, these last years, of a fair neighbor of the vivacious house of Cary, whose wit and beauty had haunted him in the very thick of campaigns upon the frontier, and who still mastered his heart now and again, with a sort of imperious charm. . . . It may well have made him glad of misadventures in the past to know his heart safe now.

Martha Custis, nee Dandridge, was eight months older than George. Her father was a planter and a member of a fairly old but not outstandingly prosperous Virginia family. Martha was the oldest daughter and as a child learned more house-keeping than spelling. She could sew a fine seam and play the spinet at least well enough to teach her granddaughter when the time came. But on the whole, her accomplishments were domestic rather than artistic or intellectual. When she was eighteen her trim little figure and really handsome brown eyes attracted the attention of thirty-seven-year-old Daniel Parke Custis.

Daniel Custis was the rather timid son of Colonel John Custis, current head of a wealthy family on the Eastern Shore. He was very much under the thumb of his cantankerous father, who had never approved of any girl in whom Daniel showed an interest; hence his bachelorhood at an age when some of his contemporaries had marriageable children. The old man threatened to disinherit his son in favor of a Negro boy if he was not obeyed; in fact, he once made a will to that effect. Inexplicably he liked Martha because of some forthright speech she addressed to him. Daniel's emissary — he was afraid to approach the Colonel directly — reported that "he is more enamored with her character than you are with her person . . . hurry down immediately for fear he should change the strong inclination he has to your marrying directly." An amusing anecdote of the Custises is that Colonel John stopped speaking to his wife, Frances Parke, shortly after their marriage and, until she died, they communicated only through servants. An epitaph which he positively ordered be put on his tomb may still be read at Arlington Cemetery:

> Aged 71 Years and yet lived but seven years
> Which was the space of time he kept
> A Bachelor's house at Arlington
> On the Eastern shore of Virginia.

There was none of Colonel John's violence in his son. Daniel and Martha lived quietly and contentedly at the White House for the eight years that he survived after their marriage in 1749. They had four children, two of whom died in infancy. Of the two remaining, Martha — called Patsy — was a sickly child and subject to fits throughout her life. The son, John Parke Custis, was good-natured but had little initiative or ambition. The children were aged two and four respectively when Washington proposed to their mother.

Daniel Parke died without leaving a will. Martha's one-third share of his estate was valued at over £23,000 not including a great deal of land which was involved in long-drawn-out litigation. Since the children's expenses could be charged against the estate until they reached their majority, Martha at the age of twenty-seven was a very wealthy and desirable widow. George badly needed a mistress for Mount Vernon. Martha badly needed a strong male hand to guide the children, the slaves, the agents and overseers, and the sprawling lands. In every respect the union of George and Martha was practical. He was undoubtedly not the first Virginia gentleman who had come to the White House to pay court to the young widow. But Martha's cool common sense dictated that he was by all means the most acceptable.

Immediately after his engagement to Martha, George left for Winchester to take part in a campaign to redeem Braddock's defeat and capture present-day Pittsburgh from the

French. When he had joined Braddock, in 1755, George had tried to induce Sally Fairfax to write to him. In one letter he said, "In order to engage your correspondence, I think it expedient just to deserve it; which I shall endeavor to do by embracing the earliest and every opportunity of writing to you." When he received no reply he penned this rather pathetic appeal:

When I had the pleasure to see you last, you expressed an inclination to be informed of my safe arrival at camp with the charge that was entrusted to my care [her horse] but at the same time desired it might be communicated in a letter to somebody of your acquaintance. This I took as a gentle rebuke and polite manner of forbidding me corresponding with you. . . . If I am right in this I hope you will excuse my present presumption. . . . If on the contrary these are fearful apprehensions only, how easy is it to remove my suspicion, enliven my [spirits?] and make me happier than the day is long, by honoring me with a correspondence which you did once partly promise.

If Sally wrote to him at this time the letters have never come to light, nor is there an explanation for her command that he write to her through a third party. This might be construed that her husband would object to her receiving letters from George; or that she feared that George might write something that would compromise her. But there is no evidence on this.

At the outset of this new campaign there is no known correspondence until September 1, 1758. On that date Sally's husband acknowledged the receipt of two letters from Washington, saying: "The first Mrs. Fairfax undertakes to answer, as I don't care to detain the bearer." The letter that Sally wrote George is missing, but his reply indicates that it must have been brief. His reply was not. In words that were sufficiently vague so that they might have been explained had the

letter fallen into other hands than Sally's, he told her that he
loved her and asked how she felt about him:

> Camp at Fort Cumberland, 12th
> September, 1758.

Dear Madam,

Yesterday I was honored with your short but very agreeable
favor of the first inst. How joyfully I catch at the happy occasion
of renewing a correspondence which I feared was disrelished on
your part, I leave to time, that never failing expositor of all
things, and to a monitor equally faithful in my own breast, to
testify. In silence I now express my joy; silence, which in some
cases, I wish the present, speaks more intelligently than the
sweetest eloquence.

If you allow that any honor can be derived from my opposition to our present system of management, you destroy the merit
of it entirely in me by attributing my anxiety to the animating
prospect of possessing Mrs. Custis. . . . 'Tis true, I profess myself
a votary of love. I acknowledge that a lady is in the case, and
further I confess that this lady is known to you. Yes, Madame, as
well as she is to one who is too sensible of her charms to deny
the power whose influence he feels and must ever submit to. I
feel the force of her amiable beauties in the recollection of a
thousand tender passages that I could wish to obliterate, till I
am bid to revive them. But experience, alas! sadly reminds me
how impossible this is, and evinces an opinion which I have long
entertained, that there is a destiny which has the control of our
actions, not to be resisted by the strongest efforts of human
nature.

You have drawn me, dear Madame, or rather I have drawn
myself, into an honest confession of a simple fact. Misconstrue
not my meaning; doubt it not, nor expose it. The world has no
business to know the object of my love, declared in this manner
to you, when I want to conceal it. One thing above all things in
this world I wish to know, and only one person of your acquaintance can solve me that, or guess my meaning. But adieu to this
till happier times, if I ever shall see them. The hours at present

[are] melancholy dull. Neither the rugged toils of war, nor the gentler conflict of A . . . B . . . [Assembly Balls?], is in my choice. I dare believe you are as happy as you say. I wish I was happy also. Mirth, good humor, ease of mind, and — what else? — cannot fail to render you so and comsumate your wishes. . . .

I cannot easily forgive the unseasonable haste of my last express, if he deprived me thereby of a single word you intended to add. The time of the present messenger is, as the last might have been, entirely at your disposal.

This letter did not come to light until 1886, in a bundle of eighty-one faded missives still in the possession of the Fairfax family. When it was first printed in the New York *Herald* it raised a storm of protest among the cult of Washingtonians who believed that their idol, whom history had dehumanized, could do no wrong nor think no evil. One "expert" blandly asserted that the letter was addressed to Martha, without attempting to explain how it got among the Fairfax papers or the reference in the text to "the animating prospect of possessing Mrs. Custis." Another attempted explanation was that it was addressed to Mary Cary; which was not really of much help in whitewashing George's reputation because Mary Cary had been Mary Ambler for six years by the time it was written.

The letter from William Fairfax saying that his wife was going to write George on September first, and the acknowledgment in the love letter of "Your short but very agreeable favor of the first inst." leave little doubt that the letter was addressed to Sally. It should be emphasized that there is no evidence of an improper relationship between Washington and his neighbor's wife. His greatest biographer, Douglas Southall Freeman, writes:

There is no reason to assume any relationship that was not kept within the strictest proprieties. It scarcely could have escaped

observation in a small society, having few subjects about which
to gossip, that Washington admired Sally and that he displayed
to her the measure of gallantry permissible on the part of a young
bachelor and neighbor to the attractive wife of a close friend. On
the other hand, scandal almost certainly would have been reported. Sally herself was of a prudent nature. Late in life she
wrote that it had been her maxim "to go without what I wanted
ever so much if I could not pay instantly, for I considered that
I robbed the seller of the interest of his money by withholding
the payment." A woman guided by that principle might want the
admiration of the tall master of Mount Vernon, who was already
the most renowned young Virginian, but she would not take any
chances with him. Washington . . . never broke out, in any other
surviving letter, as he did in this one, prompted by the receipt
of a missive in her beautiful handwriting. Even if he was engaged
and she was married, it was natural, it was youthfully human,
for him to try to find out, before he went into the wilderness
again, whether she really cared for him. Almost every man of
twenty-six has at least that measure of vanity. The language of
the letter is so involved and obscure that at best it is interpreted
as *double-entendre,* but whatever Washington's reason for writing as he did, no explanation is quite so unreasonable as one that
would deny what he certainly meant to say — that he was going
to marry Martha but was in hopeless love with Sally and wished
above everything else to know whether she loved him.

Sally's answer to Washington's appeal has never come to
light. His next letter makes it clear that it was agreeable,
albeit unsatisfactory. She wrote about what the young ladies
in her circle were doing and told him that she was going to
appear in a performance of Addison's "Cato," playing the
part of Cato's daughter, Marcia. In his reply Washington
expressed a longing to play the part of Marcia's soldier-lover,
Juba. But Sally did not tell him the "one thing above all
things" that he wanted to know, for he started his next letter
by writing "Dear Madam, Do we still misunderstand each

other's letters? I think it must appear so, though I would feign hope the contrary as I cannot speak plainer without. But I'll say no more, and leave you to guess the rest." And then continued with news and gossip of the camp. This is the total of the correspondence relating to Washington's presumably unrequited love.

George must surely have written to his fiancée during the seven months of the western campaign. The ardor of his letters will never be known, because Martha carefully burned them after his death. There is one letter from George to Martha during the days of their engagement which is included in two editions of his collected writings, but it is almost certainly a forgery. It reads, in full:

July 20, 1758

We have begun our march for the Ohio. A courier is starting for Williamsburg, and I embrace the opportunity to send a few words to one whose life is now inseparable from mine. Since that happy hour when we made our pledges to each other, my thoughts have been continually going to you as to another Self. That an all-powerful Providence may keep us both in safety is the prayer of your ever faithful and affectionate friend.

Aside from the fact that this letter is not at all in Washington's style — is more simple and direct than anything else he wrote at that period — there are several particulars that brand it a forgery. There is no salutation; every other letter written by Washington to a woman started "Dear Madam," "Honored Madam," or simply "Madam." One of his few surviving letters to his wife begins "My Dearest." There is no involved termination such as Washington invariably used; two months later he ended a letter to Sally Fairfax, "Be assured that I am, dear madame, with the most unfeigned regard, your most obedient and obliged public servant." The letter refers to a "courier." Washington never used this word; always wrote "express." It also mentions an "opportunity." If Washington spelled this word correctly on this occasion it is the only time in his life that he did so; he always wrote "oppertunity." Finally, the letter starts by saying, "We have begun our march for the Ohio." This was not a fact and other letters from Washington of about the same date show that his greatest concern was that the march to the Ohio might not be begun at all.

The march was begun; and ended in December, 1758. On the following January 6, Washington appeared at the White House to marry Martha Custis. There are many descriptions of the wedding, although none written by anyone who was there. All agree that the bride wore white and that, although she wore no veil, she was garbed more ornately than was usual for a widow. One of the earliest accounts of her costume mentions "a white satin quilted petticoat, and a heavy, corded white silk overskirt; high-heeled shoes of white satin, with diamond buckles; rich point-lace ruffles; pearl necklace, earrings, and bracelet, and pearl ornaments in her hair." The three bridesmaids wore blue.

George had put aside his uniform and wore a civilian coat of blue — possibly the blue velvet ordered from London — over an embroidered white satin waistcoat and knee breeches fastened with buckles of gold. He carried a straight dress sword, his hair was powdered, and he wore white gloves. Of this last there is no doubt; they are on display in the Masonic Museum at Alexandria; and they are huge. The wedding festivities were apparently very gay.

The Washingtons spent a seven-week honeymoon at the home of the bride, giving George a chance to get acquainted with his stepchildren. The next seven weeks were spent at the Custis home in Williamsburg, while Washington took his seat in the House of Burgesses. Then a cavalcade of bride, bridegroom, children, nurses, servants, and luggage started for Mount Vernon, which Martha had never seen. George was halfway home before he realized that he had done nothing to prepare the house to receive its new mistress. Up until this time Mount Vernon had been "bachelor hall." It had been sparsely furnished since the days when Anne, Lawrence's wife, presided there. From Fredericksburg, Washington sent an "express" galloping ahead with a note to an overseer, John Alton:

Jno: I have sent Miles on today, to let you know that I expect to be up tomorrow, and to get the key from Colonel Fairfax's house, which I desire you will take care of. You must have the house very well cleaned, and were you to make fires in the rooms below it would air them. You must get two of the best bedsteads put up, one in the hall room, and the other in the little dining room that used to be, and have beds made on them against we come. You must also get out the chairs and tables, and have them very well rubbed and cleaned; the staircase ought also to be polished in order to make it look well.

Enquire about in the neighborhood and get some eggs and chickens, and prepare in the best manner you can for our coming: you need not, however, take out any more of the furniture than the beds and tables and chairs in order that they may be well rubbed and cleaned.

In those days a wife did not own property independently of her husband. Upon their marriage the management of Martha's inheritance from Custis passed to George, and he lost no time in making the new position clear to her agents in London in this letter that he wrote before leaving Williamsburg:

The enclosed is the minister's certificate of my marriage with Mrs. Martha Custis, properly, as I am told, authenticated. You will, therefore, for the future please to address all your letters which relate to the affairs of the late Daniel Parke Custis, Esq., to me, as by marriage I am entitled to a third part of that estate, and invested likewise with the care of the other two thirds [held in trust for the Custis children]. . . .

On the other side is an invoice of some goods which I beg of you to send me by the first ship, bound either to Potomac or Rappahannock, as I am in immediate want of them.

The invoice on the back of the letter was the first of many that would go to London to convert Mount Vernon into a suitable abode for a rising country squire and his family, and to garb that family in accord with its station. Obviously when a man takes a bride the first thing he needs is furniture for a bridal chamber, so the list started:

One tester bedstead 7½ feet pitch with fashionable blue or blue-and-white curtains to suit a room laid with yellow Ireland paper.

Window curtains of the same for two windows; with either papier-mâché cornish [valances] . . . or cornish covered with the cloth.

One fine bed coverlid to match the curtains. Four chair bottoms of the same; that is, as much covering suited to the above furniture as will go over the seats of four chairs (which I have by me) in order to make the whole furniture of this room uniformly handsome and genteel.

The list further called for some books on agriculture, including one titled, *A New System of Agriculture or A Speedy Way to Grow Rich.* It ended with: "Order from the best house in Madeira a pipe of the best old wine, and let it be secured from pilferers."

For the first fifteen years of their marriage George and Martha led the peaceful lives of a gentleman farmer and his lady. George owned four separate farms near Mount Vernon, which had run down during his service in the French and Indian War. It took most of the 1760s to put them on a profitable basis. Washington's daily grind usually involved riding up to twenty miles to supervise his properties. As time passed he became a big man in the county. Before the Revolution he held, at one time or another, almost every county post except coroner and sheriff. He retained his seat in the House of Burgesses and was a vestryman and warden in the church. These latter duties were more or less required of him by his position; despite the famous picture of him praying in the snow at Valley Forge, Washington was not much of a churchgoer. As with many modern families, Martha was more regular at church attendance than her husband, who seemed to go only when his position required it or when his wife put her dainty little foot down. He would much rather hunt a fox on Sunday — and usually did.

While her husband was attending to business, private or public, riding to hounds, shooting ducks, fishing, or playing cards — all forms of recreation favored by George — Martha was more attentive to her share of the work. Like Deborah Franklin, Martha Washington was primarily a housewife — but there the comparison ends. Deborah kept her house; Martha managed hers. This involved a different kind of work, but work withal. She rose before daylight with George and made the rounds with her large bunch of keys, unlocking doors and supplies for slaves who had but weak resistance to temptation, particularly if liquor was involved.

The mistress of Mount Vernon had a large staff of house servants to supervise in the daily routine of cleaning and cooking. And, as Deborah had a shop to serve, Martha had to supervise what would normally be several commercial activities. There was a dairy and a smoke house and a spinning-and-weaving operation that rivaled a small factory. Sometimes as many as thirty-five spinning wheels were whirring at Mount Vernon and in a single year Martha turned out 815 yards of linen, 365 yards of woolen, 144 yards of linsey and forty yards of cotton — a total of 1,364 yards of cloth.

Unlike Deborah, Martha had to be ready at a moment's notice to change from a housekeeper to a hostess. She never knew how many guests might drop in for dinner, and, perhaps, to stay a night or a week. Also, unlike Deborah, she must make calls among the neighboring plantations. Of these Belvoir was the closest and Martha and Sally Fairfax, although very different in temperament and character, were presumably on the best of terms. There is nothing to indicate whether Martha knew of her husband's feelings for Sally.

There is a record of one occasion, obviously before the Revolution, when: "the whole neighborhood was thrown into a paroxysm of festivity by the anchoring of the British frigate in the river, just in front of the hospitable mansion of the Fairfaxes. A succession of dinners and breakfasts takes place at Mount Vernon and Belvoir, with occasional tea parties on board the frigate."

Two centuries before television commercials extolled sprays to purify the air, Martha knew how to make "A Perfume to Stand in A Roome." In a volume of recipes in her handwriting that still exists she wrote: "Take two or three quarts of roses buds or ye leaves of damask roses & put them in a pot with bay salt, 3 or 4 grayns of musk & as much of amber-greece, 20 or 30 drops of oyle of rodium, a little benjamin & Storeax, beat together in a cheyney pot or any other yt is handsome & keep it allways covered, but when you have a mind to have yr roome sweet you must take of ye cover."

Painting of Deborah Franklin attributed to Benjamin Wilson

Mary Stevenson Hewson, daughter of Franklin's landlady in London, was a close friend and longtime correspondent on subjects philosophical. RIGHT: Madame Helvetius, from a miniature painted many years before Franklin met her.

Courtesy Washington and Lee University

Courtesy Henry Francis du Pont Winterthur Museum

Martha Washington, painted by John Wollaston at about the time of her marriage to George. RIGHT: Mary Philipse, painted by J. S. Copley after she had become Mrs. Roger Morris.

Mrs. George Washington, painted in her later years by Edward Savage

Mrs. John Adams, painted by Gilbert Stuart in 1812, several years after her husband's retirement

Maria Cosway, from a miniature painted by her husband at about the time that Jefferson met her

Mrs. Thomas Mann Randolph, Jefferson's daughter Martha, painted by Thomas Sully

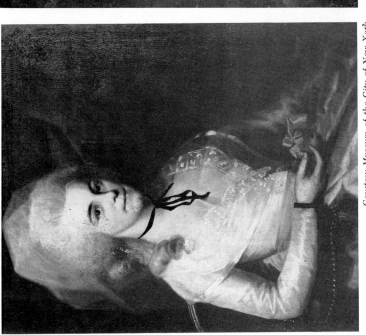

Mrs. Alexander Hamilton, painted by Ralph Earl about the time of her marriage. RIGHT: Mrs. Alexander Hamilton, painted by Daniel Huntington shortly before her death.

Dolley Madison, by James Stuart

Other present day commercial products that were manufactured at Mount Vernon to Martha's formula were described as "To Make Sweet Water to Perfum Cloaths in ye foulding after they are Washed"; "To keep ye Hayre Clean and Improve it"; "To Keep Teeth Clean and White and to Fasten Them." This last recipe advised: "Take cuttle fishbone and make it into a very fine powder & rub ye teeth with it, then wash them after with white wine and plantan water & 3 or 4 drops of spirrit of vittorell mixt with them and rub them well with a cloth & it will preserf ye teeth from putrefaction & keep them fast, white & clean & preserf from ye toothach iff it be used every day." This apparently did not work well to "fasten" George's teeth — he lost them all fairly early in life.

Much of Martha's time was devoted to her children, to whom George was a conscientious stepfather. Washington was very much the master in the home and Martha was a dutiful, though not a subservient, wife — with one exception. In matters pertaining to the children Martha stubbornly resisted interference. This is a polite way of saying that the children were badly spoiled and there was not much that George could do about it.

Martha was reluctant to leave the children to accompany her husband to Williamsburg for meetings of the Assembly. When she did go away on one visit she wrote her sister that she took Patty but "left Jackey at home for a trial to see how well I could stay without him though we ware gon but won fortnight I was quite impatiant to get home. If I at aney time heard the doggs barke or a noise out, I thought thair was a person sent for me. I often fancied he was sick or some accident had happened to him so that I think it is impossible for me to leave him as long as Mr. Washington must stay when he comes down."

The Washington properties did not start to make money until George shifted from tobacco to wheat as a main crop and diversified his activities. He acquired a schooner and went into the fishing business. He built two mills and produced and marketed G. Washington Flour. He started a distillery, but there was never a Washington Bonded Whiskey. The still produced applejack and peach brandy from the produce of the farm's orchards. This was traded or used by tenants and servants.

For most of the pre-Revolutionary period the Washingtons were strapped for cash — a situation common to many Virginia planters, whose wealth was in land and slaves. By the early 1770s Washington had over 12,000 acres in eastern Virginia and 20,000 acres in the western part of the state and Pennsylvania; and owned over 200 slaves. But that did not prevent his London factors from reminding him that he was in their debt to the amount of £1811; a letter which aroused George's ire because, he wrote, "in whatsoever light it may appear to you, it is not less evidently certain that mischances rather than misconduct hath been the causes of it."

The fact that Washington did not have money did not prevent him from spending it. For Martha there were egrets for her headdress, "One cap, handkerchief, tucker and ruffles to be made of Brussels lace, proper to wear with the above negligee, to cost £/20. . . . Six pounds of perfumed powder," and much else. "For Master Custis" there were Irish holland, fine cambric, "two laced hats, one pair handsome silver shoe and knee buckles, 10s worth of toys, six little books for children beginning to read." "For Miss Custis" there were fine printed linen and Irish holland, "two fans; two masks; two bonnets; one stiffened coat of fashionable silk, made to pack-thread stays; one fashionable-dressed baby 10s, and other toys 10s."

Jacky had a tutor until he was fourteen, when George induced Martha to let him go away to school in Annapolis. He secretly told the minister who ran the school to have the boy vaccinated against smallpox without letting his mother know, "that she might escape those tortures which suspense would throw her into." Jacky was not a model student. The minister wrote: "I must confess to you I never in my life knew a youth so exceedingly indolent, or so surprisingly voluptuous; one would suppose nature had intended him for some Asiatic Prince." George was worried about the youth's morals and wrote "the warmth of his own passions, assisted by the bad example of other youths, may prompt him to actions derogatory of virtue, and that innocence of manners which one could wish to preserve him in. For which reason I would beg leave to request, that he may not be suffered to sleep from under your own roof . . . nor allow him to be rambling about of nights." Two centuries ago the Father of his Country had exactly the same problem as the parents of today's teen-agers.

He finally put the boy in King's College in New York (now Columbia University) but not for long. On his first Christmas holiday Jacky announced that he was going to marry a girl from Maryland. George's protests were to no avail. He wrote the President of King's College that, in view of "his own inclination, [and] the desires of his mother . . . I did not care to push my opposition too far, and therefore have submitted to a kind of necessity."

Neither George nor Martha would have qualified as Puritans or Quakers in their attitude toward outward signs of luxury or affluence, but Martha's tastes were the simpler of the two. She well graced a coach and four but she probably would have been just as happy in a less ostentatious equipage. Her husband delighted in making a fine show when he went abroad. Two years before he acquired the Custis fortune, when he was merely a colonel of provincial troops, he had ordered from London this clothing for the servants who accompanied him to Boston:

Two complete livery suits for servants, with a spare cloak and all other necessary trimmings for two suits more. I would have you choose the livery by our arms; only as the field is white, I think the clothes had better not be quite so, but nearly like the inclosed. The trimmings and facings of scarlet, and a scarlet waistcoat. If livery lace is not quite disused, I should be glad to have the cloaks laced. I like that fashion best, and two silver-laced hats for the above servants. One set of horse-furniture with livery lace, with the Washington crest on the housings, etc.

In 1773, a few weeks after George had taken Jacky to New York for his short stay at King's College, tragedy struck Mount Vernon. Patsy had been sickly from early childhood; apparently she had epilepsy. As she entered her teens the malady worsened. A visit to the Warm Springs at Frederick did not help, nor did a procession of physicians. On June nineteenth Washington's diary records: "19. At home all day. About five o'clock poor Patsy Custis died suddenly." The girl was seventeen. A few days later he wrote suggesting that Martha's mother, Mrs. Dandridge, come to live at Mount Vernon.

It is an easier matter to conceive than to describe the distress of this family; especially that of the unhappy parent of our dear Patsy Custis, when I inform you that yesterday removed the sweet innocent girl entered into a more happy and peaceful abode than any she has met with in the afflicted path she hitherto has trod. She rose from dinner about four o'clock in better health and spirits than she appeared to have been in for some time; soon after which she was seized with one of her usual fits, and expired in it, in less than two minutes without uttering a word, a groan, or scarce a sign. . . . This sudden, and unexpected blow, I scarce need add has almost reduced my poor wife to the lowest ebb of misery; which is increased by the absence of her son (whom I have just fixed at the College in New York from whence I returned the 8th inst.) and want of the balmy consolation of her relations; which leads me more than ever to wish she could see them, and that I was master of arguments powerful enough to prevail upon Mrs. Dandridge to make this place her entire and absolute home. I should think as she lives a lonesome life (Betsy being married) it might suit her well, and be agreeable, both to herself & my wife; to me most assuredly it would.

Less than three weeks later Washington suffered another loss. The Fairfaxes came "to take leave of us," and the next day "Mrs. Washington and self went to Belvoir to see them take shipping." Sally and William Fairfax went to England in expectation of his becoming Lord Fairfax, but he died before this was realized. Although Sally outlived Washington, she remained in England and he never saw her again.

A few months later Jacky married Nelly Calvert at her father's home in Maryland. Martha was in deep mourning for her daughter and did not attend the wedding of her son. But she did send, with her husband, the most moving letter that she ever wrote;

My dear Nelly: God took from me a daughter when June roses were blooming — He has now given me another daughter, about her age, when winter winds are blowing, to warm my heart again. I am as happy as one so afflicted and so blest can be. Pray receive my benediction and a wish that you may long live the loving wife of my happy son, and a loving daughter of

Your affectionate mother,

M. Washington

Three months after Jacky's wedding George left his wife for what he expected would be a short session of the Burgesses in Williamsburg. His journey was not brief; it led to Philadelphia and the First Continental Congress. Then, after a short return to Mount Vernon, back to the second meeting of the Congress. From here, on June eighteenth, he penned his wife a long letter.

My Dearest,

I am now set down to write to you on a subject which fills me with inexpressible concern, and this concern is greatly aggravated and increased when I reflect upon the uneasiness I know it will give you. It has been determined in Congress that the whole army raised for the defence of the American cause shall be put under my care, and that it is necessary for me to proceed immediately to Boston to take upon me the command of it.

You may believe me, my dear Patsy, when I assure you, in the most solemn manner, that, so far from seeking this appointment, I have used every endeavor in my power to avoid it, not only from unwillingness to part with you and the family, but from a consciousness of its being a trust too great for my capacity, and that I should enjoy more real happiness in one month with you at home, than I have the most distant prospect of finding abroad, if my stay were to be seven times seven years. . . . It was utterly out of my power to refuse this appointment, without exposing my character to such censures as would have reflected dishonor upon myself, and given pain to my friends. This, I am sure, could not, and ought not, to be pleasing to you, and must have lessened me considerably in my own esteem. . . . I shall return safe to you in the fall. I shall feel no pain from the toil or the danger of the campaign; my unhappiness will flow from the uneasiness I know you will feel from being left alone. I therefore beg that you will summon your whole fortitude, and pass your time as agreeably as possible. Nothing will give me so much sincere satisfaction as to hear this, and to hear it from your own pen. My earnest and ardent desire is that you would pursue any plan that is most likely to produce content, and a tolerable degree of tranquillity; as it must add greatly to my uneasy feelings to hear that you are dissatisfied or complaining at what I really could not avoid.

As life is always uncertain, and common prudence dictates to every man the necessity of settling his temporal concerns while it is in his power and while the mind is calm and undisturbed, I have, since I came to this place (for I had not time to do it before I left home) got Colonel Pendleton to draft a will for me, by the directions I gave him, which will I now enclose. The provision made for you in case of my death will, I hope, be agreeable.

George did not come home in the fall. In fact, during the next six years he spent but three days at Mount Vernon. Martha, during this period, became a long-distance commuter. In the spring and summer, when the army was fighting, Martha stayed at Mount Vernon. When the troops went into winter quarters Martha joined her husband, first at Cambridge and later at Morristown, Philadelphia, Valley Forge, and Newburgh. Washington would accept no salary as Commander-in-Chief of the army, but he did render expense accounts, and these included Martha's expenses, and those of the servants who accompanied her on her several journeys away from Mount Vernon. George justified this, and quite properly, on the grounds that he never took the leaves to which officers were entitled.

Shortly after George left to take charge of the American troops that were holding the enemy in Boston, Martha narrowly escaped a brush with the British. Virginia's Royal Governor, Lord Dunmore, tried to organize "Lord Dunmore's own Regiment of Indians" and "Lord Dunmore's Ethiopians." With the help of a small British fleet he captured Norfolk and it was feared that he might burn Mount Vernon and hold Martha as hostage. A distant cousin of

George's, Lund Washington, was managing the plantation and George wrote him:

I can hardly think that Lord Dunmore can act so low and unmannerly a part as to think of seizing Mrs. Washington by way of revenge upon me; however as I suppose she is, before this time, gone over to Mr. Calvert's, [Jacky's father-in-law] and will soon after returning go down to New Kent, she will be out of his reach for two or three months to come, in which time matters may, and probably will, take such a turn as to render her removal either absolutely necessary, or quite useless.

Lund replied:

Dunmore has come and gone, and left us untouched except by some alarm. I sent my family many miles back in the country, and advised Mrs. Washington to do likewise, as a prudential movement. At first she said, "No; I will not desert my post"; but she finally did so with reluctance, rode only a few miles, and, plucky little woman as she is, stayed away only one night.

In November, 1775, George sent a coach and four, with a liveried outrider, to bring his wife, Jacky, and Nelly to Cambridge. The trip north, with a stopover at Philadelphia, was a regal procession. Smartly uniformed troops of mounted militia — which would have been more useful at Cambridge — escorted her into and out of cities. There was some confusion as to what she should be called. Although the patriots were supposed to abhor anything connected with nobility, a plain "Mrs." did not seem suitable for the wife of "His Excellency," the General. Whether she liked it or not the plump little housewife from Virginia was generally called Lady Washington. After the festivities in Philadelphia she wrote: "I don't know but you have seen the figure our arrival made in . . . Philadelphia proper and I left it in as great pomp as if I had been a very great somebody."

Then as today, one could not believe everything published in the press. While Martha was traveling more than five hundred miles over winter roads to be with her husband one paper commented: "Mr. Washington, we hear, is married to a very amiable lady, but it is said that Mrs. Washington, being a warm loyalist, has separated from her husband since the commencement of the present troubles, and lives, very much respected, in the city of New York."

Martha was helpful to her husband in Cambridge, where the social end of headquarters badly needed organization. There was much dissension about rank among some subordinate generals and Martha's relationship with their wives was undoubtedly a factor in smoothing things over. The wives of Generals Knox, Gates, and Mifflin were at headquarters and Martha received and paid calls upon the local ladies with the two latter. Mrs. Knox was a great favorite of Washington's. They both loved to dance, although Mrs. Knox was, to put it politely, "stout." Martha had become pleasingly plump by this time and was quite willing to have her husband display his terpsichorean talents with another partner. There is a story that George and Lucy Knox once danced four hours without sitting down.

At this stage of the war there were one, perhaps two, other women whose lives affected Washington's fortunes, although he surely did not know one and probably did not know the other. The first was a trollop named Mrs. Loring. Before he was relieved of command at Boston, British General Gates appointed a local Tory, Joshua Loring, as army commissary. When Gates' successor, General William Howe, arrived Loring wanted to keep the job and the graft. He did it, simply, by giving his wife to Howe. As one contemporary phrased it: "Joshua had a handsome wife. The General Sir William

Howe, was fond of her. Joshua made no objections. He
fingered the cash, the General enjoyed madam." Mrs. Loring
was a compulsive gambler and gambling was a favorite recreation of Howe's. Serious historians aver that had Howe
paid more attention to fighting the war and less to his gambling companion and bedmate the Americans might have
been disastrously defeated in New York or New Jersey during
1776-77. Howe was a good strategist and the British won most
of the battles. But, like Mark Antony, their General was too
anxious to get back to his American Cleopatra to follow up
his victories. A contemporary poem, "The Battle of the
Kegs," put it:

> Sir William, he, snug as a flea,
>   Lay all this time a snoring,
> Nor dream'd of harm as he lay warm,
>   In bed with Mrs. Loring.

Mrs. Loring made out quite well. One of her sons became
archdeacon of Calcutta and another was knighted and became a British vice-admiral.

The story of another woman who helped Washington may
be legendary. After the Americans were defeated at the Battle
of Long Island they retreated to lower Manhattan. As the
British fleet took station in the North and East rivers, Washington started north toward Harlem. British and Hessians
landed on the eastern shore of the island near a farm owned
by a Quaker named Robert Murray. (This part of the East
Side of Manhattan just below Forty-second Street is still
known as the Murray Hill section.) Mrs. Murray invited the
officers in for cakes and wine. The troops, according to the
story, lolled on their arms in a corn field for two or three
hours while their officers joshed with the attractive Mrs.
Murray about her American friends; although a Quaker, she

was an avowed patriot. While they sipped their wine Washington's rear guard slipped past them, along what is now Central Park West. One historian wrote: "A good body of troops with two field pieces, in about twenty minutes or less, could have taken such a position as would have necessarily cut off Putnam's retreat."

While he was at Harlem Heights George should have been grateful to Mary Philipse for his comfort; his headquarters was the home that she had built for Captain Morris, who was in England. Mary, a Tory, had fled to Yonkers to escape her former suitor.

According to her grandson, Martha said that she always heard the first cannon at the opening of a campaign and the last at the closing. Washington sent for her as each summer's campaign drew to a close and sent her away to the safety of Mount Vernon when the new season's fighting started. She spent the second winter of the war at his headquarters in Morristown, where the local ladies were surprised at her simple dress and preference for checkered aprons. She played serene hostess to Washington's official family — including his twenty-year-old aide, Alexander Hamilton — and the officers' wives who were in the camp or near it. After an early afternoon dinner George enjoyed a ride with some of his officers and their ladies. Martha seldom if ever went; perhaps that is why the wife of one young colonel could write of George: "He can be downright impudent at times — such impudence, Fanny, as you and I like."

The next year Martha was late in arriving at Valley Forge and missed the first of the misery of the winter of 1777-78. Although by other accounts things were still bad when she arrived in February, she did not seem to think so, for she wrote: "The general is in camp in what is called the great

valley on the Banks of the Schuylkill. Officers and men are
chiefly in Hutts, which they say is tolerable comfortable; the
army are as healthy as can well be expected in general. The
General's apartment is very small; he has had a log cabin
built to dine in, which has made our quarters much more
tolerable than they were at first."

Still, there was much less gaiety at Valley Forge than at
Morristown. According to one officer: "The evening was
spent in conversation over a cup of tea or coffee. There were
no levees or formal soirees, no dancing and playing, or amusements of any kind, except singing. Every gentleman or lady
who could sing was called 'upon in turn for a song.' "

A sixteen-year-old girl who saw "Lady" Washington in
camp left this picture of her in an account which she gave
when she was eighty:

I never in my life knew a woman so busy from early morning
until late at night as was Lady Washington, providing comforts
for the sick soldiers. Every day, excepting Sundays, the wives of
officers in camp, and sometimes other women, were invited to Mr.
Pott's to assist her in knitting socks, patching garments, and
making shirts for the poor soldiers when materials could be procured. Every fair day she might be seen, with basket in hand, and
with a single attendant, going among the huts seeking the keenest
and most needy sufferers, and giving all the comfort to them in her
power. I sometimes went with her, for I was a stout girl, sixteen
years old.

On one occasion she went to the hut of a dying sergeant,
whose young wife was with him. His case seemed to particularly
touch the heart of the good lady, and after she had given him
some wholesome food she had prepared with her own hands, she
knelt down by his straw pallet and prayed earnestly for him and
his wife with her sweet and solemn voice. I shall never forget the
scene.

The recollections of an octogenarian are not entirely dependable, but the story of Martha praying for the sergeant is more credible than that of her husband praying in the snow. She was very religious.

After the campaign during the summer of 1778 Martha wrote her brother: "I am uneasy at this time — I have some reason to expect that I shall take another trip to the northward — the pore Geneeral is not likely to come to see us from what I can see hear." The first stop on the next trip north was Philadelphia where George and Martha attended several balls, one in honor of Benjamin Franklin's seventy-third birthday. Sally Bache wrote to her father in France: "I have lately been several times invited abroad with the General and Mrs. Washington. He always inquires after you in the most affectionate manner, and speaks of you highly. We danced at Mrs. Powell's your birthday or night I should say, in company together, and he told me it was the anniversary of his marriage; it was just twenty years that night."

There were more balls at winter headquarters in Middlebrook, where George performed a three-hour dance marathon, this time with the wife of General Greene. Here an officer wrote what would be, on the whole, a fine epitaph for Martha.

Mrs. Washington combines, in an uncommon degree, great dignity of manner with the most pleasing affability, but possesses no striking marks of beauty. I learn from the Virginia officers that Mrs. Washington has ever been honored as a lady of distinguished goodness, possessing all the virtues which adorn her sex, amiable in her temper and deportment, full of benignity, benevolence, and charity, seeking for objects of affliction and poverty, that she may extend to the sufferers the hand of kindness and relief.

So went Martha's life throughout the war; back to another winter quarters at Morristown, meetings with George in Philadelphia, and a precious three days when her husband enter-

tained officers of his French allies at Mount Vernon while
en route to the last battle at Yorktown. Here a spectator to
Cornwallis' surrender was an emaciated Jacky Custis. Serving
as a temporary civilian aide to his stepfather, he had con-
tracted camp fever. He was taken to an aunt's house in nearby
Eltham. George rode from Yorktown, Martha and Jacky's wife
came by coach from Mount Vernon, but they had scarcely
arrived when Jacky, aged twenty-eight, died. The Washingtons later adopted two of his four children, George Washington Parke and Nelly.

Between the end of the fighting and the formal peace
Martha spent another, rather gay, winter with her husband
at Newburgh. She returned home and, after the peace was
signed, George went to Philadelphia to resign his commission
and then rode hard to fulfill a promise that he would have
Christmas dinner with his wife at Mount Vernon. On the
morning of December 25, 1783, he flung himself off his horse
at his own doorway to be greeted by Martha and the excited
squeals of Jacky's younger children. Even that homecoming
day there were guests. One visitor recorded: "All Christmas
afternoon people came to pay their respects and duty. Among
them were stately dames and gay young women. The General
seemed very happy and Mistress Washington was from daybreak making everything as agreeable as possible for everybody."

The next five and a half years — from the end of 1783 to
the spring of 1789 — were probably the happiest in the lives
of George and Martha. The plantations had again run down
and George took up his old labor of restoring them. Martha
returned to the life that she liked best, housekeeper and
hostess under her own roof. If she was not entirely pleased

that so much of her time was spent in the latter capacity she gave no indication of it.

George was the great hero of the new country, and visitors from far and wide flocked to Mount Vernon — some invited, many unexpected and often unknown. George wrote that Mount Vernon "may be compared to a well-resorted tavern, as scarcely any strangers who are going from North to South, or from South to North, do not spend a day or two at it." And it was a year and a half after their return from the wars before he could write in his diary that he and Martha had dined alone. That indefatigable traveler, the Marquis de Chastellex, reported that, at Mount Vernon: "Your apartment was your house, the servants of the house were yours; and while every inducement was held out to bring you into the general society of the drawing room, or at the table, it rested with yourself to be served or not with everything in your own chamber."

Life at Mount Vernon was gay. There were a half dozen members of the immediate family, including a younger brother of George's, a niece of Martha's, and two of her grandchildren. With the children and their friends, plus the stream of visitors, there was seldom a dull moment. Martha managed all of this with calm dignity. George, if some visitors can be believed, was becoming somewhat pompous as a result of the excessive adulation.

During the immediate postwar years Martha lived with the constant sound of the hammer and the saw. Prewar Mount Vernon had been adequate for the needs of a country squire and his family — but not to those of a national hero. Starting in the summer of 1784 alterations were begun that doubled the size of the house. The portico, now its most distinguishing feature, was added as was the large dining room in which Martha flowered as a hostess.

Skillful and dedicated as she was, Martha could not carry the total burden of housekeeping and entertaining. Her husband wrote to Samuel Fraunces, keeper of the New York tavern in which he had said farewell to his officers, asking for a reliable steward who could be "recommended for honesty, sobriety, and knowledge of their profession, which is in a word to relieve Mrs. Washington of the drudgery of seeing the table properly covered and things economically used."

In 1787 Washington left home to preside over the Constitutional Convention. Then, in April, 1789, the Secretary of Congress dismounted at Mount Vernon to inform him officially that he had been elected President. He said several times that he was a reluctant President; and it may very well be true that, were it not for his deep sense of duty, he would rather have stayed at Mount Vernon. There is no doubt that Martha was not entirely happy during her eight years as First Lady. Before she started to play that role she wrote:

I little thought when the war was finished that any circumstances could possibly happen which would call the General into public life again. 1 had anticipated that . . . we should be suffered to grow old together, in solitude and tranquillity . . . I will not, however, contemplate with too much regret disappointments that were inevitable.

Later, after she had a taste of being the wife of a President, she described George's feelings and her own by writing to Mercy•Warren:

Though the General's feelings and my own were perfectly in unison with respect for our predilection for private life, yet I cannot blame him for acting according to his ideas of duty in obeying the voice of his country. The consciousness of having

attempted to do all the good in his power, and the pleasure of
finding his fellow citizens so well satisfied with the disinterested-
ness of his conduct, will doubtless be some compensation for the
great sacrifice which I know he has made. With respect to myself,
I sometimes think the arrangement is not quite as it ought to
have been; that I, who had much rather be at home, should
occupy a place with which a great many younger and gayer
women would be prodigiously pleased. . . . I know too much of
the vanity of human affairs to expect felicity from the splendid
scenes of public life. I am still determined to be cheerful and to
be happy in whatever situation I may be; for I have also learned
from experience that the greater part of our happiness or misery
depends upon our dispositions, and not upon our circumstances.

In another letter she wrote:

I live a very dull life hear, and know nothing that passes in
the town — I never goe to any public place — indeed I think I am
more like a state prisoner than anything else; there is a certain
bounds set for me which I must not depart from — and as I cannot doe as I like, I am obstinate and stay at home a great deal.

Martha considered the house in New York "a very good
one . . . handsomely furnished all new for the General." The
elegance and luxury of its furnishings led it to be called "The
Palace." It was staffed by fourteen white servants and seven
slaves. But it was the "General's" house, rather than Martha's.
It was he would hire Fraunces as the steward and fire him for
extravagance. He meticulously wrote out the duties of a
successor; graciously allowing that Mrs. Washington might
be consulted as to details:

In the first place I am to inform you, that all the liquors —
the groceries — and other shop articles of consequence, will be
laid in by my secretary. Trifling articles, which are only wanted
occasionally, will be provided by yourself. . . . From Mr. Dandridge you will obtain the money to defray my expenses, and
render accounts weekly. . . . Ready money is to be paid for every-

thing you purchase. I want no credit and am averse to after-reckonings. The multiplicity of my public duties leaves me but little leisure to suggest domestic arrangements. . . . For this reason I require that you would advise with Mrs. Washington on the several points and be governed by her directions. My general ideas on this subject are shortly these: 1st. that my table be handsomely but not extravagantly furnished on the days that company are entertained; 2nd. that a decent and economical board be spread at other times. . . . As we never have suppers nor sudden calls for extra dinners; it should not be a difficult matter to ascertain with certainty to what any expenses (agreeably to the prevailing mode of living) may be reduced. . . . In consequence of your performing these services — and in full expectation of your paying particular attention to the cookery seeing that everything appertaining to it is conducted in a handsome style, but without waste or extravagance, I agree to allow you fifty guineas a year.

Throughout the Presidency the Washingtons had servant trouble. During their first winter in New York George ran this advertisement in the local papers:

A Cook

Is wanted for the family of the President of the United States. No one need apply who is not perfect in the business, and can bring indubitable testimonials of sobriety, honesty, and attention to the duties of the station.

When they moved to Philadelphia Fraunces had to be re-hired, despite his extravagance, and the President had to raise the wages of house maids, kitchen maids and washerwomen from four dollars to five dollars a month.

Martha, during this time, had other problems. The amenities of her position required almost full-time attention to her social calendar. Visits had to be acknowledged and returned; for which she must be flawlessly garbed with hair dressed every day. In Mount Vernon it was sufficient that she be clean and neat.

There is some evidence that the busy President took a hand in grooming the First Lady on her social responsibilities, at least on her correspondence. Martha was always an atrocious speller, even by the lax standards of the eighteenth century. At Mount Vernon there are several interesting pairs of letters from Martha. One of each, unsigned, is in Washington's hand; the other is an exact copy in Martha's. When she was the wife of a Virginia planter who wrote only to her family or close friends Martha's spelling did not matter much. But now she was in the eyes of the world and George apparently felt that she needed lessons in social correspondence. He wrote some of her letters, which she copied.

Although she did not relish the position, Martha emerged as a new personality as the First Lady, and George had seldom found himself more fortunate in his consort than during the early part of his first term. Washington did not know how to behave as the President of the United States, which is not surprising because nobody had ever been President; there were no rules nor traditions to follow. He quickly learned that he could not hold open house in the presidential mansion as he had in Mount Vernon. Except on business he could see people only at a weekly levee. Also, although democracy was a fine theory, he believed that the office of President should have some dignity, which he expressed with liveried footman at the door and a coach with six cream-colored horses to go abroad. Vice-President John Adams and some members of the Senate wanted to call him "His Highness the President of the United States and Protector of Their Liberties." The House of Representatives put their collective foot down on this, but there was much criticism that Washington and his Federalist supporters were aping nobility. When Thomas Jefferson arrived to take office as Secretary of State he was appalled at "the levees, birthdays, pompous cavalcade to the statehouse on the meeting of Congress, the formal speech from the throne, the procession of Congress in a body to re-echo the speech in answer, etc., etc." He recorded: "I took occasion, at various times, of expressing to General Washington my disappointment at these symptoms of a change of principle, and that I thought them encouraged by the forms and ceremonies which I found prevailing, not at all in character with the simplicity of republican government, and looking as if wishfully to those of European courts."

Martha, too, held a weekly levee on Friday evening. These were decorous affairs in which Martha sat "with Mrs. Knox near the fireplace; other ladies were seated on sofas, and gentlemen stood in the center of the room conversing." If George came into the room — as he usually did before the evening was over — and found Mrs. Knox seated at Martha's right he tactfully led her to another place in the room. That was the seat for Mrs. Adams, wife of the Vice-President.

Abigail Adams left a description of Martha, shortly after her arrival in New York. She wrote:

I took the earliest opportunity . . . to go and pay my respects to Mrs. Washington. She received me with great ease and politeness. She is plain in her dress, but that plainness is the best of every article. She is in mourning. Her hair is white, her teeth beautiful, her person rather short than otherwise. . . . Her manners are modest and unassuming, dignified and feminine, not the tincture of hauteur about her. . . . Mrs. Washington is one of those unassuming characters which create love and esteem. A most becoming pleasantness sits upon her countenance and an unaffected deportment which renders her the object of veneration and respect. With all these feelings and sensations I found myself much more deeply impressed than I ever did before their Majesties of Britain.

Since the puritancial Abigail considered most Virginians as only slightly less immoral than the French — whom she considered very immoral indeed — this vignette of Martha was high praise.

Martha was somewhat happier after the government moved to Philadelphia, although before leaving New York she again wrote to Mercy Warren:

I contrive to be as happy here as I could be at any place except Mount Vernon. In truth, I should be very ungrateful if I did not acknowledge that everything has been done which politeness, hospitality, or friendship could suggest to make my situation as satisfactory and agreeable as possible.

The city of Philadelphia had procured the mansion of Robert Morris for the use of the President, probably the handsomest house in the city. Washington did not find it satisfactory. He wrote his secretary, Tobias Lear: "It is, I believe, the best *single house* in the city; yet, without additions it is inadequate to the *commodious* accommodation of my family." He then went to Mount Vernon and deluged Lear with a flood of letters telling him in great detail how the house in Philadelphia was to be enlarged, decorated, and furnished. In all of this there is no indication that he consulted Martha or considered her wishes or plans for the presidential mansion. He was usually considerate of Martha's comfort — although not necessarily of her opinion. But he apparently felt that this was the President's house, not hers.

The ladies of the members of the government and the diplomatic corps were generally the same in Philadelphia as in New York but Martha seemed to be more at ease here. Perhaps she was getting used to her role; or perhaps the fact that they were much nearer to Mount Vernon and could get home more frequently had something to do with it. George always enjoyed the theater, which was better in Philadelphia, and he and Martha were regular patrons.

Then there were balls, frequent and glittering, which George attended with relish and Martha with, at least, good will. At one she is described as sitting next to "the wives of the foreign ambassadors, glittering from the floor to the summit of their head dress. One of the ladies wore three large ostrich feathers. Her brow was encircled by a sparkling fillet of diamonds; her neck and arms were almost covered with jewels, and *two* watches were suspended from her girdle." Martha did not practice such ostentation but she accepted it in others with resignation and without criticism.

The big event of each Philadelphia season was the Washington Birthday Ball on February 22 — although Washington always said that his birthday was February 11, as it was under the calendar in use when he was born. These celebrations became more and more elaborate as the years passed. When he and Martha were sixty-four in 1796, the festivities started at one minute after midnight with the pealing of bells, followed by cannon and more bells at daybreak. Throughout the day open house was held at the Executive Mansion to entertain well wishers from Congress, the Pennsylvania Legislature, the guilds, and others. In the evening there was a supper at Oeller's Hotel followed by a grand ball at Rickett's amphitheatre, which was decorated with candelabra, transparencies, and emblematic paintings. Five hundred citizens attended and the President, as usual, danced every dance. Said one Congressman: "The ladies were elegantly dressed in white and waving plumes on their heads. . . . The President and Mrs. Washington mixed with the company and conversed sociably with everyone."

Such goings on led Benjamin Franklin Bache, publisher-grandson of the old sage, to write that the President behaved "with all the insolence of an Emperor of Rome." By this time, as the end of Washington's second term neared, the opposition press had become sufficiently bold to openly criticize the great hero. Unlike her successor, Abigail Adams, Martha kept herself above politics and made no recorded comment on criticisms of her husband. In only one instance is she known to have lost her poise; she accused the "filthy Democrats" who came to the Executive Mansion of leaving dirty fingermarks on her wall paper. This is about the only vicious thing that Martha is ever known to have said, and she may have been moved by the manners of the opposition, rather than their politics. Most of the Republican-Democrats who supported Jefferson were from the new lands to the west or represented the farmers and artisans. They did not have the polish of Virginia gentlemen, the only men whom Martha had ever known until she started to visit her husband's headquarters.

The last birthday ball of Washington's presidency was in 1797, after Adams had been elected. This was also an "elegant entertainment" at Rickett's amphitheatre at which the obvious esteem and affection for her husband aroused Martha's deep emotions. "Mrs. Washington was moved even to tears, with the mingled emotions of gratitude for such strong proofs of public regard and the new prospect of the uninterrupted enjoyment of domestic life. . . . I never saw the President look better, or in finer spirits, but his emotions were too powerful to be concealed. He could sometimes scarcely speak."

A few weeks later, after the Washingtons were resettled at Mount Vernon, Martha wrote Mrs. Knox:

I cannot tell you how much I enjoy home after being deprived of one so long. . . . The General and I feel like children just released from school or from a hard taskmaster. . . . We are so penurious with our enjoyment that we are loath to share it with anyone but dear friends. . . . I am again fairly settled down to the pleasant duties of an old-fashioned Virginia housekeeper, steady as a clock, busy as a bee, and cheerful as a cricket.

The next two and a half years were a quiet time in the lives of the old couple; except, of course, for the stream of visitors, which never ceased. They came singly, in pairs and in groups as they had after the Revolution. On one occasion Washington wrote a note to his ex-secretary saying; "I am alone at *present,* and shall be glad to see you this evening. Unless someone pops in, unexpectedly — Mrs. Washington and myself will do what I believe has not been done within the last twenty years by us — that is to set down to dinner by ourselves." (Apparently he had forgotten that, fifteen years before, he had noted in his diary that he and Martha had dinner alone — but both records indicate what an infrequent occurrence this was.)

Most of the visitors gazed on George with awe and reverence. A few were critical of his coolness or aloof manner. All were charmed by Martha. The comments of everyone who ever stopped at Mount Vernon were in the same vein as Albert Gallatin's in a letter to his wife: "Our most gracious queen . . . continues to be a very good-natured and amiable woman." Nelly summarized life with her grandparents at Mount Vernon during the last two and a half years of George's life by writing: "We have spent our summer and autumn very happily here . . . and are now contentedly seated round our winter fireside. I never have a dull or lonesome hour, never find a day too long. Indeed, time appears to fly."

Another female visitor, Eliza Carrington, described how Martha integrated her duties as hostess into her daily routine. There were servants to do most of the manual labor but, said Martha, "these require instruction in some cases and looking after in all." After "looking after" the downstairs servants, Martha took her guest to her own chamber and visited while she supervised other domestics. A chambermaid sat at one side of the room knitting; an "old decent woman" cut out winter clothes for the Negroes; a "little colored pet" was in a corner learning to sew. And while Martha directed all this she knitted stockings herself. She gave Mrs. Carrington, on this occasion, "a pair half done, which she begs I will finish and wear for her sake." Nelly Custis later wrote that "Grand-mamma made all my stockings and Washington's herself until we went to New York."

Some days were better than others. Neither George nor Martha were quite happy on the day that he had to answer a letter from the President of Princeton that contained disquieting reports about sixteen-year-old George Washington Parke Custis. Washington had to admit that Martha's grandson had an "almost unconquerable disposition to indolence in everything that did not tend to his amusements," in spite of repeated parental "admonition, encouragement or advice." He must have remembered writing a very similar letter about the boy's father when he was a teen-ager. There is no record as to what the disquieting reports dealt with except a reference, in a letter from the youngster, to "the late contest with the passions," which he concluded by saying that he was a "sincere penitent."

The day that Nelly was married to Lawrence Lewis, a

relative of George's, was a happier day, particularly since it was Washington's sixty-seventh birthday. He had recently been reappointed as Commander-in-Chief of the American forces when war with France threatened, and wanted to wear the gorgeous gold embroidered uniform that he had ordered. But it did not come in time so he wore his old Continental buff and blue. If he missed the "elegant" birthday balls of Philadelphia, Martha surely did not.

Then there was a day in 1798 when, after a lapse of twenty-five years, George sat down and wrote another letter to Sally Fairfax. He mentioned the passage of time and then continued abruptly: "During this period so many important events have occurred, and such changes in men and things have taken place, as the compass of a letter would give you but an inadequate idea of. None of which events, however, nor all of them together, have been able to eradicate from my mind the recollection of those happy moments, the happiest of my life, which I have enjoyed in your company."

Martha was recurrently ill during much of this time. She had repeated colds and a swelling in her face that may have been neuralgia. Possibly fatigue had something to do with it. Running an establishment like Mount Vernon and playing the gracious hostess to a shifting crowd of visitors must have put a physical strain on a woman in her late sixties. George considerately advertised for a competent housekeeper to whom he would pay $150 a year.

On December 12, 1799, George Washington made the rounds of his farms on horseback, through a steady rain. The next day he had a cold and a sore throat. Before they retired Lear suggested that he take something for it, but the General said that the best way to treat a cold was to "let it go as it came." Between two and three o'clock on the morning of

December 13, George woke Martha and told her he was ill. She wanted to rouse the house, but her husband insisted that she should not get up in the cold room. George was breathing with difficulty and Martha's anxiety must have matched his physical discomfort as they waited the sunrise, when a housemaid came to light the morning fire. Martha sent her for Tobias Lear and, at George's request, for an overseer from one of the farms to come and bleed him.

The Washingtons' physician, Dr. Craik, was a very old man who had been with the General during the Revolution. At Martha's insistence a second doctor was sent for, and then a third. Although George insisted on getting dressed, the three doctors, Martha, and Lear hovered around him all day. None of the medical ministrations of the late eighteenth century — bleeding, blistering, poultices, and massage with sal volatile — brought relief. By nightfall Washington could scarcely speak. Martha, Lear, Dr. Craik, and his body servant, Christopher, watched as he struggled for breath. A little after ten that night Lear was holding his hand when the General pulled it away to take his own pulse. While he was doing it he died without "a struggle or a sigh." There was silence for a few moments until Martha asked, quietly from the foot of the bed, "Is he gone?" Lear nodded and Martha added: " 'Tis well. All is now over. I have no more trials to pass through. I shall soon follow him."

Two days later George was buried, rather quietly, in the family vault. Apparently Martha did not attend the actual burial; at least there is no reference to her in any of the accounts. When it was proposed that the vault be resealed Martha objected to its being bricked up. Instead she insisted that a door be made because "it will soon be necessary to open it again." When Congress proposed to remove the remains to the new Federal City, which would be named for him, Martha reluctantly consented, saying that experience "taught me the great example which I have so long before me never to oppose my private wishes to the public will — I must consent to the request made by Congress . . . and in doing this I need not — I cannot say what a sacrifice of individual feeling I make to a sense of public duty." Nothing came of this proposal.

After George's death Martha moved into a small attic bedroom above the chamber she had shared with her husband. Here she spent much of the two remaining years of her life; although she was by no means a recluse. She still kept a hand on the tiller at Mount Vernon and continued to play hostess to the but slightly smaller stream of guests who visited the mansion. One such guest wrote this final description of her shortly before her death at the age of seventy:

Mrs. Washington appears much older than when I saw her last in Philadelphia, but her countenance very little wrinkled and remarkably fair for a person of her years. She conversed with great ease and familiarity, and appeared as much rejoiced at receiving our visit as if we had been of her nearest connections. She regretted that we had not arrived sooner, for she always breakfasted at seven, but our breakfast would be ready in a few minutes. In a short time she rose, and desired us to walk into another room, where a table was elegantly spread with ham, cold corn beef, cold fowl, red herring, and cold mutton, the dishes ornamented with sprigs of parsley and other vegetables from the garden.

At the head of the table was the tea and coffee equipage, where she seated herself, and sent the tea and coffee to the company. We were all Federalists, which evidently gave her particular pleasure. Her remarks were frequently pointed and sometimes sarcastic, on the new order of things, and the present administration. . . . She appeared in good health, but like one who has sustained a loss that will always remain fresh in her mind. She spoke of the General with great affection, and observed that, though she had many favors and mercies, for which she desired to bless God, she felt as if she was become a stranger among her friends, and could welcome the time when she should be called to follow her deceased friend.

Martha died quietly in her little room after a seventeen-day fever, during which she burned most of George's letters to her. Her most appropriate epitaph is probably a line in a letter that her husband had written forty-two years before, when he said: "I am fixed . . . in this seat with an agreeable consort for life." An agreeable consort she surely was. Shortly before his death, her husband had written to another woman of the "happy moments — the happiest in my life . . . I have enjoyed in your company." If Martha knew that the happiest moments in George's life were spent in Sally's company — not hers — she never let it influence her affection for or duty to her husband.

CHAPTER IV

The One Woman for John Adams

According to John Adams' later recollections, as expressed in his autobiography, he started to take an interest in the opposite sex when he was ten or eleven, an age at which most modern youths regard girls with loathing or, at best, consider them as soft boys. But Adams, with his strict puritanical background and his own high moral precepts, kept a strong curb on his youthful passions and limited his contact with the opposite sex to conversation. Later he wrote this rather smug essay on the subject:

Here it may be proper to recollect something which makes an article of great importance in the life of every man. I was of an amorous disposition and very early from ten or eleven years of age was very fond of the society of females. I had my favorites among the young women and spent many of my evenings in their company and this disposition, although controlled for seven years after my entrance into college, returned and engaged me too much till I was married. I shall draw no characters nor give any enumeration of my youthful flames. It would be considered as no compliment to the dead or the living. This I will say — they were all modest and virtuous girls and always main-

tained this character through life. No virgin or matron ever had
cause to blush at the sight of me, or to regret her acquaintance
with me. No father, brother, son, or friend ever had cause of
grief or resentment for any intercourse between me and any
daughter, sister, mother, or any other relation of the female sex.
My children may be assured that no illegitimate brother or sister
exists or ever existed. These reflections, to me consolatory beyond
all expression, I am able to make with truth and sincerity and I
presume I am indebted for this blessing to my education. My
parents held every species of libertinage in such contempt and
horror, and held up constantly to view such pictures of disgrace,
of baseness, and of ruin, that my natural temperament was always
overawed by my principles and sense of decorum. This blessing
has been rendered the more precious to me, as I have seen
enough of the effects of a different practice. Corroding reflections
through life are the never-failing consequence of illicit amours,
in old as well as in new countries. The happiness of life depends
more upon innocence in this respect than upon all philosophy of
Epicurus or of Zeno without it. I could write romances, or his-
tories as wonderful as romances, of what I have known or heard
in France, Holland, and England, and all would serve to confirm
what I learned in my youth in America, that happiness is lost
forever if innocence is lost, at least until a repentance is under-
gone so severe as to be an overbalance to all the gratifications of
licentiousness. Repentance itself cannot restore the happiness of
innocence, at least in this life.

He then added: "I soon perceived a growing curiosity, a
love of books and a fondness for study, which dissipated all
my inclination for sports, and even for the society of the
ladies." This, in effect, is the story of the women in his life
except for Abigail, his wife for fifty-four years.

The only record of a particular woman in John's life, other
than Abigail, concerns a wily female named Hannah Quincy
who almost ensnared the young lawyer when he was twenty-
four. John rode to Germantown frequently to visit Hannah,

with whose mind he was enchanted. He enjoyed talking to her about Shakespeare's concept of kingship or the merits of Pope's translation of Homer. These were subjects on which Hannah could converse intelligently, but her mind was fixed on matrimony, and she was adept at switching the conversation into that area. John was often surprised to find himself talking about marriage when he had started to talk about books.

Hannah's person, too, attracted John and he mentions in his diary that he lay awake most of the night thinking about her; but he was not ready for marriage. Still, he had a narrow escape from the designing Hannah, which he described by writing:

Accidents, as we call them, govern a great part of the world, especially marriages. Sewall and Esther broke in upon H. and me and interrupted a conversation that would have terminated in a courtship, which would, in spite of the Dr. have terminated in a marriage, which marriage might have depressed me to absolute poverty and obscurity to the end of my life. But the accident separated us, and gave room for Lincoln's addresses, which have delivered me from very dangerous shackles, and left me at liberty, if I will but mind my studies, of making a character and a fortune.

The "Dr." and "Lincoln" whom he mentions was a Dr. Bela Lincoln who quickly stepped in and satisfied Hannah's craving for a husband.

Two years later John Adams met another girl who interested him: Abigail Smith, a cousin of Hannah's and the daughter of Reverend William Smith. John's friend, Richard Cranch, was courting Abigail's older sister Mary, and John frequently rode to Weymouth with him and chatted with the younger Smith girls, Abigail and Eliza, while Richard sparked Mary. Soon, he was coming on his own to court the second daughter. Abigail was seventeen when John started to take her seriously, nine years younger than her future husband.

John left no record of his original impression of Abigail, beyond a cryptic diary comment in which he mentioned that Hannah Quincy was "fond . . . and tenderly pitiful." He then added: "Parson Smith's Girls have not this fondness, nor this tenderness." And later: "Are the Smith girls either frank or fond, or even candid — not fond, not frank, not candid."

But whether or not she was fond or frank, Abigail was beguiling. She had no formal education, but as a sickly child she had spent much time with her Grandmother Quincy, which was an education in itself. Both of the Smith and Quincy households were bookish, and Abigail's classical knowledge made her an interesting conversationalist to the young lawyer who took himself so seriously. Her mind was, possibly, even more energetic than John's and she did not hesitate to express her opinions. But Abigail had a ready wit that compensated for her forthright manner and made her conversation more interesting, to a man like John, than that of the flirtatious Hannah. Although she was no great beauty, a portrait painted at about the time of her marriage indicates that she was rather pretty.

Soon John had revised his early estimate of Abigail's tenderness and told his diary that she was "a constant feast. Tender, feeling, sensible, friendly. A friend. Not an imprudent, not an indelicate, not a disagreeable word or action. Prudent, modest, delicate, soft, sensible, obliging, active.

> Where all was full, possessing and posset
> No craving Void left Aching in the Breast."

Theirs was no whirlwind courtship; it lasted almost four years and apparently received little encouragement from Abigail's family except, possibly, from her father. The Quincys were a power in the commonwealth and did not consider an Adams as a very good catch. John had stood fourteenth in his class at college in a listing which, in the true Harvard manner, placed the students in the order of their social, rather than their academic, position. Had his mother not been a Boylston he undoubtedly would have been closer to the foot of the class. Further, John was a lawyer — a calling which many in mid-eighteenth-century Massachusetts considered as scarcely honest. There is a legend that the Reverend Mr. Smith, after marrying John and Abigail, answered the criticisms of some of his flock on the score of John's occupation by preaching a sermon drawn from Luke vii; 33: "For John came neither eating bread nor drinking wine, and, ye say, he hath a devil."

The young couple were separated during much of their courtship while John rode the court circuit and when, in 1763, he went to Boston to be inoculated against smallpox. Abigail started her career as the outstanding American female correspondent of the times during this period. Her letters over more than half a century are more interesting than her husband's — and at least as profound. Many years later John would write:

It is a little remarkable that you never heard the literary character of my consort. There have been few ladies in the world of a more correct or elegant taste. A collection of her letters, for the forty-five years that we have been married, would be worth ten times more than Madame de Sévigné's, though not so perfectly measured in syllables and letters, and would, or at least ought to, put to the blush Lady Mary Wortley Montagu and all her admirers. So much you will say, for conjugal complaisance. So much, I say, for simple justice to her merit.

There is every reason to believe that the long courtship of the two young Puritans was on the highest moral plane; but while they were patient they were also panting. Their letters soon dealt more with kisses than with books and both admitted the temptations that courtship involved. John referred to a storm that kept them apart as cruel but perhaps blessed "to you or me or both for keeping me *at my distance.*" In another letter he admits that; "itches, aches, agues (and repentance) might be the consequences of a contact in present circumstances." Abigail, too, thought that it might be well that a wise Providence had ordained their separation for "we might, if we had been together, have been led into temptation."

Finally, they were married on October 25, 1764, an event that Adams described in his autobiography as "a connection which has been the source of all my felicity." Unlike Franklin and Washington there is no indication that money was a factor in Adams' choice of a mate; although his legal practice immediately benefited by a connection with the Quincys. But it is possible that, as with Franklin and Washington, an empty house had some bearing on John's marital plans. He had inherited a farm from his father shortly before he started to court Abigail, and it was here that they set up housekeeping.

Considering the health of the bride and groom, one would not have expected the match to last, as it did, for more than half a century. True, John's ailments were more fancied than real. He was a food faddist and a hypochondriac who was resigned to an early death. Abigail was actually in delicate health throughout her life, suffering from migraine headaches, chronic insomnia, and unaccountable fevers.

For the next ten years Abigail's life was that of a New

England farm housewife, except for a brief period when they lived in Boston. Her husband was with her when he was not on the circuit and, at home, he was a farmer as well as lawyer; doing much of the work himself. The Adamses were not as poor as the Franklins nor as affluent as the Washingtons. Abigail did much of her own housework, but even before they were married, John sought a girl to help her with the chores. There is no evidence that she spun the yarn and wove the cloth for her husband's clothes, as did Deborah Franklin, nor that she supervised servants in such activities as did Martha Washington. Although she would later manage the farm while John was in Europe and run a little business of selling articles that he sent her from France, using friends as commission agents, Abigail's forte was not for such enterprises — yet she was far more than a housekeeper. To a much greater extent than the consorts of the other Founding Fathers, she was her husband's intellectual companion and helpmate.

During the first seven years of her marriage Abigail bore five children — a sixth was stillborn in 1777. One daughter, Susanna, died as an infant. Of the remaining four, two made out well, two not so well. The oldest child, Abigail (called Nabby), made an unfortunate marriage and, after years of poverty on a western farm, returned home to die of cancer. The second son, Charles, died a debt-ridden drunkard at the age of thirty. The youngest son had a model and unspectacular career as a judge. And the eldest son, John Quincy, followed in his father's footsteps to become the sixth President of the United States.

The second ten years of her life with John were the most difficult for Abigail, mainly because she was seldom with John. In late 1774 he rode to Philadelphia to attend the first

Continental Congress, leaving Abigail to mind the farm and raise four children, then aged two to nine. For the next three and one half years her husband spent most of his time in Congress. Then in early 1777 he sailed for France to replace Silas Deane as one of the three American Commissioners to that country. Except for his brief return in 1779 Abigail was alone until she joined him in France in 1784. To make matters somewhat worse for the mother, he took ten-year-old John Quincy Adams with him on the first trip and both John Quincy and Charles on the second.

Abigail's life during this period is well documented by her pen in scores of letters to her absent husband. Sometimes she wrote daily, occasionally thrice daily. John was a faithful correspondent, but she never had enough letters from him. Her letters, marked by wit, a high intellect, deep concern for her husband, and replete with biblical or classical allusions, touched on many subjects. During a few months in the fall of 1774 she wrote of the following topics.

The farm:

The drought has been very severe. My poor cows will certainly prefer a petition to you, setting forth their grievances and informing you that they have been deprived of their ancient privileges, whereby they are become great sufferers, and desiring that they may be restored to them.

Her children's early education:

I have always thought it of very great importance that children should, in the early part of life, be unaccustomed to such examples as would tend to corrupt the purity of their words and actions, that they may chill with horror at the sound of an oath, and blush with indignation at an obscene expression. These first principles, which grow with their growth, and strengthen with their strength, neither time nor custom can totally eradicate.

Words of encouragement:

You will perhaps be tired. No. . . . You have before you, to express myself in the words of the Bishop, the greatest national concerns that ever came before any people; and if the prayers and petitions ascend unto heaven which are daily offered for you, wisdom will flow down as a stream, and righteousness as the mighty waters, and your deliberations will make glad the cities of our God.

Personal needs:

I have a request to make of you; something like the barrel of sand, I suppose you will think it, but really of much more importance to me. It is, that you . . . purchase me a bundle of pins and put them in your trunk for me. The cry for pins is so great that what I used to buy for seven shillings and sixpence are now twenty shillings, and not to be had for that.

Her country's welfare:

The great anxiety I feel for my country, for you, and for our family renders the day tedious and the night unpleasant. The rocks and quicksands appear upon every side. What course you can or will take is all wrapped in the bosom of futurity. Uncertainty and expectation leave the mind great scope. Did ever any kingdom or state regain its liberty, when once it was invaded, without bloodshed? I cannot think of it without horror. Yet we are told that all the misfortunes of Sparta were occasioned by their too great solicitude for present tranquillity, and, from an excessive love of peace, they neglected the means of making it sure and lasting. They ought to have reflected, says Polybius, that, "as there is nothing more desirable or advantageous than peace, when founded in justice and honor, so there is nothing more shameful, and at the same time more pernicious, when attained by bad measures and purchased at the price of liberty.

Boston gossip:

General Burgoyne lives in Mr. Sam Quincy's house. A lady, who lives opposite, says she saw raw meat cut and hacked upon her mahogany tables, and her superb damask curtain and cushions exposed to the rain, as if they were of no value. . . . As to Burgoyne, I am not master of language sufficient to give you a true idea of the horrible wickedness of the man. His designs are dark; his dissimulation of the deepest dye; for, not content with deceiving mankind, he practices deceit on God himself. . . . An abandoned, infamous gambler, of broken fortune, and the worst and most detestable of the Bedford gang, who are wholly bent on blood and tyranny and spoil.

And mingled with all this and much more were cries of longing for the man she loved so deeply:

My much loved Friend, — I dare not express to you, at three hundred miles' distance, how ardently I long for your return. I have some very miserly wishes, and cannot consent to your spending one hour in town, till, at least, I have had you twelve. The idea plays about my heart, unnerves my hand whilst I write; awakens all the tender sentiments that years have increased and matured, and which, when with me, every day was dispensing to you. The whole collected stock of ten weeks' absence knows not how to brook any longer restraint, but will break forth and flow through my pen. May the like sensations enter thy breast, and (spite of all the weighty cares of state) mingle themselves with those I wish to communicate.

When independence for the colonies became more than a remote possibility, late in 1775, her letters contained shrewd political comments that forecast the difficulties of the about-to-be-born country; and equally astute opinions on human nature. In one she wrote:

I wish I knew what mighty things were fabricating. If a form of government is to be established here, what one will be assumed? Will it be left to our Assemblies to choose one? And will not many men have many minds? And shall we not run into dissensions among ourselves?

I am more and more convinced that man is a dangerous creature; and that power, whether vested in many or a few, is ever grasping, and, like the grave, cries, "Give, give!" The great fish swallow up the small; and he who is most strenuous for the rights of the people, when vested with power, is as eager after the prerogatives of government. . . .

The reins of government have been so long slackened that I fear the people will not quietly submit to those restraints which are necessary for the peace and security of the community. If we separate from Britain, what code of laws will be established? How shall we be governed so as to retain our liberties? Can any government be free which is not administered by general stated laws? Who shall frame these laws? Who will give them force and energy?

Abigail was ready to declare for independence before Congress was. Exactly one month before Richard Lee of Virginia offered a resolution "that these united colonies are, and of a right ought to be free and independent," Abigail told her husband:

A government of more stability is much wanted in this colony, and they are ready to receive it from the hands of the Congress. And since I have begun with maxims of state, I will add another, namely, that a people may let a king fall, yet still remain a people; but, if a king let his people slip from him, he is no longer a king. And as this is most certainly our case, why not proclaim to the world, in decisive terms, your own importance? Shall we not be despised by foreign powers, for hesitating so long at a word?

Abigail had other ideas on independence that she expressed facetiously, although they surely stemmed from a serious conviction.

I long to hear that you have declared an independency. And, by the way, in the new code of laws which I suppose it will be necessary for you to make, I desire you would remember the

ladies and be more generous and favorable to them than your
ancestors. Do not put such unlimited power into the hands of
the husbands. Remember, all men would be tyrants if they could.
If particular care and attention is not paid to the ladies, we are
determined to foment a rebellion, and will not hold ourselves
bound by any laws in which we have no voice or representation. . . .

Why . . . not put it out of the power of the vicious and the
lawless to use us with cruelty and indignity with impunity? Men
of sense in all ages abhor those customs which treat us only as
the vassals of your sex; regard us then as beings placed by Providence under your protection, and in imitation of the Supreme
Being make use of that power only for our happiness.

John answered this with one of his rather rare humorous
letters:

As to your extraordinary code of laws, I cannot but laugh.
We have been told that our struggle has loosened the bonds of
government everywhere; that children and apprentices were dis-
obedient; that schools and colleges were grown turbulent; that
Indians slighted their guardians, and Negroes grew insolent to
their masters. But your letter was the first intimation that another
tribe, more numerous and powerful than all the rest, were grown
discontented. . . . Depend upon it, we know better than to repeal
our masculine systems. . . . We have only the name of masters,
and rather than give up this, which would completely subject us
to the despotism of the petticoat, I hope General Washington and
all our brave heroes would fight.

Abigail retreated from her demand for the legal emancipa-
tion of women, but she had the last word:

I cannot say that I think you are very generous to the ladies;
for, whilst you are proclaiming peace and good will to men,
emancipating all nations, you insist upon retaining an absolute
power over wives. But you must remember that arbitrary power
is like most other things which are very hard, very liable to be
broken; and, notwithstanding all your wise laws and maxims, we

have it in our power, not only to free ourselves, but to subdue
our masters, and, without violence, throw both your natural and
legal authority at our feet —

>   Charm by accepting, by submitting sway,
>   Yet have our humor most when we obey.

Despite her views of women's rights, Abigail Adams has
never been numbered among America's feminists; she was
basically feminine rather than feminist. Franklin likened a
man without a wife to one half of a pair of scissors. Abigail
felt equally incomplete without her husband. But she was
never a clinging vine. When Washington lost New York she
wrote John: "We are no wise dispirited here. We possess a
spirit that will not be conquered. If our men are all drawn
off and we should be attacked, you would find a race of
Amazons in America." She reminded him that when the
Saracens turned their backs upon the foe they were slain by
their women, and said that if the men of America surrendered to Howe, "an army of women would oppose him."

Although her husband was her principal correspondent
during the Revolution, he was not the only one. She had an
interesting and, for a Puritan matron, a rather surprising
exchange of letters with James Lovell, another of the Massachusetts delegation to Congress. It started when she asked
John for a map so that she could follow the military campaign and her husband asked Lovell to get it for him. Lovell
sent it directly to Abigail, with a note that said that he could
have handed the map to her husband but: "I could not with
delicacy have told him to *his face* that your having given your
heart to *such* a man is what, most of all makes me yours."
This he followed with more seeming compliments for John
which he twisted into avowals of affection or admiration for
Abigail. Although it may have made her a little uneasy there

was nothing in this letter to which Abigail could take offense. When she answered it with a brief thank-you note, and mentioned "the very polite letter" to John, Lovell started to write more or less frequently.

Lovell's letters, in which he addressed Abigail as Portia, became increasingly bold. He was a master of the *double-entendre* and trod agilely on the brink of impropriety; but in such a way that he could always maintain his innocence if Abigail took offense. He was probably playing the same type of slightly risqué game that delighted Franklin in his correspondence with many women, but Abigail Adams was a less suitable partner for such play than the women to whom Franklin wrote.

In one of Lovell's boldest letters he wrote: "How *do* you do, lovely Portia, these very cold days? Mistake me not willfully; I said days." He added that though it was cold in Philadelphia too, he would not covet his neighbor's blankets. "But really I doubt," he added, "whether I shall be able to keep myself void of all covetousness. I suspect I shall covet to be in the arms of Portia [here the page ended, and Abigail, turning over, read] 's friend and admirer — the wife of my bosom. . . . There was not room," he continued, "to write *turn over*. I hope, however, that you did not stop long without doing so, madam, because a quick turnover alone could save the tenth commandment entire; and you must now see plainly that I had not the smallest suspicion of my being driven by my present sufferings to make a frantic breach there." He then referred Portia to Ecclesiastes iv; 11. Abigail's curiosity sent her to the Bible and she was aghast to read: "Again if two lie together, then they have heat; but how can one be warm alone."

Throughout all this Abigail chided him as "a wicked man"

and told him that he must not say such things — but she kept on writing. In the case of the letter above she chose to think that his remarks were a satire of Sterne's *Tristam Shanty,* which they had mentioned earlier and which Abigail considered "too vile" to read. "But," she added, "I have charity enough for the writer to believe that his associates have been wholly of his own sex for three years past, or he could not have so offended." She also cautioned him to destroy her letter and assured him that she had burned his. This was not true. Apparently puritanical Abigail found Lovell exciting — at a distance of four hundred miles. In any event she carefully saved all of his letters, which are today in the vaults of the Massachusetts Historical Society.

John and his oldest son left for France in February, 1778. Abigail did not hear from her husband until June. This was due to the uncertainty of shipping rather than delinquency on John's part, but his wife suffered agonies of apprehension, particularly when word reached Braintree that Adams' ship, the *Boston,* had been captured by a British frigate. When she received his first letter she wrote: "Shall I tell my dearest that tears of joy filled my eyes this morning at the sight of his well-known hand?" Then, after a few more sentences, she broached a subject that may possibly have given her some concern — French women. She asked her husband to tell her of all his adventures; "though, methinks, I would not have them in all respects too similar to those related of your venerable colleague, [Franklin] whose Mentor-like appearance, age, and philosophy most certainly lead the politico-scientific ladies of France to suppose they are embracing the god of wisdom in a human form; but I, who own that I never yet 'wished an angel, whom I loved, a man,' shall be full as content if those divine honors are omitted." But she had no doubts about her husband's fidelity. She knew that: "The whole heart of my friend is in the bosom of his partner. More than half a score of years have so riveted it there that the fabric which contains it must crumble into dust ere the particles can be separated."

If Abigail was not worried about the ladies of France she was much worried about the depreciated Continental currency. "Our money is very little better than blank paper." She wrote: "It takes forty dollars to purchase a barrel of cider; fifty pounds lawful for a hundred of sugar, and fifty dollars for a hundred of flour; four dollars per day for a laborer, and find him, which will amount to four more. . . . No article that can be named, foreign or domestic, but what costs more than double in hard money what it once sold for." She added: "The articles sent by Captain Tucker have arrived safe, and will be of great service to me." These were things that she had asked John to send her so that she might sell them for a profit through friends in Boston.

But mostly she longed for the man she loved. "How lonely are my days! how solitary are my nights! secluded from all society but my two little boys and my domestics. . . . Can the best of friends recollect that for fourteen years past I have not spent a whole winter alone? . . . How insupportable the idea that three thousand miles and the vast ocean now divide us!" Then she told him of a Scotch song that she had found and which eight-year-old Charles had learned to sing to her.

It has beauties in it to me which an indifferent person would not feel, perhaps.

> His very foot has music in't,
> As he comes up the stairs.

> How oft has my heart danced to the sound of that music!
>> And shall I see his face again?
>> And shall I hear him speak?

Gracious Heaven! hear and answer my daily petition, by banishing all my grief.

In another letter she again employed poetry to tell of her love:

> Should at my feet the world's great master fall,
> Himself, his world, his throne, I'd scorn them all.

No. Give me the man I love; you are neither of an age or temper to be allured by the splendor of a Court or the smiles of princesses. I never suffered an uneasy sensation on that account. I know I have a right to your whole heart, because my own never, never knew another lord . . .

On their wedding anniversary in 1782 Abigail wrote of their love as follows:

Look to the date of this letter, and tell me, what are the thoughts which arise in your mind? Do you not recollect, that eighteen years have run their circuit since we pledged our mutual faith to each other, and the hymeneal torch was lighted at the altar of Love? Yet, yet it burns with unabating fervor. Old Ocean has not quenched it, nor old Time smothered it in this bosom. It cheers me in the lonely hour; it comforts me even in the gloom which sometimes possesses my mind.

It is, my friend, from the remembrance of the joys I have lost, that the arrow of affliction is pointed. I recollect the untitled man, to whom I gave my heart, and, in the agony of recollection, when time and distance present themselves together, wish he had never been any other. Who shall give me back time? Who shall compensate to me those years I cannot recall? How dearly have I paid for a titled husband? Should I wish you less wise, that I might enjoy more happiness? I cannot find that in my heart. Yet Providence has wisely placed the real blessings of life within the reach of moderate abilities.

His wife had nothing to worry about in John's relationship with other women in France. The very thought of infidelity — his or anyone else's — filled him with horror. And what he considered the immorality of the French shocked him. When he visited Bellevue, the palace that Louis XV had built for his mistress, Madame de Pompadour, Adams was moved to comment:

Instead of wondering that the licentiousness of women was so common and so public in France, I was astonished that there should be any modesty or purity remaining in the kingdom. . . . Could there be any morality left among such a people, where such examples were set up to the view of the whole nation? . . . What havoc, said I to myself, would these manners make in America! Our governors, our judges, our senators or representatives, and even our ministers, would be appointed by harlots, for money; and their judgments, decrees, and decisions be sold to repay themselves, or, perhaps, to procure the smiles of profligate females.

While Adams, together with Franklin and John Jay, negotiated peace terms with Great Britain in 1783 he repeatedly urged Abigail to join him in France, but it was not until June, 1784, after the treaty was signed, that his wife and daughter set sail. Abigail had feared a winter crossing, and well she might for she proved to be a very bad sailor, even in balmy spring weather. She described her miseries during the first two weeks of the voyage in a letter to her sister.

'Tis said of Cato, the Roman Censor, that one of the three things, which he regretted during his life, was going once by sea when he might have made his journey by land. I fancy the philosopher was not proof against that most disheartening, dispiriting malady, seasickness. Of this I am very sure, that no lady would ever wish a second time to try the sea, were the objects of her pursuit within the reach of a land journey. I have had frequent occasion, since I came on board, to recollect an observation of my best friend's, "that no being in nature was so disagreeable as a lady at sea," and this recollection has in a great measure reconciled me to the thought of being at sea without him; for one would not wish, my dear sister, to be thought of in that light by those to whom we would wish to appear in our best array. The decency and decorum of the most delicate female must in some measure yield to the necessities of nature; and, if you have no female capable of rendering you the least assistance, you will feel grateful to any one who will feel for you, and relieve or compassionate your sufferings.

And this was truly the case of your poor sister and all her female companions, when not one of us could make her own bed, put on or take off her shoes, or even lift a finger. As to our other clothing, we wore the greater part of it until we were able to help ourselves. . . .

The vessel is very deep loaded with oil and potash. The oil leaks, the potash smokes and ferments. All adds to the flavor. When you add to all this the horrid dirtiness of the ship, I am sure you will be thankful that the pen is not in the hand of Swift or Smollet, and still more so that you are far removed from the scene.

John was at the Hague when Abigail and Nabby reached London. When he heard of their arrival he sent John Quincy to bring them on, writing Abigail that he was sending "a son who is the greatest traveler of his age and, without partiality, . . . as promising a youth as is in the world." Then, learning that Jefferson had arrived in Paris to succeed Franklin, he decided to follow his son to London and take the family to France.

Abigail and Nabby spent several pleasant weeks in the British capital, entertained by the American colony, before John Briesler, a servant whom they had brought from America, excitedly announced: "Young Mr. Adams has come." Mother and daughter ran to the door, but there was no son; he had stopped next door to get his hair dressed. When he did arrive a few minutes later his mother scarcely recognized him. She had not seen him for four years, and a boy changes much between the ages of thirteen and seventeen. Seeing him and Nabby together she wrote her sister: "Were I not their mother I would say a likelier pair you will seldom see in a summer's day."

John arrived a few days later and the family set out for Paris. For much of the next sixteen years the Puritan matron would live in a number of great cities — London, Paris, New York, Philadelphia and, finally, the new Federal City, Washington, D.C. In her mind none equalled her familiar haunts in Massachusetts, and in none of the palatial homes that she occupied was she as contented as on the farm in Braintree — when John was there.

In France, the Adamses settled in Auteuil, a suburb of Paris, and Abigail wrote of the deficiencies of the first large house in which she had ever lived:

The house we have taken is large, commodious, and agreeably situated, near the woods of Boulogne, which belong to the King, and which Mr. Adams calls his park, for he walks an hour or two every day in them. The house is much larger than we have need of; upon occasion, forty beds may be made in it. . . .

But with an expense of thirty thousand livres in looking glasses, there is no table in the house better than oak board, nor a carpet belonging to the house. The floors I abhor, made of red tiles in the shape of Mrs. Quincy's floor-cloth tiles. These floors will by no means bear water, so that the method of cleaning them is to have them waxed, and then a man-servant with foot brushes drives round your room dancing here and there like a Merry Andrew. This is calculated to take from your foot every atom of dirt and leave the room in a few moments as he found it. . . . The servants' apartments are generally upon the first floor, and the stairs which you commonly have to ascend to get into the family apartments are so dirty that I have been obliged to hold up my clothes, as though I was passing through a cow-yard.

The expense of the establishment frightened the economical New Englander. The rent was two hundred guineas a year and "firing" alone would cost another hundred with wood at two and a half guineas a cord and coal at three livres a bushel. But the greatest problem was servants. They had brought two from America, John and Esther, but Abigail found that:

It is the policy of this country to oblige you to a certain number of servants, and one will not touch what belongs to the business of another, though he or she has time enough to perform the whole. In the first place, there is a coachman who does not an individual thing but attend to the carriages and horses; then the gardener, who has business enough; then comes the cook; then the *Maitre d'hotel;* his business is to purchase articles in the family, and oversee that nobody cheats but himself; a *valet de chambre* — John serves in this capacity; a *femme de chambre* — Esther serves in this line, and is worth a dozen others; a *coiffeuse* — and for this place, I have a French girl about nineteen, whom I have been upon the point of turning away, because Madame will not brush a chamber; "it is not de fashion, it is not her business." I would not have kept her a day longer, but found, upon inquiry, that I could not better myself, and hairdressing here is very expensive, unless you keep such a madame in the house. She sews tolerably well, so I make her as useful as I can. . . . There is another indispensable servant, who is called a *frotteur;* his business is to rub the floors. . . .

Thus with seven servants and hiring a charwoman upon occasion of company, we may possibly make out to keep house; with less, we should be hooted at as ridiculous, and could not entertain any company. To tell this in our own country would be considered as extravagance; but would they send a person here in a public character to be a public jest?

The American servants, used to simple farm life, objected to the more formal atmosphere of Paris; particularly to having their hair dressed.

Esther had several crying fits upon the occasion, that she should be forced to be so much of a fool; but there was no way to keep them from being trampled upon but this; and, now that they are *à la mode de Paris,* they are much respected. To be out of fashion is more criminal than to be seen in a state of nature, to which the Parisians are not averse.

Abigail was undoubtedly determined not to like France or the French before she arrived. John had given her bad reports of the country's moral climate; and the French had not treated her husband well. As a diplomat in France during the war Adams had been frankly a failure because he disagreed so thoroughly with Franklin, whom the French adored. The French Foreign Minister had finally refused to deal with him. Although Abigail might, on occasion, disagree with her husband, nobody else was allowed to; and the country that had not accepted her genius could have little to recommend it.

She expressed her first impressions of the French countryside and of Paris by writing:

The civilization is by no means equal to that of England; the villages look poor and mean, the houses all thatched, and rarely a glass window in them; their horses, instead of being handsomely harnessed, as those in England are, have the appearance of so many old cart-horses. Along you go, with seven horses tied up with ropes and chains, rattling like trucks; two ragged postilions, mounted, with enormous jack boots, add to the comic scene. And this is the style in which a duke or a count travels through this kingdom. You inquire of me how I like Paris. Why, they tell me I am no judge, for that I have not seen it yet. One thing, I know, and that is that I have smelt it. . . . It is the very dirtiest place I ever saw.

Abigail enjoyed the serious theater, in which Paris led the world; and she came to accept the ballet because of the beauty of the dance. But she never resigned herself to the indecent exposure and supposed immorality of the dancers, or to much else that she considered immoral in the Old World.

I have seen many of the beauties, and some of the deformities, of this old world. I have been more than ever convinced, that there is no summit of virtue, and no depth of vice, which human nature is not capable of rising to, on the one hand, or sinking into, on the other. I have felt the force of an observation, which I have read, that daily example is the most subtile of poisons. I have found my taste reconciling itself to habits, customs, and fashions, which at first disgusted me; the first dance which I saw upon the stage shocked me; the dresses and beauty of the performers were enchanting; but, no sooner did the dance commence, than I felt my delicacy wounded, and I was ashamed to be seen to look at them. Girls, clothed in the thinnest silk and gauze, with their petticoats short, springing two feet from the floor, poising them-selves in the air, with their feet flying, and as perfectly showing their garters and drawers as though no petticoat had been worn, was a sight altogether new to me. . . . Shall I speak a truth, and say that repeatedly seeing these dances has worn off that disgust, which I at first felt, and that I see them now with pleasure? Yet, when I consider the tendency of these things, the passions they must excite, and the known character, even to a proverb, which is attached to an opera girl, my abhorence is not lessened, and neither my reason nor judgment has accompanied my sensibility in acquiring any degree of callousness. . . .

As soon as a girl sets her foot upon the floor of the opera, she is excommunicated by the Church, and denied burial in holy ground. She conceives nothing worse can happen to her; all restraint is thrown off, and she delivers herself to the first who bids high enough for her. But let me turn from a picture, of which the outlines are but just sketched; I would willingly veil the rest, as it can only tend to excite sentiments of horror.

Yet despite the dirt of Paris and what she considered the decadence that surrounded her, Abigail was happier in Auteuil than she had been for ten years, because she was with her husband. She presided when John entertained French diplomats, members of the American colony and his colleagues, Franklin and Jefferson. She was charmed by the latter, a friend of her husband's from the days when they served on the Congressional Committee to write the Declaration of Independence, whom Abigail first met in Europe. But she never ceased to complain about the expense of entertainment. She told her sister:

We make it a pretty general rule to entertain company once a week. (I do not call a transient friend or acquaintance dining, by that name.) Upon those occasions, our company consists of fifteen, eighteen, or twenty, which commonly costs us as many guineas as there are persons. You will naturally be surprised at this, as I was when I first experienced it; but my weekly bills, all of which pass through my hands, and are paid by me, convince me of it. . . . Believe me, my dear sister, I am more anxious for my situation than I was before I came abroad. I then hoped that my husband, in his advanced years, would have been able to have laid up a little without toiling perpetually; and, had I been with him from the first, he would have done it when the allowance of Congress was more liberal than it now is; but cutting off five hundred [guineas] at one blow, and at the same time increasing our expenses, by removing us from place to place, is more than we are able to cope with, and I see no prospect but we must be losers at the end of the year.

She made the calls required of a diplomat's wife, handicapped by her halting French, which she learned to read and write passably, but never could speak. She was particularly charmed by the Marquise de Lafayette who "met me at the door, and with the freedom of an old acquaintance, and the rapture peculiar to the ladies of this nation, caught me by the hand and gave me a salute upon each cheek, most heartily rejoiced to see me. You would have supposed I had been some long absent friend, whom she dearly loved."

Jefferson was decidedly pro-French; Adams pro-English to the extent that he could be pro-anything that was not American. Abigail of course endorsed her husband's view and had many arguments with the well-mannered Virginian on the subject. Most things, she believed, were better in England, although she was captivated by French politeness. The French men were gracious, charming, attentive, full of compliments and courtesies that made a woman conscious of her femininity. She finally admitted that even the French women were "very easy in their manners, eloquent in their speech, their voices soft and musical, and their attitude pleasing. I fancy they must possess the power of persuasion and insinuation beyond any other females."

But neither country had the moral stamina to please a Puritan. To Mercy Warren she wrote:

Which of the two countries can you form the most favorable opinion of, and which is the least pernicious to the morals? That where vice is licensed; or where it is suffered to walk at large, soliciting the unwary and unguarded, as it is to a most astonishing height in the streets of London, and where virtuous females are frequently subject to insults. . . . The stage is in London made use of as a vehicle to corrupt the morals. In Paris no such thing is permitted. They are too polite to wound the ear. In one country vice is like a ferocious beast, seeking whom it may devour; in the other like a subtle poison, secretly penetrating and working destruction.

If Abigail preferred England she soon had cause for rejoicing. Early in 1785 John was appointed Ambassador to the Court of St. James and the couple moved to England with

Nabby, John Quincy going home to Harvard. One of Abigail's first fearsome ceremonies was a formal presentation to the Queen, of which she wrote:

Congratulate me, my dear sister, it is over. I was too much fatigued to write a line last evening. At two o'clock we went to the drawing room of the Queen. . . . We were placed in a circle round the drawing room, which was very full, I believe two hundred persons present. Only think of the task! . . . The lord in waiting presents you to the King; and the lady in waiting does the same to her Majesty . . . The circle was so large that the company were four hours standing. The Queen was evidently embarrassed when I was presented to her. I had disagreeable feelings too. She, however, said, "Mrs. Adams, have you got into your house? Pray, how do you like the situation of it?" . . . The Queen was in purple and silver. She is not well shaped nor handsome. As to the ladies of the Court, rank and title may compensate for want of personal charms; but they are, in general, very plain, ill-shaped, and ugly; but don't you tell anybody that I say so.

Most of the upper class British did not reciprocate Abigail's good will to her country's former enemies. Their attitude toward the Adamses was exemplified by one paper which editorialized: "An Ambassador from America! Good Heavens, what a sound! The *Gazette* surely never announced anything so extraordinary before. . . . This will be such a phenomenon in the corps diplomatique that 'tis hard to say which can excite indignation most, the insolence of those who appoint the character, or the meanness of those who receive it." John's salary was so picayune that Abigail had to count every shilling to avoid bankruptcy, and their economies were the subject of much sarcastic press comment. It was said that "The American minister has not yet paid his way, that is given a diplomatic dinner to the ministers, because Congress' paper [money] will not pass here." When, in the interest of further economy, Abigail undertook to do the food shopping herself, one paper wrote that she looked like a farmer's wife "going in an old chaise to market with a little fresh butter."

Another concern of Abigail's was that her husband had changed somewhat from the small town farmer-lawyer of earlier days. Always, at home, he had taken an active interest in her domestic arrangements. Now the cares of state supplanted such homely concerns. He had no interest in household servants, the furnishings, or food. It was Abigail who found and rented the mansion in Grosvenor Square which became the first American embassy in London. John even left to her the long-range negotiations for the purchase of a larger house in Braintree.

The three years that they spent in London were a constant frustration to John. His principal objectives as Ambassador were to negotiate a treaty of commerce with the British and to induce them to live up to the terms of the peace treaty; specifically to evacuate the posts in the northwest that they were still occupying. The British minister refused to discuss any of this until the Americans would talk about compensation to Tories whose estates had been expropriated during the war. Since Congress could not compel the various states to take such action, Adams had no authority to discuss this and his principal negotiations were stalemated from the day of his arrival until the day of his departure.

The most important event of the stay in London was Nabby's marriage to her father's secretary, Colonel William Smith. Before Abigail and Nabby left America the mother, and to a greater extent John, had been concerned about Nabby's involvement with a young man named Royall Tyler.

Nabby claimed that she loved him dearly, but her parents considered him a wastrel. He was no end charming and this had a softening influence on Abigail — at times it seemed that it was not quite clear whether he was courting the mother or the daughter. There was nothing really wrong with Tyler, except that he preferred to spend the money that he had inherited rather than add to it by honest toil. The parents were very happy when Nabby, in London, switched her affections to the gallant but sober Smith, who showed a great deal more promise than Tyler. Ironically, the promise was not performed. Nabby's husband spent much time following the will-of-the-wisp of various get-rich-quick schemes, none of which succeeded. Tyler mended his ways and became a highly respected judge. Before she left London Abigail was a grandmother, although she wrote her sister: "I do not feel so ancient as that event will make me."

Abigail penned many letters of advice to her son, John Quincy, at Harvard. The oldest boy was unquestionably the favorite son, and her pen had lectured him on moral precepts since he first went to Europe with his father. In a typical letter from London she told him:

It is said of Hannibal, that he wanted nothing to the completion of his martial virtues, but that, when he had gained a victory, he should know how to use it. It is natural to the human heart to swell with presumption when conscious of superior power; yet all human excellence is comparative, and he who thinks he knows much today will find much more still unattained, provided he is still eager in pursuit of knowledge. . . .

It is an old adage, that a man at thirty must be either a fool or a physician. Though you have not arrived at that age, you would do well to trust to the advice and experience of those who have. Our bodies are framed of such materials as to require constant exercise to keep them in repair, to brace the nerves, and give vigor to the animal functions. Thus do I give you "line upon line, and precept upon precept."

Although Abigail did not believe that the English theatre equalled the French, she looked forward to seeing:

> the celebrated actress Mrs. Siddons. . . . The first piece I saw her in was Shakespeare's *Othello*. She was interesting beyond any actress I had ever seen; but I lost much of the pleasure of the play, from the sooty appearance of the Moor. Perhaps it may be early prejudice; but I could not separate the African color from the man, nor prevent that disgust and horror which filled my mind every time I saw him touch the gentle Desdemona.

In many of her letters back home Abigail was the typical American tourist. She could see little merit in the Old World as compared to the "good old U.S.A." To her niece she wrote:

> Were you to be a witness to the spectacles of wretchedness and misery which these old countries exhibit, crowded with inhabitants, loaded with taxes, you would shudder at the sight. I never set my foot out without encountering many objects whose tattered parti-colored garments hide not half their nakedness and speak, as Otway expresses it, "variety of wretchedness." Covered with disease and starving with hunger they beg, with horror in their countenances. Besides these, what can be said of the wretched victims who are weekly sacrificed upon the gallows in numbers sufficient to astonish a civilized people? I have been credibly informed that hundreds of children from four years and upwards, sleep under the trees, fences, and hedges of Hyde Park nightly, having nowhere else to lay their heads and they subsist by day upon the charity of the passengers. . . . There must be some essential defect in the government and morals of a people, when punishments lose their efficacy and crimes abound. But I shall make you sick with my picture of wretchedness.

To her friend Mercy Warren she wrote:

> I have resided in this country nearly two years, and, in that

time, I have made some few acquaintances whom I esteem, and shall leave with regret; but the customs and manners of a metropolis are unfriendly to that social intercourse which I have ever been accustomed to. Amusement and diversion may always be purchased at the theaters and places of public resort, so that little pains are taken to cultivate that benevolence and interchange of kindness which sweetens life, in lieu of which more visits of form are substituted to keep up the union. Not only the wrinkled brow of age is grasping at the card table, and even tricking with mean avarice, but the virgin bloom of innocence and beauty is withered at the same vigils. I do not think I should draw a false picture of the nobility and gentry of this metropolis, if I were to assert that money and pleasure are the sole objects of their ardent pursuit; public virtue, and, indeed, all virtue, is exposed to sale, and as to principle, where is it to be found, either in the present administration or opposition? Luxury, dissipation, and vice, have a natural tendency to extirpate every generous principle, and leave the heart susceptible of the most malignant vices.

She concluded by saying, "I long, my dear madam, to return to my native land. My little cottage, encompassed with my friends, has more charms for me than the drawing room of St. James, where studied civility and disguised coldness cover malignant hearts."

Abigail's wish to return home was granted early in 1788 when her husband's resignation as Minister to Great Britain was accepted by Congress. Before she left London she wrote lengthy instructions for the redecoration of their new home in Braintree. One room was to be French grey with red-figured wallpaper to match the upholstery of the furniture that they were bringing from London. The furniture for another room was green and it would be best "to have the paper conformable to it." There was dark mahogany paneling in the sitting room and she could not decide whether to paint this a lighter color or to cut two windows to brighten the room. She wanted to build an addition for her husband's books, but finances dictated that this would have to wait until the boys' schooling was finished. The house was important because, she wrote: "Mr. Adams means to retire to Braintree as a private man. Nor need anyone fear that he will become a competitor with them for offices."

When they arrived home Abigail was surprised that the house, which she remembered as a mansion, looked "like a wren's house" after years in the spacious houses in France and England. The repairs were not complete, some of the furniture had been broken during the voyage and, to complicate his wife's problems and symbolize his intention to return to the life of a farmer, John promptly bought six cows and presented them to Abigail.

Adams did not remain a private man for long. Nine months after his return he was elected Vice President of the United States. He journeyed to New York to be sworn in, while Abigail stayed home to tend the farm. She wrote one of her few letters of complaint at this time, mainly because of those six cows which John had bought so precipitantly, and which Abigail now had difficulty getting rid of. She had to trade three heifers and ten sheep to Dr. Tufts in return for a promise to pay the boys' quarter tuition at Harvard. The season was backward; the trees had not leafed; the cows had not calved; and, "really everything seems to have gone awry, veal has got to twopence per pound."

Adams was having his troubles too. He was ill-suited to preside over the Senate, a position in which he was not supposed to enter into debate. John could not keep still and was frequently out of order himself when he should have been keeping order. He had advocated a high and mighty title for

Washington, and this aroused the ire of the fiercely democratic members of the House of Representatives. He was also
plagued with petitions for Federal appointments from friends
and relatives, including one from Ebenezer Storer, the second
husband of the Hannah Quincy who would have liked to
have been Mrs. Adams many years before. John said that
Storer's letter describing the poverty of his family caused him
"many anxious reflections and . . . many melancholy hours."
But Storer did not get the job.

John was living with John Jay in New York, but he missed
his creature comforts — and his Abigail. He had been in New
York little more than a month when he wrote his wife:

> If you think it best, leave Thomas at college, but I pray you to
> come on with Charles, as soon as possible. As to the place, let my
> brother plough and plant as he will, as much as he will. He may
> send me half of the butter, cheese, etc., here. As to money to
> bear your expenses, you must, if you can, borrow of some friend,
> enough to bring you here. If you cannot borrow enough, you
> must sell horses, oxen, sheep, cows, anything at any rate rather
> than not come on. If no one will take the place, leave it to the
> birds of the air and beasts of the field, but at all events break up
> that establishment and that household.

Before the end of June, 1789, Abigail was ensconced in a
house at Richmond Hill in New York, which she described
by writing:

> I have a situation here, which, for natural beauty, may vie with
> the most delicious spot I ever saw. It is a mile and a half distant
> from the city of New York. The house is situated upon an
> eminence; at an agreeable distance flows the noble Hudson, bear-
> ing upon its bosom the fruitful productions of the adjacent
> country. On my right hand, are fields beautifully variegated with
> grass and grain. . . . Upon my left, the city opens to view, inter-
> cepted, here and there, by a rising ground, and an ancient oak. In

front, beyond the Hudson, the Jersey shores present the exuberance of a rich, well-cultivated soil. The venerable oaks and broken ground, covered with wild shrubs, which surround me, give a natural beauty to the spot, which is truly enchanting. A lovely variety of birds serenade me morning and evening, rejoicing in their liberty and security; for I have, as much as possible, prohibited the grounds from invasion, and sometimes almost wished for game laws, when my orders have not been sufficiently regarded.

But the old problems remained. Congress neglected to vote a salary for the Vice President for some time, and when they did it was a pittance — John called it "a curiosity." The Adamses were required to do much official entertaining, but John had no expense account. Servants were again a vexation. Said Abigail:

I cannot find a cook in the whole city but what will get drunk, and as to the Negroes, I am most sincerely sick of them, and I can do no more without Mr. Brisler [a servant from home] than a coach could go without wheels or horse to draw it. I can get hands, but what are hands without a head, and their chief object is to be as expensive as possible.

To top it all, shortly after her arrival she was playing nurse to her son, two of Nabby's children, and two servants:

Mrs. Smith's two children with the whooping cough, Charles with the dysentery, Louisa and Polly with a complaint similar. To Charles I gave a puke last night and his complaints have abated. Louisa and Polly are to take one tonight. If we had not been so fortunate in our situation I do not know how we could have lived. It is very sickly in the city.

The question of titles, levees, ceremonies, and general pomp caused much unpleasantness for the Adamses. The most rabid democrats interpreted some of John's political writings as proving that he had monarchical tendencies.

Washington's mode of life — his coach and six, liveried postilions, etc. — caused some resentment. Since the Republican press did not dare criticize the President, the Vice-President became the whipping boy — a situation that would obtain until the latter years of Washington's second term. Typical of the slanderous attacks on John is this poem that appeared in a Massachusetts paper:

> Be grateful then, YE CHOSEN! mod'rate wise,
> Nor stretch your claims to such preposterous size,
> Lest your too partial country — wiser grown —
> Should on your native dunghills set you down.
> Ape not the fashions of the foreign great,
> Nor make your betters at your *levees* wait —
> Resign your awkward pomp, parade and pride,
> And lay that useless *etiquette* aside;
> Th' unthinking laugh, but all the thinking hate
> Such vile, abortive mimickry of State;
> Those idle lackeys, saunt'ring at your door.

Of this Abigail rather pathetically wrote: "The Vice-President ten times to one goes to Senate in a one-horse chaise, and levee's we have had none. The President only, has his powdered lackies waiting at the door."

Another minor grievance was the preaching of the Congregational ministers of New York, whose sermons did not please Abigail. She thought that the clergymen sought to make up with thundering theatrics what their sermons lacked in content and said that she wanted to hear "liberal good sense . . . true piety without enthusiasm, devotion without grimace, and religion upon a rational system." Generations of Puritan Boylstons, Quincys, et al. must have turned in their graves when Abigail switched to St. Paul's, an Episcopal Church.

After fifteen months in New York the Adamses had again

to move when Philadelphia became the nation's capital. Abigail had her usual problems with servants. In the course of eighteen months she had seven cooks; "not a virtuous woman amongst them all; the most of them drunkards." And there was the ever-present concern over money. The Quaker merchants strove to make a good thing, financially, from the temporary presence of the national government in their midst. But Abigail was reasonably happy because they could return to Braintree — which was now renamed Quincy — between sessions of Congress. In Philadelphia her social life was even more hectic than in New York:

I should spend a very dissipated winter if I were to accept of one half the invitations I receive, particularly to the routes, or tea and cards. Even Saturday evening is not excepted, and I refused an invitation of that kind for this evening. I have been to one assembly. The dancing was very good; the company of the best kind. The President and Madam, the Vice-President and Madam, Ministers of State, and their Madams, etc.; but the room despicable; the etiquette — it was difficult to say where it was to be found. Indeed, it was not New York; but you must not report this from me. . . . I have been to one play, and here again we have been treated with much politeness. The actors came and informed us that a box was prepared for us. The Vice-President thanked them for their civility, and told them that he would attend whenever the President did. And last Wednesday we were all there. The house is equal to most of the theaters we meet with out of France. It is very neat, and prettily fitted up; the actors did their best . . . upon the whole it was very well performed. On Tuesday next I go to a dance at Mr. Chew's, and on Friday sup at Mr. Clymer's; so you see I am likely to be amused.

Ill health and the exigencies of the farm kept Abigail in Quincy during some sessions of Congress and her letters, said John, kept him alive. They were "a feast," "a rich treasure." They were more important than all the speeches he heard in the Senate and: "There is more good thoughts, fine strokes and mother wit in them than I hear in the whole week." Among other things Abigail's letters contained a day-to-day account of the farm: "a newborn lamb was sick with the mumps and couldn't eat" and Abigail had its throat rubbed daily with "goose oil." She needed two wheelbarrows, two spades, two forks, two shovels, two oxen, two hoes and, if John wanted to expand their dairy operation, she needed more pails, tubs, and stools. Wagon wheels needed to be repaired; there were over a hundred loads of manure to spread when the plowing was finished. She had not tarred the trees for six weeks and "the slugs still crawl." To all of this John replied:

The more I am charmed with your bravery and activity in farming, the more I am mortified that my letters in answer to yours are so insignificant and insipid. I must leave all your agriculture to your judgment and the advice of your assistants. I sent you more grass seeds with the furniture, which I hope has arrived before now. . . . You are so valorous and noble a farmer that I feel little anxious about agriculture. Manure in hills if you think best, but manure your barley ground and harrow it well.

By the end of John's first term as Vice-President the two-party system had crystallized. Washington was, presumably, above party. Adams was the recognized leader of the Federalists, although he did not consider himself as a "party" man. Jefferson was emerging as the leader of the Anti-Federalists, who became known as Democrat-Republicans and, finally, as Democrats. During the second election, in which John was returned to office by a narrower margin, he was the particular target of the rabid Anti-Federalist press. In a letter, Abigail fumed at the injustice to her husband:

Few old countries have exhibited more intrigue and false-hood than the anti-federal party has done in the late election. . . . Several of the States were . . . duped by the artifice and lies of the Jacobins, particularly North Carolina. The cry of rights of man, liberty, and equality were popular themes. Their object was to represent the Vice-President as inimical to them, and as a man whose object was to introduce a government of King, Lords, and Commons, and a hereditary nobility. For this purpose they made unfair extracts from his writings, upon which they put their own comments. In one company in Virginia they roundly asserted that he had recommended to Congress to make a son of George the Third, King of America. In another, that he was opposed to the President and that all the difficulty which he had met with from the Senate originated with him. This story the President himself contradicted. . . .

In a country where property is so equally distributed; where no clergy fatten upon the spoils of the people; where no nobility exists for the Jacobins to level, but where every man, be he ever so poor, is protected by the laws, and not a real cause of com-plaint exists, yet do we daily see in embryo all the seeds of discord springing up . . . which, in the course of a few years, will throw this nation into a civil war, and write in letters of blood those very truths which one of their best friends has forwarned them of, and that at the expense of his present popularity. . . . It has been a subject of no small satisfaction to me that the bitterest party-writer has never dared to impeach either the honor, the honesty, or the integrity of the Vice-President, or fix a blemish upon his private character. Though they have not been so honest as Robert R. Livingston of New York who said nothing vexed him so much in all the French Revolution and the horrid cruel-ties they committed as to see the fools by their conduct playing the game into the hands of that Mr. Adams, and proving the truth of his books. Why, said Benson, to whom the observation was made, "Mr. Adams reads the Scriptures, and he reads there that man is as stupid as the wild ass's colt. Mr. Adams does not write the Scriptures; he only reads and believes."

Four years later, when John's election as the second President seemed probable, she wrote her son Thomas on the same theme:

At this eventful period, I can judge of your solicitude to learn through a channel upon which you could depend, whatever affects the interests of our country. In a quotation from the *Chronicle* you cannot expect truth. Falsehood and malevolence are its strongest features. It is the offspring of faction, and nursed by sedition, the adopted bantling of party. It has been crying monarchy and aristocracy. . . .

One writer asserts that "Mr. Adams has immortalized himself as an advocate for hereditary government, as much as Mr. Jefferson has distinguished himself, in and out of office, as a true republican. Mr. Adams has sons placed in high offices and who are no doubt understood to be what he calls the well-born; and who, following his own principle, may, as he hopes, one time become the seigneurs or lords of this country. Mr. Jefferson has daughters only, and had he the wish, has no male successor." By such false and glaring absurdities do these miserable beings endeavor to deceive and delude the people into a distrust of their most disinterested friends, the real guardians of their liberties and defenders of their privileges. . . .

I feel perhaps too keenly the abuse of party. Washington endured it; but he had the support of the people and their undiminished confidence to the hour of his resignation, and a combination of circumstances which no other man can look for. . . . What is the expected lot of a successor? He must be armed as Washington with integrity, with firmness, with intrepidity. These must be his shield and his wall of brass; and religion too, or he never will be able to stand sure and steadfast. . . .

During his sixteen years of public office Abigail's support was vital to John. One recent biographer, Page Smith, said simply: "Abigail insured his sanity." John was a political philosopher rather than a politician, statesman, or diplomat. He could not compromise with his ideals nor condone others who did not live by his stern Puritan principles. Putting it more bluntly, he could not get along with anybody who did not agree with him. At one time or another he fought bitterly with every one of the principal Founding Fathers except Washington; and he even criticized the great national hero. He lashed out at Jefferson, Hamilton, Madison — and Franklin was his particular *bête noire*. The old doctor once said of Adams: "He means well for his country, is always an honest man, often a wise one, but sometimes, and in some things, absolutely out of his senses."

Constant strife marked John's public career and it is possible that he could not have withstood the slings and arrows with which he was temperamentally ill equipped to cope had it not been for the help and support of his wife. His enemies were her enemies — although she could never completely overcome her early reverence for Franklin. When Mercy Warren wrote a history of the Revolution that criticized John, Abigail became coldly formal toward her long-time close friend.

John was subject to moods ranging from bright optimism to black pessimism. The latter state was more usual. At times he was convinced that true democracy was impossible because man was not perfectible. He had frequent periods of self-doubt as to his own capabilities — but not his convictions. He was sure that the whole world was against him and that neither his contemporaries nor posterity would appreciate his efforts in behalf of his country nor the purity of his motives. Through all this Abigail was, at times, a balance wheel; at others a source of encouragement and consolation. And always she was a source of strength to her husband. Her faith in John never wavered. On the day when his election as President was assured she proclaimed that faith in this moving letter:

The sun is dressed in brightest beams
to give thy honors to the day.

And may it prove an auspicious prelude to each ensuing season. You have this day to declare yourself head of a nation. "And now, O Lord, my God, thou hast made thy servant ruler over the people. Give unto him an understanding heart, that he may know how to go out and come in before this great people; that he may discern between good and bad. For who is able to judge this thy so great a people?" These were the words of a royal sovereign; and not less applicable to him who is invested with the chief magistracy of a nation, though he wear not the crown, nor the robes of royalty.

My thoughts and my meditations are with you, though personally absent; and my petitions to Heaven are that "the things which make for peace may not be hidden from your eyes." My feelings are not those of pride nor ostentation upon the occasion. They are solemnized by a sense of the obligations, the important trusts, and numerous duties connected with it. That you may be enabled to discharge them with honor to yourself, with justice and impartiality to your country, and with satisfaction to this great people, shall be the daily prayer of your   AA.

Abigail did not start for Philadelphia until two months after her husband's inauguration. She paused at Eastchester to visit Nabby, who was already impoverished by her husband's speculations. Abigail wrote to her sister: "My reflections upon prospects there took from me all appetite to food and depressed my spirits, before too low. The Colonel gone on a journey, I knew not where. I could not converse with her. I saw her heart too full. Such is the folly and madness of speculation and extravagance. To her no blame is due. Educated in different habits, she never enjoyed a life of dissipation." Then she went on to New York to see her son Charles who "lives prettily but frugally. He has a lovely babe and a discreet woman I think for his wife, quite different from many of the family." En route she recorded her reactions to her new responsibilities.

My thoughts are continually like Noah's dove, returning to the ark I have left. Whether like that I shall return no more, must be left with that Being, in whose hands my breath is. I consider myself following where duty leads and trust the event.

> Is Heav'n tremendous in its frowns? Most sure;
> And in its favours formidable too:
> Its favours here are trials, not rewards;
> A call to duty, not discharge from care;
> And should alarm us, full as much as woes;
> Awake us to their cause, and consequence;
> O'er our scann'd conduct give a jealous eye;
> And make us tremble.

Such appears to me the situation in which I am placed, enviable no doubt in the eyes of some, but never envy'd nor coveted by me. That I may discharge my part with honour, and give satisfaction is my most earnest wish.

A few days after her arrival in Philadelphia the new First Lady held her first reception for "32 ladies and near as many gentlemen. I shall have the same ceremony to pass through today, and the rest part of the week. As I am not prepared with furniture for a regular drawing Room, I shall not commence one I believe, as the summer is so near at hand, and my health very precarious." As a postscript to the above she wrote:

Evening eight o'clock: The day is past, and a fatiguing one it has been, The Ladies of Foreign Ministers and the Ministers, with our own Secretaries and Ladies have visited me today, and add to them, the whole levee today of Senate and House. Strangers etc. making near one hundred asked permission to visit me, so that from half past twelve till near four, I was rising up and sitting down. Mr. Adams will never be too big to have his friends.

A week later she outlined her routine as the President's wife.

I keep up my old habit of rising at an early hour. If I did not I should have little command of my time. At five I rise. From that time till eight I have a few leisure hours. At eight I breakfast, after which until eleven I attend to my family arrangements. At that hour I dress for the day. From twelve until two I receive company, sometimes until three. We dine at that hour unless on company days which are Tuesdays and Thursdays. After dinner I usually ride out until seven. I begin to feel a little more at home, and less anxiety about the ceremonious part of my duty, though by not having a drawing room for the summer I am obliged every day to devote two hours for the purpose of seeing company. Tomorrow we are to dine the Secretaries of State etc. with the whole Senate.

The Adamses entertained on a scale much less lavish than their predecessors, but Abigail constantly bemoaned the expense of their position: "We give for this very house a thousand pounds a year. President Washington never gave more than five hundred. And everything else in the same proportion, nay more than double." Washington had established the practice of holding open house on July 4, and Abigail complained that: "As we are here we cannot avoid the trouble nor the expense. I have been informed the day used to cost the late President five hundred dollars. More than two hundred wt of cake used to be expended, and two quarter casks of wine besides spirit. You will not wonder that I dread it, or think President Washington to blame for introducing the custom, if he could have avoided it."

Abigail was a very different First Lady from Martha Washington, who had confined herself to domestic and social duties. Abigail shared with John his political burdens and forcefully expressed her opinions of those who criticized or disagreed with him. She had described Martha as "modest and unassuming, dignified and feminine, not the tincture of hauteur about her." Of these adjectives only "dignified" and "feminine" could be applied to Abigail. She was often sarcastically referred to as "Her Majesty," and there were those who said that she made the President's decisions for him. This was not true — although she did have something to say about many of them.

The great problem of Adams' administration was the undeclared war with France; a situation for which he received the blame but which he had actually inherited from Washington, who had done much to alienate the French. Adams finally cut the Gordian knot by dispatching new envoys to France without consulting his cabinet. This was a surprise to the Democrats and a political blow to both parties that caused great consternation. Abigail, who was in Quincy at the time, wrote her husband that the measure had "universally electrified the public. . . . It comes so sudden, was a measure so unexpected, that the whole community were like a flock of frightened pigeons: nobody had their story ready; some called it a hasty measure; others condemned it as an inconsistent one; some swore, some cursed."

John was amused by a comment that Mrs. Adams would never have let him take such a step had she been in Philadelphia and wrote her: "This ought to gratify your vanity enough to cure you." Her son Thomas reported similar opinion in Boston, to the effect that "they wished the old woman had been there; they did not believe it would have taken place." Abigail wrote John: "This was pretty saucy but the old woman can tell them they are mistaken, for she considers the measure a master stroke of policy. . . . It is a measure which strikes in the head Jacobinism. It came as unexpected to them as to the Federalists." She ended by saying that the country's defenses should be kept up and that "We should hold the sword in one hand and the olive branch in the other . . . Pray am I not a good politician?"

Ironically, Adams' settlement of the difficulties with France probably prevented his re-election. The Federalists were riding high on anti-French public opinion until their own President cut the ground from under their feet and deprived them of a campaign issue. Also, the people had accepted the Alien and Sedition Acts that the Federalists had passed as a war measure, but with the war scare abated they listened to the charge of the Democrats that Adams had interfered with the sacred freedom of the press. He was handsomely defeated by his Vice-President, Jefferson. Of his defeat Abigail wrote to her son Thomas:

The consequence to us, personally, is that we retire from public life. For myself and family, I have few regrets. At my age, and with my bodily infirmities, I shall be happier at Quincy. Neither my habits, nor my education or inclinations have led me to an expensive style of living, so that on that score I have little to mourn over. If I did not rise with dignity, I can at least fall with ease, which is the more difficult task. I wish your father's circumstances were not so limited and circumscribed, as they must be, because he cannot indulge himself in those improvements upon his farm which his inclination leads him to, and which would serve to amuse him and contribute to his health. I feel not any resentment against those who are coming into power, and only wish the future administration of the government may be as productive of the peace, happiness, and prosperity of the nation as the two former ones have been. I leave to time the unfolding of a drama. I leave to posterity to reflect upon the times past; and I leave them characters to contemplate. My own intention is to return to Quincy as soon as I conveniently can.

As the wife of the lame-duck President, Abigail had one

more move to make before she could return to private life. Between the election and Jefferson's inauguration the Government moved to its permanent home in Washington D.C. and Abigail became the first Lady to occupy the White House. She described the Federal City and the President's mansion by writing:

I arrived here on Sunday last, and without meeting with any accident worth noticing, except losing ourselves when we left Baltimore, and going eight or nine miles on the Frederick road, by which means we were obliged to go the other eight through woods, where we wandered two hours without finding a guide, or the path. Fortunately, a straggling black came up with us, and we engaged him as a guide, to extricate us out of our difficulty; but woods are all you see, from Baltimore until you reach *the city*, which is only so in name. Here and there is a small cot, without a glass window, interspersed amongst the forests, through which you travel miles without seeing any human being. In the city there are buildings enough, if they were compact and finished, to accommodate Congress and those attached to it; but as they are, and scattered as they are, I see no great comfort for them. The river, which runs up to Alexandria, is in full view of my window, and I see the vessels as they pass and repass.

The house is upon a grand and superb scale, requiring about thirty servants to attend and keep the apartments in proper order, and perform the ordinary business of the house and stables. . . . The lighting the apartments, from the kitchen to parlors and chambers, is a tax indeed; and the fires we are obliged to keep to secure us from daily agues is another very cheering comfort. To assist us in this great castle, and render less attendance necessary, bells are wholly wanting, not one single one being hung through the whole house, and promises are all you can obtain. This is so great an inconvenience, that I know not what to do, or how to do. . . . But no comparisons — if they will put me up some bells, and let me have wood enough to keep fires, I design to be pleased. I could content myself almost anywhere three months; but, surrounded with forests, can you believe that wood is not

to be had, because people cannot be found to cut and cart it! . . . .
You must keep all this to yourself, and, when asked how I like
it, say that I write you the situation is beautiful, which is true.
The house is made habitable, but there is not a single apartment
finished. . . . We have not the least fence, yard, or other convenience, without, and the great unfinished audience-room I
make a drying-room of, to hang up the clothes in. The principal
stairs are not up, and will not be this winter. . . . If the twelve
years, in which this place has been considered as the future seat
of government, had been improved as they would have been if
in New England, very many of the present inconveniences would
have been removed. It is a beautiful spot, capable of every im-
provement, and the more I view it, the more I am delighted
with it.

Since I sat down to write, I have been called down to a servant
from Mount Vernon, with a billet from Major Custis, and a
haunch of venison, and a kind, congratulatory letter from Mrs.
Lewis, upon my arrival in the city, with Mrs. Washington's love,
inviting me to Mount Vernon, where, health permitting, I will
go, before I leave this place.

When the family returned to Quincy, Abigail threw herself into the work of the farm. She gave her son-in-law a
message for Nabby: "Tell her I have commenced my opera-
tions of dairy-woman; and she might see me, at five o'clock in
the morning, skimming my milk." John too, although in his
sixty-fifth year, did much of the manual work of the farm.
The time was a little difficult for Abigail because her husband sulked for two or three years. His normally busy pen
was idle while he brooded about the injustices he had suffered. Abigail continued to write long letters to nephews,
nieces, children, and grandchildren full of exhortations to
be industrious, virtuous, devout, and thrifty; and to get
plenty of exercise and say their prayers.

To others she wrote in defense of her husband. She renewed her correspondence with Mercy Warren to justify something John had written a quarter century before. In 1775 a letter of John's to Mercy's husband had been intercepted and published in the British press. At the time he was disputing the subject of independence with John Dickenson, a Quaker representative in the Continental Congress. Without mentioning Dickenson by name, Adams, in the intercepted letter, had referred to "a certain piddling genius." Abigail had never forgotten how unfairly the British press had twisted John's meaning and in 1801 she wrote to Mercy:

The design of the publisher appears from the introduction of the letter to make it believed that the person alluded to as "a piddling genius" was General Washington, and that the supposed writer was engaged in a plot to get him removed from the command of the army; that he possessed a sanguinary, revengeful temper . . . without adverting to the period when the letter was written, and the state of the country at that time. . . . The old actors are gone off the stage. Few remain who remember the perils and dangers to which we were then exposed, and fewer still who are willing to do justice to those who hazarded their lives and fortunes to secure to them the blessings which they now possess, and upon which they riot and scoff. Little regard is paid to that prohibition, "Thou shalt not bear false witness," or to that system of benevolence which teaches us to "love one another"; and which I trust we, my dear Madam, shall never lose sight of, however reviled and despitefully used.

The "Adams Mansion" was a busy place during the early years of the nineteenth century, constantly filled with children — nieces, nephews, grandchildren and, finally greatgrandchildren. Son Charles had died and his widow with her two small children were permanent residents. John Quincy came home from his Ambassadorship to Berlin in 1801 with a foreign-born wife, Louisa Catherine, and their infant,

George Washington Adams, Abigail's seventh grandchild. Louisa Catherine, brought up in England and France, did not know what to make of the New England farm of her husband's parents. She wrote: "Had I stepped into Noah's Ark I could not have been more utterly astonished." She was pleased that "the old gentleman took a fancy to me," but between the second First Lady and the daughter-in-law who would become the sixth in this succession there was always a certain wariness. Both were strong-willed women.

The children around the house did much to cheer John up, and this created something of a problem for Grandma, who was a rather strict disciplinarian. Her husband's indulgence with the children caused some near quarrels. In fact, there is evidence from some of Abigail's letters to her sister that she was getting a little "fed up" with her spouse's temperament in their old age. She wrote her sister that, during their long life, "I have some times insisted upon my own way and sometimes yielded silently." Her sister Eliza, too, had a husband who was sometimes inflexible, and Abigail continued: "You know all this, who is always in the right? Yet after half a century, I can say my first choice would be the same if I again had youth and opportunity to make it." She recalled a query their parson had raised: "What is an old woman good for?" She replied "that she would do to set off against an old man."

In 1804 Abigail was torn between two allegiances. Her husband and Thomas Jefferson had been close friends since the Declaration of Independence days and in London and France. Before Adams left the White House they had become estranged, and would neither speak nor write to each other for more than twelve years. In 1804 Jefferson's daughter died. Abigail had taken care of the child, when she was eight years old, in London. Although she supported her husband in his quarrel with the Virginian, Abigail could not forebear sending the President a letter of condolence.

Had you been no other than the private inhabitant of Monticello, I should, ere this time, have addressed you with that sympathy which a recent event has awakened in my bosom; but reasons of various kinds withheld my pen, until the powerful feelings of my heart burst through the restraint, and called upon me to shed a tear of sorrow over the departed remains of your beloved and deserving daughter — an event which I most sincerely mourn. . . .

I know how closely entwined around a parent's heart are those cords which bind the parental to the filial bosom; and when snapped asunder, how agonizing the pangs! I have tasted of the bitter cup, and bow with reverence and submission before the great Dispenser of it, without whose permission and overruling providence not a sparrow falls to the ground. That you may derive comfort and consolation in this day of your sorrow and affliction from that only source calculated to heal the wounded heart, a firm belief in the being, perfections, and attributes of God, is the sincere and ardent wish of her, who once took pleasure in subscribing herself your friend.

In replying Jefferson expressed his unhappiness in the estrangement with John, saying that their differences were political, not personal. During his last days as President, Adams had appointed a number of Federalists to lifetime judgeships. Jefferson referred to this, saying that "one act of Mr. Adams' life, and one only, ever gave me a moment's personal displeasure. I did consider his last appointments to office as personally unkind. They were from among my most ardent political enemies, from whom no faithful cooperation could ever be expected." Abigail replied: "As this act, I am certain, was not intended to give any personal pain or offence, I think it a duty to explain it, so far as I then knew his views and designs. The Constitution empowers the President to fill up offices as they become vacant. It was in the exercise of this power that appointments were made, and characters selected, whom Mr. Adams considered as men faithful to the constitution. . . . No offence was given by it and no personal unkindness thought of. . . . so far was Mr. Adams from harboring such a sentiment, that he had not any idea of the intolerance of party spirit at that time."

The irate Abigail did not leave it at this. Jefferson had criticized her husband and he must be shown that it was he and his Democratic supporters who were in the wrong, not her John. Her letter continued at length. "I have never felt any enmity toward you, Sir, for being elected President of the United States. But the instruments made use of and the means which were practised to effect a change have my utter abhorrence and detestation, for they were the blackest calumny and the foulest falsehoods." After more in this vein she added: "And now, Sir, I will freely disclose to you what has severed the bonds of former friendship, and placed you in a light very different from what some viewed you in.

"One of the first acts of your administration was to liberate a wretch, who was suffering the just punishment of his crimes for publishing the basest libel, the lowest and vilest slander which malice could invent or calumny exhibit, against the character and reputation of your predecessor." This referred to a publisher named Callander, a bitter critic of John's, who had been convicted under the Sedition Act and whom Jefferson had promptly pardoned. Abigail concluded: "There is one other act of your administration which I considered as personally unkind, and which your own mind will easily suggest to you; but as it neither affected character nor reputation, I forbear to state it."

Jefferson replied that he had released Callander, as he had

others convicted under the Sedition Act because that law was a nullity under the Constitution, "as absolute and palpable as if Congress had ordered us to fall down and worship a graven image." He added that, "on his honor," he had not the remotest idea of any other act of his that could be construed as a personal unkindness toward the Adamses. In a third long letter, mainly devoted to the iniquities of party politics — by which Abigail meant Democratic party politics — she enlightened him. "Soon after my eldest son's return from Europe, he was appointed by the District Judge to an office in which no political concerns entered. Personally known to you, and possessing all the qualifications, you yourself being judge, which you had designated for office, as soon as Congress gave the appointments to the President, you removed him. . . . With pleasure I say, that he is not a blind follower of any party." She then brusquely terminated the correspondence by concluding: "I have written to you with a freedom which only former friendship would warrant; and to which I would gladly return, could all causes but mere difference of opinion be removed. I wish to lead a tranquil and retired life under the administration of the government, disposed to heal the wounds of contention, to cool the raging fury of party animosity, to soften the rugged spirit of resentment, and desirous of seeing my children and grandchildren heirs to that freedom and independence which you and your predecessor united your efforts to obtain. With these sentiments, I reciprocate my sincere wishes for your health and happiness." This would be the last letter to Jefferson from Quincy until Dr. Benjamin Rush reconciled the old friends eight years later.

The second decade of the nineteenth century brought much grief to Abigail. Her contemporaries were starting to die off — relations, friends, and neighbors. Among the first to go were her sister Mary and her husband, William Cranch — the same with whom John had ridden to the Smith house when he was courting. Of her sister's passing she wrote to her nephew:

> I passed the three last days of her life chiefly with her, in two of which she appeared wandering; in one of them she did not mention your father, in the other she talked much of him, and in a kind of ecstasy said, "He has only stepped behind the scene; I shall know where to find him"; . . . Once, after a silence of some time, she broke out into an apostrophe — "O my son, my son" — and said no more. I presumed she had been thinking of the grief which the death of your father would occasion to you.

The year 1813 was particularly hard. Nabby came home to die a lingering, painful death from cancer. Abigail nursed her in one room and her daughter-in-law Sally, Charles' widow, in the next with an advanced case of consumption. She was frequently ill herself but her wit and spirits did not desert her. She wrote a long, gay letter to her granddaughter Caroline detailing life in Quincy:

> Your neat, pretty letter, looking small, but containing much reached me this day. I have a good mind to give you the journal of the day.
> Six o'clock. Rose, and, in imitation of his Britannic Majesty, kindled my own fire. Went to the stairs, as usual, to summon George and Charles. Returned to my chamber, dressed myself. No one stirred. Called a second time, with voice a little raised.
> Seven o'clock. Blockheads not out of bed. Girls in motion. Mean, when I hire another manservant, that he shall come for *one* call.
> Eight o'clock. Fires made, breakfast prepared . . . Mrs. A. at the tea-board. Forgot the sausages. Susan's recollection brought them upon the table.
> *Enter* Ann. "Ma'am, the man is come with coals."

"Go, call George to assist him." *Exit* Ann.

Enter Charles. "Mr. B— is come with cheese, turnips, etc. Where are they to be put?" "I will attend to him myself." *Exit* Charles.

Just seated at the table again.

Enter George with "Ma'am, here is a man with a drove of pigs." A consultation is held upon this important subject, the result of which is the purchase of two spotted swine.

Nine o'clock. *Enter* Nathaniel, from the upper house, with a message for sundries; and black Thomas's daughter, for sundries. Attended to all these concerns. A little out of sorts that I could not finish my breakfast. Note; never to be incommoded with trifles. . . .

At twelve o'clock, by a previous engagement, I was to call at Mr. G—'s for Cousin B. Smith to accompany me to the bridge at Quincy-port, being the first day of passing it. The day was pleasant; the scenery delightful. Passed both bridges, and entered Hingham. Returned before three o'clock. Dined, and,

At five, went to Mr. T. G—'s, with your grandfather; the third visit he has made with us in *the week;* and let me whisper to you he played at whist with Mr. J. G—, who was as ready and accurate as though he had both eyes to see with. Returned.

At nine, sat down and wrote a letter.

At eleven, retired to bed. . . . By all this, you will learn that Grandmother has got rid of her croaking, and that Grandfather is in good health, and that both of us are as tranquil as that bald old fellow, called Time, will let us be.

And here I was interrupted in my narrative.

I reassume my pen upon the twenty-second of November, being this day sixty-eight years old. How many reflections occur to me upon this anniversary!

What have I done for myself or others in this long period of my sojourn, that I can look back upon with pleasure, or reflect upon with approbation? Many, very many follies and errors of judgment and conduct rise up before me, and ask forgiveness of that Being, who seeth into the secret recesses of the heart, and from whom nothing is hidden. I think I may with truth say, that in no period of my life have the vile passions had control over me. I bear no enmity to any human being; but, alas! as Mrs. Placid said to her friend, by which of thy good works wouldst thou be willing to be judged? I do not believe, with some divines, that all our good works are but as filthy rags; the example which our great Master has set before us, of purity, benevolence, obedience, submission, and humility, are virtues which, if faithfully practised, will find their reward; or why has he pronounced so many benedictions upon them in his Sermon on the Mount?"

The old woman did not lose touch with affairs outside of Quincy. She disagreed with most of New England, which opposed the War of 1812. To Mercy Warren she wrote:

We have our firesides, our comfortable habitations, our cities, our churches, and our country to defend, our rights, privileges, and independence to preserve. And for these are we not justly contending? Thus it appears to me; yet I hear from our pulpits and read from our presses that it is an unjust, a wicked, a ruinous, and unnecessary war. If I give an opinion with respect to the conduct of our native State, I cannot do it with approbation. She has had much to complain of as it respected a refusal of naval protection, yet that cannot justify her in paralyzing the arm of government when raised for her defence and that of the nation. A house divided against itself — and upon that foundation do our enemies build their hopes of subduing us. May it prove a sandy one to them.

In 1816 Abigail had the pleasure of hearing that her son John Quincy had been appointed Secretary of State in James Monroe's cabinet. She surely speculated on the fact that Jefferson had started as Secretary of State and ended as President and that Monroe had held this position in Madison's cabinet before his elevation to the presidency. But Abigail did not live to see John Quincy in the White House. In October 1818 she fell seriously ill. A stroke deprived her of speech and movement for a few days, until she quietly died at the age of seventy-three. John wrote to John Quincy: "The bitterness of death is past, the grim spoiler so terrible to human nature has no sting left for me." From Monticello Jefferson wrote to express his sympathy to his old friend and remind him that the time was not distant when both of them "must ascend in essence to an ecstatic meeting with friends we have loved and lost, and whom we shall still love and never lose again. God bless and support you under your heavy affliction."

John lived for eight years longer; he and Jefferson died within hours of each other on July 4, 1826. In his final years an old flame re-entered his life. The widowed Mrs. Ebenezer Storer — nee Hannah Quincy — called on him. The old man — he was nearing ninety — said: "Madam, shall we not walk in Cupid's Grove together?" To which Hannah replied, "Ah, sir, it would not be the first time that we have walked there." Josiah Quincy, who observed the meeting, recorded that: "The flash of old sentiment was startling from its utter unexpectedness."

CHAPTER V

The Tragic Loves of Thomas Jefferson

A MINOR FRUSTRATION of American history is Thomas Jefferson's reticence about his private life. He wrote many thousands of letters on subjects ranging from agriculture to zoology; but virtually none about himself. His autobiography is almost exclusively a political document. In it he devoted pages to the causes of the French Revolution and to a verbatim account of the Congressional discussion on the Declaration of Independence. But his only references to his wife are the date of their marriage and a passing comment on her death. He said that he refused a Congressional appointment to go to France with Franklin in 1776 because "such was the state of my family that I could not leave it"; and, when he was first appointed to the peace commission at the end of the Revolution, "the same reasons obliged me still to decline." But what these reasons were will never be known.

One of the few things about which Jefferson was not so reticent was his earliest love. The first of his letters that have been preserved, with one exception, are to a friend, John Page. They were written over a period of two years, from the time he was nineteen until he was twenty-one, and tell of his love for Rebecca Burwell, whom he called Belinda. He had met Rebecca, when she was sixteen, while he was attending William and Mary College in Williamsburg. She remained there while he went back to Shadwell to read law.

The first letter in which Thomas mentioned Rebecca was written on Christmas day, 1762, from the estate of relatives with whom he was spending the holiday. It is a humorous epistle describing how rats in his bedroom were inspired by the devil to

eat up my pocketbook, which was in my pocket, within a foot of my head. And not contented with plenty for the present, they carried away my jemmy-worked silk garters, and half a dozen new minuets I had just got, to serve, I suppose, as provision for the winter. . . .

You know it rained last night, or if you do not know it, I am sure I do. When I went to bed, I laid my watch in the usual place, and going to take her up after I arose this morning, I found her in the same place, it's true! but all afloat in water, let in at a leak in the roof of the house, and as silent and still as the rats that had eaten my pocketbook. Now, you know, if chance had had anything to do in this matter, there were a thousand other spots where it might have chanced to leak as well as this one, which was perpendicularly over my watch. But I'll tell you; it's my opinion that the Devil came and bored the hole over it on purpose. Well, as I was saying, my poor watch had lost her speech. I should not have cared much for this, but something worse attended it; the subtle particles of the water with which the case was filled had, by their penetration, so overcome the cohesion of the particles of the paper, of which my dear picture and watch paper were composed, that in attempting to take them out to dry them, Good God! *Mens horret referre!* My cursed fingers gave them such a rent, as I fear I never shall get over. This, cried I, was the last stroke Satan had in reserve for me; he knew I cared not for anything else he could do to me, and was determined to

try this last most fatal expedient. . . . However, whatever misfortunes may attend the picture of lover, my hearty prayers shall
be that all the health and happiness which heaven can send may
be the portion of the original, and that so much goodness may
ever meet with what may be most agreeable in this world, as I
am sure it must in the next. And now, although the picture may
be defaced, there is so lively an image of her imprinted in my
mind, that I shall think of her too often, I fear, for my peace of
mind.

The picture in the watch was of Rebecca, and Thomas
asked Page to try to get another from her. He seemed to rely
on Page to represent him in his love affair. In a subsequent
letter he wrote:

How does R.B. do? What do you think of my affair, or what
would you advise me to do? Had I better stay here and do
nothing, or go down and do less? Or in other words had I better
stay here while I am here, or go down that I may have the pleasure of sailing up the river again in a full-rigged flat? Inclination
tells me to go, receive my sentence, and be no longer in suspense;
but, reason says if you go and your attempt proves unsuccessful
you will be ten times more wretched than ever.

Later in this same letter his mind wandered from Rebecca
and he asked his friend:

Have you an inclination to travel, Page? Because if you have I
shall be glad of your company. For you must know that as soon
as the Rebecca (the name I intend to give the vessel above mentioned) is completely finished I intend to hoist sail and away. I
shall visit particularly England, Holland, France, Spain, Italy
(where I would buy me a good fiddle), and Egypt and return
through the British provinces to the northward home. This, to
be sure, would take us two or three years and if we should not
both be cured of love in that time I think the devil would be in it.

Page apparently told Thomas that he had a rival in Williamsburg, of whom Jefferson wrote:

The rival you mentioned I know not whether to think formidable or not as there has been so great an opening for him during my absence. I say "has been" because I expect there is one no longer since you have undertaken to act as my attorney. You advise me to "go immediately and lay siege in form." You certainly did not think at the time you wrote this of that paragraph in my letter wherein I mentioned to you my resolution of going to Britain. And to begin an affair of that kind now, and carry it on so long a time in form is by no means a proper plan. No, no. Page, whatever assurances I may ask in return from her, depend on it they must be kept in private. . . . If I am to succeed the sooner I know it the less uneasiness I shall have to go through: if I am to meet with a disappointment the sooner I know it the more of life I shall have to wear it off. . . . If Belinda will not accept of my service it shall never be offered to another.

He then asked Page to speak to Rebecca about his plan to travel:

I should be scared to death at making her so unreasonable a proposal as that of waiting untill I returned from Britain, unless she could be first prepared for it. I am afraid it will make my chance of succeeding considerably worse. But the event at last must be this, that if she consents, I shall be happy; if she does not, I must endeavor to be as much so as possible.

Thomas finally got around to speaking to Rebecca himself, late in 1763, and reported the incident to Page as follows:

In the most melancholy fit that ever any poor soul was, I sit down to write to you. Last night, as merry as agreeable company and dancing with Belinda in the Apollo could make me, I never could have thought the succeeding sun would have seen me so wretched as I now am! I was prepared to say a great deal: I had dressed up in my own mind such thoughts as occurred to me, in as moving language as I knew how, and expected to have performed in a tolerably creditable manner. But, good God! When I had an opportunity of venting them, a few broken sentences,

uttered in great disorder, and interrupted with pauses of un-
common length, were too visible marks of my strange confusion!
The whole confab I will tell you, word for word, if I can, when
I see you.

Another letter indicates that he had a further conversation
with Rebecca in which he proposed that she wait until he
finished his travels and then they might reach an understanding. He was toying with the idea of marriage; and "toying"
is the right word. He was not ready to commit himself until
he had a fling at the world; but nothing ever came of his
travel plans. In 1764 Rebecca apparently became disgusted
with her vacillating suitor and married a man named Jac-
quelin Ambler. She had no further influence on Jefferson's
life, but many years later her daughter married John Marshall, the Supreme Court Chief Justice who caused Jefferson
much trouble when he was President.

After the Burwell affair there were apparently no women
in Jefferson's life until his marriage eight years later. Although his devotion to Rebecca may have been in the nature
of puppy love it seems to have turned him into a misogynist
during his twenties. Thomas had a habit of copying excerpts
that interested him into a notebook and during this period
several of them were to the effect that marriage and women
were no good. There was this quote from a play by Ottway:

> Wed her!
> No! were she all Desire could wish, as fair
> As the vainest of her sex be thought,
> With Wealth beyond what woman's pride could waste,
> She should not cheat me of my Freedom. Marry!
> When I am old & weary of the World,
> I may grow desperate,
> And take a Wife to mortify withal.

And this antifeminine quote from *Paradise Lost:*

> O! why did God,
> Creator wise! that Peopl'd highest Heav'n
> With spirits masculine, create at last
> This Novelty on Earth, this fair Defect
> Of Nature? And not fill the world at once
> With Men, as Angels, without feminine?
> Or find some other Way to generate
> Mankind?

There are other antifeminine quotes from Euripides, including these from *Medea:* "Mortals should beget children from some other source and there should be no womankind; thus there would be no ill for men." And again: "O Zeus, why hast thou established women, a curse deceiving men, in the light of the sun?"

His notebook also contained a rather curious document delineating the conduct that should be expected from a wife which Jefferson either composed or copied from an unknown source:

Sweetness of temper, affection to a husband, and attention to his interests constitute the duties of a wife and form the basis of matrimonial felicity.

The charms of beauty and the brilliancy of wit, though they may captivate in the mistress will not long delight in the wife; they will shorten even their own transitory reign if, as I have often seen, they shine more for the attraction of everybody else than their husbands. Let the pleasing of that one person be a thought never absent from your conduct. . . .

Never consider as a trifle what may tend to please him. The great articles of duty he will set down as his own; but the lesser attentions he will mark as favors; trust me there is no feeling more delightful to one's self, than that of turning those little things to so precious a use.

But wedlock, even in its happiest lot, is not exempted from

the common fate of all sublunary blessings. The rapture of extravagant love will evaporate and waste; the conduct of the wife must substitute in its room, other regards, as delicate and more lasting. I say the conduct of the wife; for marriage, be a husband what he may, reverses the prerogative of sex; his will expect to be pleased, and ours must be sedulous to please. This privilege a good-natured man may waive: he will feel it, however, his due; and third persons will have penetration enough and may have malice enough to remark the want of it in his wife.

[The word "ours" in the second sentence above may be a slip of the pen or may indicate that this was originally written by a woman.]

The office of a wife includes the exertion of a friend. There are situations where it will not be enough to love, to cherish, to obey; she must teach her husband to be at peace with himself, to be reconciled to the world, etc., etc. —

There are afflictions less easy to be endured. Those which a husband inflicts, and the best wives feel most severely. The fortitude that can resist can only cure. Complaints debase her who suffers, and harden him who aggrieves. Let not a woman always look for their cause in the injustice of her Lord: They may proceed from many trifling errors in her own conduct. . . .

Above all, let a wife beware of communicating to others any want of duty or tenderness she may think she has perceived in her husband. This untwists, at once, those delicate cords which preserve the unity of the marriage engagements. Its sacredness is broken forever, if third parties are made witnesses of its failings.

I am astonished at the folly of many women who are still reproaching their husbands for leaving them alone, preferring this or that company to theirs, for treating them with this or the other mark of disregard or indifference, when to speak the truth, they have themselves in a great measure to blame. Not that I would justify the men in anything wrong on their part; but had you behaved to them with a more respectful observance, and a more equal tenderness, studying their humors, overlooking their mistakes, submitting to their opinions in matters indifferent, passing by little instances of unevenness, caprice, or passion, giv-

ing soft answers for hasty words, complaining as seldom as possible and making your daily care to relieve their anxieties. . . .

In 1767 Jefferson started to build a home for himself. The
idea of moving from the parental home, Shadwell, went back
several years. While he was still studying law he had written
Page that he wanted to build "a small house, which shall
contain a room for myself and another for you, unless Belinda
should think proper to favor us with her company, in which
case I will enlarge the plan as much as she pleases." The site
of the new residence, across from Shadwell, was the crest of
a hill which provided a view of the Blue Ridge Mountains.
At first he planned to call it The Hermitage. An entry in an
account book in 1767 read: "Work to be done at Hermitage.
Plant raspberries — gooseberries — currants — strawberries —
asparagus — artichokes — fill up trees — sow grass — hen house
— cherry tree — lucerne — road — wagoning wood and sand."
The word "Hermitage" is crossed out and the name "Monticello" written in. He first moved to the "little mountain" —
monticello in Italian — in 1771. He described it by writing:
"I have lately removed to the mountain from whence this is
dated. . . . I have here but one room which, like the cobbler's,
serves me for parlor, for kitchen, and hall. I may add, for
bedchamber and study, too. . . . I have hope, however, of
getting more elbow room this summer."

Perhaps, as with Franklin, Washington, and Adams, an
empty house turned Jefferson's thoughts to marriage. In any
event, less than a year after he moved to the mountain top
he married, on New Year's day, 1772, a twenty-three-year-old
widow, Martha Skelton, daughter of wealthy attorney John
Wayles. Nothing is known of this courtship, which apparently
lasted over a year. In October, 1770, his account book shows
that he paid a "Smith at Wayles 1/3." He was back in early

December and spent Christmas with his future bride. Two months later he commented on a friend who "is wishing to take to himself a wife, and nothing obstructs but the unfeeling temper of a parent." He added: "I too am in that way; and have still greater difficulties to encounter not from the forwardness of parents, nor perhaps want of feeling in the fair one, but from other causes as unpliable to my wishes as these."

Although Mr. Wayles did not seem to object to Jefferson as a suitor, Thomas may have sought to prove his social worthiness, for early in 1771 he wrote to a London bookseller to get him a coat of arms: "One further favor and I am done; to search the Herald's office for the arms of my family. I have what I have been told are the family arms, but on what authority I know not. It is possible there may be none. If so, I would with your assistance become a purchaser, having Sterne's word for it that a coat of arms may be purchased as cheap as any other coat."

The couple seem to have been engaged by the middle of 1771. In June Thomas wrote to London, referring to a previous order: "I wrote therein for a clavichord. I have since seen a fortepiano and am charmed with it. Send me this instrument then instead of the clavichord; let the case be of fine mahogany, solid not veneered . . . and the workmanship of the whole very handsome and worthy of the acceptance of a lady for whom I intend it."

On December 16, Jefferson "pd Richard Scott in part for a bed £3/16/3, the remainder £4, I am to pay Robt. Baine." On the thirtieth he paid forty shillings for a marriage license and two days later was married at Martha's home, The Forest, by two ministers, to each of whom he paid £5. It was apparently a gay wedding, the festivities lasting several days; or so it would seem from the amount that he paid to the fiddlers, and the size of the tips to the servants. To pay all this he borrowed twenty shillings back from one of the ministers. It is characteristic of Jefferson that the only record of his courtship and marriage must be gleaned from his meticulously kept account book.

The newlyweds started for Monticello on January 18, stopping off for a short visit at Tuckahoe en route. Many years later Jefferson's oldest daughter wrote an account of the journey of the bride and groom to the one-room home atop the mountain, as she had apparently heard it from her parents.

They left The Forest after a fall of snow, light then, but increasing in depth as they advanced up the country. They were finally obliged to quit the carriage and proceed on horseback. Having stopped for a short time at Blenheim, where an overseer only resided, they left it at sunset to pursue their way through a mountain track rather than a road, in which the snow lay from eighteen inches to two feet deep, having eight miles to go before reaching Monticello. They arrived late at night, the fires all out and the servants retired to their own houses for the night. The horrible dreariness of such a house, at the end of such a journey, I have often heard both relate.

Jefferson's garden book records: "The deepest snow we have ever seen; in Albemarle it was about three feet deep."

Martha Jefferson is a shadowy figure in history. Jefferson wrote nothing of her. Her oldest child was but ten when she died. There are few comments from contemporaries. Henry Randall wrote a fine biography of Jefferson in 1858, while some who knew the great Virginian were still alive. In it he penned this description — but did not say where he obtained his information:

Mrs. Skelton, left a widow when scarcely advanced beyond her girlhood, was distinguished for her beauty, her accomplishments, and her solid merit. In person, she was a little above medium height, slightly but exquisitely formed. Her complexion was brilliant — her large expressive eyes of the richest shade of hazel — her luxuriant hair of the finest tinge of auburn. She walked, rode, and danced, with admirable grace and spirit — sung, and played the spinet and harpischord (the musical instruments of the Virginia ladies of that day) with uncommon skill. The more solid parts of her education had not been neglected. She also was well read and intelligent; conversed agreeably; possessed excellent sense and a lively play of fancy; and had a frank, warm-hearted, and somewhat impulsive disposition. Last, not least, she had already proved herself a true daughter of the Old Dominion in the department of housewifery.

All of the meager accounts indicate that the first few years of the marriage of Martha and Thomas were idyllic. The wife was a capable pianist, the husband more than a passable violinist, and they both sang. Jefferson was busy enlarging the house that would one day be one of America's most famous mansions. Martha's father died within two years after their marriage and Jefferson, through his wife, inherited some 11,000 acres and 135 slaves. Thomas noted that this inheritance, "after the debts should be paid, which were very considerable, was about equal to my own patrimony, and consequently doubled the ease of our circumstances."

As soon as the honeymoon was over Martha set out to be a good housewife by following in the footsteps of her methodical husband. She took an old notebook in which Thomas had recorded early law cases, turned it upside down, and began at the back to record household events and expenses. She dutifully inscribed: "1772, Feb. 10, opened a barrel of Col. Harrison's flour; 13, a mutton killed; 17, two pullets killed; 27, a cask of small beer brewed, 15-gallon cask." She noted that she had supervised the making of forty-six pounds of soft soap and an equal amount of hard soap. She inventoried the household linen and made "a list of our clothes." The latter included, in part, for Mr. Jefferson: "9 ruffled shirts and 18 plain ditto, 20 old cambric stocks, 15 old rags of pocket handkerchiefs, 3 pr. of English corded breeches, 4 of Virginia ditto, 6 Virginia corded dimity waistcoats, 13 pr. white silk stockings, 5 red waistcoats, 2 buff 1 white flannel ditto, 1 green coat, 1 black princes ditto." Mrs. Jefferson had "16 old shifts, 4 new ditto, 6 old fine aprons, 4 Virginia petticoats, 9 pr. of silk stockings, 10 pr. of old cotton, 8 silk gowns, 6 washing ditto old and 2 new to make up, 2 suits of brussels lace, one suit of worked muslin." At this point she apparently found such humdrum accounting boring and drew two gay little birds perched on a branch.

Only two letters by Martha have survived, written in a neat, angular hand and showing a proficiency in spelling far above most of the other ladies of the Founding Fathers. In 1780, when her husband was Governor of Virginia, the women of Philadelphia had organized a fund of clothing and money to relieve the distress of the Continental troops. It was proposed to extend this to other states, and the help of the wife of Virginia's Governor was invoked. Martha replied, to an unknown addressee:

Madame, Mrs. Washington has done me the honor of communicating the inclosed proposition of our sisters of Pennsylvania and of informing me that the same grateful sentiments are displaying themselves in Maryland. Justified by the sanction of her letter in handing forward the scheme I undertake with cheerfulness the duty of furnishing to my countrywomen an opportunity of proving that they also participate of those virtuous feelings which gave birth to it. I cannot do more for its promotion than by inclosing to you some of the papers to be disposed of as you think proper. I am with the greatest respect, Your most humble servant, Martha Jefferson.

The first of the six children that Martha bore during her ten years as a wife was born in 1772, a girl. She would have four more girls and a boy before her death; which was presumably brought on, or at least hastened, by her last confinement. Only two of the girls survived infancy. Jefferson wanted a son desperately and it was probably a proud day when he recorded, on May 28, 1777, "our son born 10 o'clock P.M."; and a dreadfully sad one when he wrote, on June 14 of the same year, "our son died 10:20 P.M."

There is no contemporary account of life at Monticello in those early years. Because of its relatively remote location it probably did not, like Mount Vernon, serve as a "well resorted tavern." But after the house became fully habitable in the early 1770s there was surely much entertaining of family, neighbors, and travelers. When his brother-in-law, Dabney Carr, died Jefferson's sister and her six children were added to the household. On the relatively rare occasions when Martha was not pregnant she sometimes accompanied her husband to Williamsburg during sessions of the House of Delegates. At other times she stayed at The Forest while Thomas was at the capital.

The most frequent adjective applied to Martha by visitors who left a record of their sojourn at Monticello was "amiable." Phillip Mazzei, an Italian to whom Jefferson gave land in the neighborhood to start a vineyard, called her "angelic." When invited to stay at Monticello while getting organized, Mazzei turned up with a "traveling companion," Mrs. Martin, whom he had just married. From all accounts, Martha must have been angelic to put up with her; Thomas was led to one of his rare discourtesies by referring to her as "that bitch."

The Jeffersons had interesting neighbors in 1780 when the "Convention Army" which Burgoyne had surrendered at Saratoga was quartered nearby. The men stayed in barracks but Jefferson was helpful in getting houses for some of the officers and there was much visiting, particularly with one of the German officers of the Hessians, General von Riedesel. Martha took a particular fancy to the von Riedesel children, one of whom was about the age of her daughter Martha, whom they called Patsy. After he left Virginia, von Riedesel wrote Jefferson: "The little ones are all well and have not yet forgot the amiable Mrs. Jefferson, which, permit me to say for children, is no small proof of the impression her kindness had made."

An unknown Hessian officer left this slight description of Monticello, and reference to Martha, which was published in a Hamburg newspaper:

> My only recuperation at present, is to learn the English language. I have free access to a copious and well-chosen library of Colonel Jefferson, Governor of Virginia. . . . The Governor possesses a noble spirit in building. He is now finishing an elegant building projected according to his own fancy. In his parlor he is erecting in the ceiling a compass of his own invention by which he can know the strength as well as the direction of the winds. I have promised to paint the compass for it. He was much pleased with a fancy painting of mine. . . . As all Virginians are fond of music, he is particularly so. You will find in his house an elegant harpsichord, pianoforte, and some violins. The latter he performs well upon himself, the former his lady touches very skillfully, and who is in all respects a very agreeable, sensible, and accomplished lady.

Martha's health started to fail within two or three years after her marriage, and it was probably his concern for his wife and his desire to be with her that induced Jefferson to withdraw from the national scene during the entire Revolution. He served in the General Assembly of Virginia and as Governor, but he was never far from his native state after August, 1776, when he resigned from Congress, until after her death. Less than three weeks after the Declaration of Independence was signed he wrote to Richard Henry Lee to come to Philadelphia and replace him in the Congress, saying: "I receive by every post such accounts of the state of Mrs. Jefferson's health that it will be impossible for me to disappoint her expectation of seeing me at the time I have promised, which supposed my leaving this place on the eleventh of next month. . . . I pray you to come, I am under a sacred obligation to go home."

Martha's last child was born in May, 1782. Only two other daughters were still living. Martha clung to life for four months after her last delivery. Then, on September 6, Jefferson wrote brusquely in his account book: "My wife died this day at 11:45 A.M." This seeming casualness on his wife's death is belied by an account that his daughter Martha wrote years later. She was only ten when her mother died, but she clearly remembered her father's inconsolable grief. She recalled:

During my mother's life, he bestowed much time and attention on our education — our cousins the Carrs and myself — and after her death, during the first month of desolation which followed, I was his constant companion while we remained at Monticello.

As a nurse, no female ever had more tenderness or anxiety. He nursed my poor mother in turn with Aunt Carr and her own sister — sitting up with her and administering her medicines and drink to the last. For four months that she lingered, he was never out of calling; when not at her bedside, he was writing in a small room which opened immediately at the head of her bed. A moment before the closing scene, he was led from the room almost in a state of insensibility by his sister Mrs. Carr, who, with great difficulty, got him into his library, where he fainted, and remained so long insensible that they feared he never would revive. The scene that followed I did not witness; but the violence of his emotion, when almost by stealth I entered his room at night, to this day I dare not trust myself to describe. He kept to his room three weeks, and I was never a moment from his side. He walked almost incessantly night and day, only lying down occasionally, when nature was completely exhausted, on a pallet that had been brought in during his long fainting fit. My aunts remained constantly with him for some weeks, I do not remember how many. When at last he left his room, he rode out, and from that time he was incessantly on horseback, rambling about the mountain, in the least-frequented roads, and just as often through the woods. In those melancholy rambles, I was his constant companion, a solitary witness to many a violent burst of grief, the remembrance of which has consecrated particular scenes of that lost home beyond the power of time to obliterate.

Perhaps the best relic of the deep love of Martha and Thomas Jefferson is a few lines from Laurence Sterne's *Tristam Shandy* — the book that Abigail Adams considered "too vile" to read. The Jeffersons may have been reading it together shortly before her death, for Martha, in a weak hand, wrote a quotation from it; probably from memory as there are minor errors:

> time wastes too fast: every letter
> I trace tells me with what rapidity
> life follows my pen, the days and
> hours of it are flying over our heads
> like clouds of windy day never to
> return — more everything presses on —

Martha's pen stops here. Then or later Thomas finished the paragraph.

... and every
time I kiss thy hand to bid adieu, every absence
which follows it, are preludes to that eternal separation
which we are shortly to make!

Jefferson's reticence on his wife's death broke only once, in a letter to her sister, Elizabeth Eppes, in which he started by telling her about the children:

The girls being unable to assure you themselves of their welfare, the duty devolves on me and I will undertake it the more willingly as it will lay you under the necessity of sometimes letting us hear from you. They are in perfect health and as happy as if they had had no part in the immeasurable loss we have sustained. Patsy rides with me five or six miles a day and presses me for permission to accompany me on horseback to Elkhill, whenever I shall go there. When that may be, however, I cannot tell, finding myself absolutely unable to attend to anything like business. This miserable hand of existence is really too burthensome to be borne and were it not for the infidelity of deserting the sacred charge left to me, I could not wish its continuance a moment. For what could it be wished? All my plans of comfort and happiness reversed by a single event and nothing arising in prospect before me but a gloom, unabridged with one cheerful expectation. The care and instruction of our children indeed affords some temporary abstractions from wretchedness, and nourishes a soothing reflection that if there be beyond the grave any [concern?] for the things of this world, there is one angel at least, who views these attentions with pleasure and wishes continuance of them, while she must pity the miseries to which they confine me.

But I forgot that I began this correspondence on behalf of the children and am afflicting you at the distance of seventy or eighty miles with sorrows which you had a right to . . . [illegible].

I will endeavor to correct myself and keep what I feel to myself that I may not dispirit you from a communication with us. . . . I say nothing of coming to Eppington. I promised you this should not be until I could support such a countenance as might not cast a damp on the cheerfulness of others.

Thomas mentioned his wife in only one other letter: to the Marquis de Chastellux, who had visited Monticello a few months before Martha's death. To the Frenchman he wrote: "I received your friendly letters of — and June 30, . . . It found me a little emerging from the stupor of mind which had rendered me as dead to the world as was she whose loss occasioned it. Your letter recalled to my memory that there were persons still living of much value to me."

Martha was buried in the graveyard at Monticello beside her children and Dabney Carr. Her husband marked her grave with this inscription:

To the memory of
Martha Jefferson
Daughter of John Wayles;
Born October 19th, 1748, O.S.
Intermarried with
Thomas Jefferson
January 1st, 1772
Torn from him by death
September 6, 1782:
This monument of his love is inscribed.

Then he added a quotation from the *Iliad* as an epitaph. Characteristically, this portion was carved in Greek. His loss was personal. His feelings would not be disclosed to the casual passerby:

If in the melancholy shades below,
The flames of friends and lovers cease to glow,
Yet mine shall sacred last; mine undecayed
Burn on through death and animate my shade.

For what it is worth, the manager of the Jefferson plantation recorded that Martha exacted a death-bed promise from her husband that he would never give their children a step-mother. He said: "Mr. Jefferson promised her solemnly that he would never be married again." There is no other evidence for this dramatic legend; but Thomas did not marry again. This was quite unusual for the times, when many wives died young after bearing numerous children and most widowers promptly remarried to get somebody to care for their brood.

The most important woman in Jefferson's life after his wife's death — and for the remainder of his life — was the other Martha, his eleven-year-old daughter, called Patsy. Two months after the older Martha died James Madison noted in his record of the debates of Congress that Jefferson's reappointment as "Minister Plenipotentiary for negotiating peace was agreed to unanimously and without a single adverse remark. The act took place in consequence of its being suggested that the death of Mrs. Jefferson had probably changed the sentiments of Mr. Jefferson with regard to public life."

Jefferson carried Patsy to Philadelphia, leaving the new-born baby, Lucy Elizabeth, and four-year-old Mary — called Polly — with Martha's sister, Mrs. Eppes. His proposed voyage to France at this time was frustrated by delays until the provisional peace was signed. Then he was elected to Congress, which was meeting in Annapolis. He left Patsy with a Mrs. Hopkinson in Philadelphia and arranged for several tutors to advance her education. His letters to her from Annapolis, written when she was just turned twelve, combine expressions of his love, concern, and never-failing courtesy with parental advice on moral ideas, social ideals, and education. They make delightful reading, and one wonders how many of today's twelve-year-olds would appreciate them. He wrote the first as soon as he arrived at Annapolis.

Dear Patsy, — After four days' journey, I arrived here without any accident, and in as good health as when I left Philadelphia. The conviction that you would be more improved in the situation I have placed you than if still with me has solaced me on my parting with you, which my love for you has rendered a difficult thing. The acquirements which I hope you will make under the tutors I have provided for you will render you more worthy of my love; and if they cannot increase it, they will prevent its dimunition. Consider the good lady who has taken you under her roof, who has undertaken to see that you perform all your exercises, and to admonish you in all those wanderings from what is right or what is clever to which your inexperience would expose you: consider her, I say, as your mother, as the only person to whom, since the loss with which Heaven has pleased to afflict you, you can now look up. . . .

With respect to the distribution of your time, the following is what I should approve:

From 8 to 10, practice music.

From 10 to 1, dance one day and draw another.

From 1 to 2, draw on the day you dance, and write a letter next day.

From 3 to 4, read French.

From 4 to 5, exercise yourself in music.

From 5 till bedtime, read English, write, etc. . . .

I expect you will write me by every post. Inform me what books you read, what tunes you learn, and inclose me your best copy of every lesson in drawing. . . . Take care that you never spell a word wrong. Always before you write a word, consider how it is spelt, and, if you do not remember it, turn to a dictionary. It produces great praise to a lady to spell well. I have placed my happiness on seeing you good and accomplished; and no distress this world can now bring on me would equal that of your disappointing my hopes. If you love me, then strive to be good under every situation and to all living creatures, and to acquire those accomplishments which I have put in your power, and which will go far towards ensuring you the warmest love of your affectionate father.

P.S. — Keep my letters and read them at times, that you may always have present in your mind those things which will endear you to me.

A few days later he gave the child an earnest lecture on dress:

I omitted in that letter to advise you on the subject of dress, which I know you are a little apt to neglect. I do not wish you to be gaily clothed at this time of life, but that your wear should be fine of its kind. But above all things, and at all times, let your clothes be neat, whole, and properly put on. Do not fancy you must wear them till dirt is visible to the eye. You will be the last one who is sensible of this. Some ladies think they may, under the privileges of the dishabille, be loose and negligent in their dress in the morning. But be you, from the moment you rise till you go to bed, as cleanly and properly dressed as at the hour of dinner or tea. A lady who has been seen as a sloven or slut in the morning, will never efface the impression she then made with all the dress and pageantry she can afterwards involve herself in. Nothing is so disgusting to our sex as a want of cleanliness and delicacy in yours. I hope, therefore, the moment you rise from bed, your first work will be to dress yourself in such style as you may be seen by any gentleman without his being able to discover a pin amiss, or any other circumstance of neatness wanting.

In thanking a French friend, the Marquis de Marbois, for recommending a tutor for Patsy he explained the plan of education that he had developed for his daughter, with an adverse comment on his own sex that was undoubtedly facetious:

The plan of reading I have formed for her is considerably different from that which I think would be most proper for her sex in any country but America. I am obliged in it to extend my views beyond herself, and consider her as possibly the head of a little family of her own. The chance that in marriage she will draw a blockhead I calculate to about fourteen to one, and of course that the education of her family will probably rest on her ideas and direction without assistance. With the poets and prose writers I shall therefore combine a certain extent of reading in the graver sciences.

Jefferson, aged forty-one, finally left for France as Minister Plenipotentiary to replace Franklin in May, 1784, taking Patsy with him. The girl left the only record of their arrival in France.

I fear we should have fared as badly at the arrival for Papa spoke very little French and I not a word, if an Irish gentleman, an entire stranger to us, who, seeing our embarrassment, had not been so good as to conduct us to a house and was of great service to us. . . . It is amazing to see how they cheat the strangers. It cost Papa as much to have the baggage brought from the shore to the house, which was about half a square, as the bringing it from Philadelphia to Boston. From there [Havre] we should have had a very agreeable voyage to Paris, for Havre de Grace is built at the mouth of the Seine and we follow the river all the way through the most beautiful country I ever saw in my life — it is a perfect garden — if the singularity of our carriage had not attracted the attention of all we met and whenever we stopped we were surrounded by beggars. One day I counted no less than nine where we stopped to change horses.

Upon reaching Paris, Patsy, the little country girl from Virginia, needed to be dressed and groomed *à la mode;* something that, at the age of twelve, she did not relish. She wrote:

I wish you could have been with us when we arrived. I am sure you would have laughed for we were obliged to send immediately for the stay maker, the mantua maker, the milliner and even the shoemaker before I could go out. I have never had the *friseur* but once, but I soon got rid of him and turned down my hair in spite of all they could say, and I defer it now as much as possible for I think it always too soon to suffer.

Through the good offices of the Marquise de Lafayette a place was secured for Patsy in a convent, the Abbaye de Panthemont, the most exclusive school for young ladies in Paris. There were undoubtedly some raised Protestant eyebrows when Jefferson put his daughter in a Catholic school but he was assured that "The Abbess in charge is a woman of the world who understands the direction of young Protestant girls. . . . It is understood that one does not talk to them about religion." This may have been so, but four years later sixteen-year-old Patsy announced that she wanted to become a nun. Her father was not unduly disturbed; he had been brought up among six sisters and undoubtedly knew the vagaries of the adolescent female mind. But he promptly took her out of the convent and brought her to live with him. There is no record that Patsy had any further interest in becoming a nun.

While she was in the convent Jefferson visited Patsy regularly and, when she was a little older, took her to dinner at the Marquise de Lafayette's and elsewhere. When he was out of Paris he wrote the child long letters. Apparently his only fear for his oldest daughter was that she had a certain indolence; a fear which, from her later life, seems to have been unfounded. But he was always exhorting her to greater industry so that she might make full use of her capabilities and be a credit to him. And he repeatedly made it clear how much she meant to him. This short passage is an example.

My expectations from you are high — yet not higher than you may attain. Industry and resolution are all that are wanting. Nobody in this world can make me so happy, or so miserable, as you. Retirement from public life will ere long become necessary for me. To your sister and yourself I look to render the evening of my life serene and contented. Its morning has been clouded by loss after loss, till I have nothing left but you. I do not doubt either your affection or dispositions. But great exertions are necessary, and you have little time left to make them. Be industrious, then, my child. Think nothing unsurmountable by resolution and application, and you will be all that I wish you to be.

After they had been in France for a couple of years her father was quite satisfied in every way with his oldest daughter. He wrote Mrs. Eppes:

She has grown much the last year or two, and will be very tall. . . . Her dispositions give me perfect satisfaction, and her progress is well. She will need, however, your instruction to render her useful in her own country. Of domestic economy she can learn nothing here, yet she must learn it somewhere, as being of more solid value than anything else.

The second daughter, Polly, was a different story. The baby, Lucy Elizabeth, died shortly after Jefferson reached France, and from then on he wanted to have Polly with him. She was only seven when he first wrote her to this effect:

I wish so much to see you, that I have desired your uncle and aunt to send you to me. I know, my dear Polly, how sorry you will be, and ought to be, to leave them and your cousins; but your sister and myself cannot live without you, and after a while we will carry you back again to see your friends in Virginia. In the meantime you shall be taught here to play on the harpischord, to draw, to dance, to read and talk French, and such other things as will make you more worthy of the love of your friends. . . . When you come here you shall have as many dolls and playthings as you want for yourself, or to send to your cousins whenever you shall have opportunities.

Apparently Jefferson had already learned that the child did not want to come to France — hence the bribe of "as many dolls and playthings as you want." But Polly would not be bribed. Her answers to this and subsequent invitations follow in full:

Dear Papa — I long to see you, and hope that you and sister Patsy are well; give my love to her and tell her that I long to see her, and hope that you and she will come very soon to see us. I hope that you will send me a doll. I am very sorry that you have sent for me. I don't want to go to France, I had rather stay with Aunt Eppes. . . . Your most happy and dutiful daughter Polly Jefferson.

Dear Papa — I should be very happy to see you, but I can not go to France, and hope that you and sister Patsy are well. Mary Jefferson.

Dear Papa — I want to see you and sister Patsy, but you must come to Uncle Eppes' house. Polly Jefferson.

Polly finally arrived in Europe in July 1787, alone except for a teen-age Negro slave maid. She landed in England, not France, and was met by Abigail Adams, who had difficulty getting her off the ship. The child had become attached to the captain, in whose care she had been placed. Abigail tried to cheer her up, saying: "Come, such a big girl! I know your sister well and I have never seen her cry." "My sister is older and ought to be better," Polly replied between sniffles, "and besides she has her papa with her."

After the child quieted down Abigail wrote to Jefferson: "Miss Polly sends her duty to you and love to her sister and says she will try to be good and not cry. She has wiped her eyes and laid down to sleep." Abigail suggested that it would be well if Jefferson himself, or Patsy, came to London for the girl. To her sister Abigail wrote:

I have had with me for a fortnight a little daughter of Mr. Jefferson's who arrived here with a young Negro girl, her servant, from Virginia. Mr. Jefferson wrote me some months ago that he

expected them, and desired me to receive them. I did so, and
was amply repaid for my trouble. A finer child of her age I never
saw. So mature an understanding, so womanly a behavior, and
so much sensibility, united, are rarely to be met with. I grew so
fond of her, and she was so attached to me, that, when Mr. Jefferson sent for her, they were obliged to force the little creature
away. She is but eight years old. She would sit sometimes and
describe to me the parting with her aunt who brought her up,
the obligations she was under to her, and the love she had for her
little cousins, till the tears would stream down her cheeks; and
how I had been her friend, and she loved me. Her papa would
break her heart by making her go again. She clung round me so
that I could not help shedding a tear at parting with her. She was
the favorite of every one in the house. I regret that such fine
spirits must be spent in the wall of a convent. She is a beautiful
girl, too.

Jefferson did not come to London to meet Polly. Public
affairs held him in Paris and he sent his *maître d'hotel*. He
surely would have liked to come because at the time there
was another woman in his life, much older than Polly, who
was then in the British capital. This was a beautiful, blond,
Anglo-Italian with the mellifluous name of Maria Louisa
Catherine Cecilia Cosway.

Maria had been brought up in an Italian convent where
she had studied painting and music under the leading
masters. After her father's death in 1778 she came to England
with her mother and a letter of introduction to the celebrated
Angelica Kauffmann, who sponsored her with the *haute
monde* who patronized artists and writers in London. Her
sponsor also procured for her a particular patron, an older
man named Charles Townley. Maria hoped for an independent career as an artist but, according to one biographer:

Alas! these expectations failed, and the money which the father
had gained in Florence was quickly spent in England, and the

family was soon in some degree of distress. This change, to her so very great, she bore with admirable fortitude and magnanimity most highly to her credit, but in the end, after having refused better offers in her better days, she from necessity married Cosway, the miniature painter, who at that time adored her, though she always despised him.

Another biographer described her as

the embodiment of the eighteenth-century ideal of grace and beauty — a slim, graceful figure, fashionably, almost extremely dressed; an oval face crowned with great masses of golden curls caught up into an elaborate coiffure with frothy gauze. Her deep violet-blue eyes mirrored her thoughts almost too transparently, whether responding to the stale gallantries of one of her husband's wealthy patrons, or reflecting deeply upon some more profound conversation that turned on animal magnetism, or perhaps the rights of man. Her voice was musical and soft — her speech an appealing melange of five or six languages which she spoke fluently but somewhat imperfectly.

A contemporary described her as: "a golden-haired, languishing Anglo-Italian, graceful to affectation and highly accomplished, especially in music."

Maria's husband, Richard Cosway, was a monkey-faced, foppish little man who was the ranking miniaturist of his day in London and was as popular as an artist as he was unpopular as an individual. Gossip had it that he had a number of flagrant affairs with ladies who posed for him. Maria, too, was a favorite subject for the scandalmongers. It was said that Charles Townley's interest was not entirely fatherly. A biographer admits that

Her name was also connected with those of Marchesi, the singer, who once certainly accompanied her abroad; Vincent Lunardi; the secretary to the Neopolitan ambassador; and J. L. Dussek the pianist. . . . There is, however, nothing to account for these statements but the breath of scandal which attacked every notorious person; and after examining many letters and much correspondence, I am distinctly of the opinion that Mrs. Cosway in the midst of her very difficult life lived honorably to her husband and was always a person of very strong religious opinions.

The gossips made much of a private passageway which was supposed to connect the Cosway residence on Pall Mall with Carleton House, the abode of the lecherous Prince of Wales. If such a passage existed, it may have been of more convenience to Richard than to Maria. Cosway did a continuing business with his Royal Highness, painting miniatures of the Prince for his mistresses and of the mistresses for the Prince. Mrs. Fitzherbert clasped a Cosway miniature of her lover in her dying hand, and her predecessor, Perdita Robinson, had one that was engraved, ironically, *"Je ne chance qu'en mourant."*

Shortly after Jefferson arrived in Paris, John Trumbull, a young American artist, was drawn to the same scene. He carried a letter of introduction to Jefferson from Abigail Adams. Thomas, who had a great interest in all of the arts, was enthusiastic about Trumbull's project to perpetuate on canvas the great scenes of the American Revolution and invited the artist to live with him. Trumbull knew Cosway and introduced Jefferson to the painter and his wife.

Maria was a very capable artist in her own right, although her husband would not permit her to work professionally. She had exhibited twenty-two paintings in the Royal Academy in the five years before she came to Paris, most of which received some critical acclaim. She was also a composer of minor note and a competent musician. She was adept at those things for which Jefferson's soul longed. She was beautiful, vivacious, intelligent, and very probably willing. It is not surprising that the lonely widower was immediately smitten. For a time, Thomas undoubtedly believed himself in love with Maria; but, as with Washington and Sally Fairfax, there is absolutely no evidence that there was anything improper in their relationship.

On the day of his first meeting with the Cosways Jefferson threw aside all business of state to stay with them. He sent "lying messengers" with excuses to cancel his appointments, including a dinner date with the Duchess de la Rochefoucauld d'Anville which he said he could not keep because of "urgent dispatches." Instead, Maria and Thomas, with her husband and Trumbull, drove off to St. Cloud to dine and visit the gallery.

For the next month Thomas saw Maria almost daily. Her husband was usually occupied painting miniatures of the family of the Duc d'Orleans. Sometimes the couple were accompanied by Trumbull, sometimes by Jefferson's young secretary, William Short. But the happiest days were those that they spent alone, days that he described by writing:

The day we went to St. Germain's. How beautiful was every object! the Port de Neuilly, the hills along the Seine, the rainbows of the machine of Marly, the terrace of St. Germain's, the chateau, the gardens, the statues of Marly, the *pavillon of Lucienne*. Recollect, too, *Madrid, Bagatelle,* the King's garden, the *Desert*. How grand the idea excited by the remains of such a column! The spiral staircase too was beautiful. Every moment was filled with something agreeable. The wheels of time moved on with a rapidity of which those of our carriage gave but a faint idea. And yet in the evening when one took a retrospect of the day, what a mass of happiness had we traveled over! Retrace all those scenes to me, my good companion.

The idyllic month ended when Cosway finished his work for the Orleans family and took his wife on to Antwerp.

Jefferson saw them off and then went home to write a long letter to Maria which is one of the few that he penned, other than his boyhood missives to Page, that exposes deep personal feelings or emotions. The letter is in the form of a supposed dialogue between his Head and his Heart. During his month with Maria, Jefferson had broken his right wrist and the lengthy epistle was laboriously written with his left hand.

My dear Madam,

Having performed the last sad office of handing you into your carriage, at the Pavillon de St. Denis, and seen the wheels get actually in motion, I turned on my heel and walked, more dead than alive, to the opposite door, where my own was awaiting me. . . . I was carried home. Seated by my fireside, solitary and sad, the following dialogue took place between my Head and my Heart.

Head. Well, friend, you seem to be in a pretty trim.

Heart. I am indeed the most wretched of all earthly beings. Overwhelmed with grief, ever fiber of my frame distended beyond its natural powers to bear, I would willingly meet whatever catastrophe should leave me no more to feel or to fear.

Head. These are the eternal consequences of your warmth and precipitation. This is one of the scrapes into which you are ever leading us. You confess your follies, indeed, but still you hug and cherish them, and no reformation can be hoped where there is no repentence.

Heart. Oh! My friend! This is no moment to upbraid my foibles. I am rent into fragments by the force of my grief! If you have any balm, pour it into my wounds; if none, do not harrow them by new torments. Spare me in this awful moment! At any other I will attend with patience to your admonitions.

Head. On the contrary, I never found that the moment of triumph with you was the moment of attention to my admonitions. While suffering under your follies you may perhaps be made sensible of them, but, the paroxysm over, you fancy it can never return. Harsh therefore as the medicine may be, it is my office to administer it. You will be pleased to remember that when our friend Trumbull used to be telling us of the merits and talents of these good people, I never ceased whispering to you that we had no occasion for new acquaintances; that the greater their merits and talents, the more dangerous their friendship to your tranquillity, because the regret at parting would be greater.

Heart. . . . Sir, this acquaintance was not the consequence of my doings. It was one of your projects, which threw us in the way of it.

Heart went on to remind Head that they had met the Cosways at a firm of architects where they had gone, at Head's behest, to study the dome of a Paris market to consider its adaptation for a like edifice in Richmond. Head then pointed out the folly of becoming involved with these new friends because, said Head:

. . . I often told you during the course that you were imprudently engaging your affections under circumstances that must cost you a great deal of pain; that the persons indeed were of the greatest merit, possessing good sense, good humor, honest hearts, honest manners, and eminence in a lovely art; that the lady had moreover qualities and accomplishments belonging to her sex, which might form a chapter apart for her, such as music, modesty, beauty, and that softness of disposition which is the ornament of her sex and charm of ours. But that all these considerations would increase the pang of separation; that their stay here was to be short; that you rack our whole system when you are parted from those you love, complaining that such a separation is worse than death.

Heart replied that they had promised to come back or, perhaps, they might come to America. There followed a plea for Maria to cross the ocean, starting with a description of the natural beauties of America — and Monticello — that would appeal to her as an artist. This was followed by a fervent portrait of the fine political system in America, a subject that

Jefferson could not ignore even in a love letter — if this was such. Then in a lengthy dialogue, Head and Heart presented a picture of Jefferson's innermost feelings that show him as, basically, a pathetically lonely man.

Head. . . . This is not a world to live at random in as you do. To avoid those eternal distresses to which you are forever exposing us, you must learn to look forward before you take a step which may interest our peace. Everything in this world is a matter of calculation. Advance then with caution, the balance in your hand. Put into one scale the pleasures which any object may offer; but put fairly into the other the pains which are to follow, and see which preponderates. . . . Do not bite at the bait of pleasure till you know there is no hook beneath it. The art of life is the art of avoiding pain, and he is the best pilot who steers clearest of the rocks and shoals with which it is beset. Pleasure is always before us, but misfortune is at our side; while running after that, this arrests us. The most effectual means of being secure against pain is to retire within ourselves, and to suffice for our own happiness. Those which depend on ourselves are the only pleasures a wise man will count on; for nothing is ours which another may deprive us of. Hence the inestimable value of intellectual pleasures. Ever in our power, always leading us to something new, never cloying, we ride, serene and sublime above the concerns of this mortal world, contemplating truth and nature, matter and motion. . . . Let this be our employ. Leave the bustle and tumult of society to those who have not talents to occupy themselves without them. Friendship is but another name for an alliance with the follies and the misfortunes of others. Our own share of miseries is sufficient; why enter then as volunteers into those of another? Is there so little gall poured into our own cup that we must need help to drink that of our neighbor?

Heart. And what more sublime delight than to mingle tears with one whom the hand of heaven hath smitten! . . . When heaven has taken from us some object of our love, how sweet it is to have a bosom whereon to recline our heads, and into which we may pour the torrent of our tears! Grief, with such a comfort, is almost a luxury! In a life where we are perpetually exposed to want and accident, yours is a wonderful proposition, to insulate ourselves, to retire from all aid, and to wrap ourselves in the mantle of self-sufficiency! . . . Let the gloomy monk, sequestered from the world, seek unsocial pleasures in the bottom of his cell! Let the sublimated philosopher grasp visionary happiness while pursuing phantoms dressed in the garb of truth! Their supreme wisdom is supreme folly and they mistake for happiness the mere absence of pain. Had they ever felt the solid pleasure of one generous spasm of the heart, they would exchange for it all the frigid speculations of their lives. . . . When nature assigned us the same habitation, she gave us over it a divided empire. To you she allotted the field of science, to me that of morals. When the circle is to be squared, or the orbit of a comet to be traced; when the arch of greatest strength, or the solid of least resistance is to be investigated, take you the problem, it is yours; nature has given me no cognizance of it. In like manner in denying to you the feelings of sympathy, of benevolence, of gratitude, of justice, of love, of friendship, she has excluded you from their control. To these she has adapted the mechanism of the heart. Morals were too essential to the happiness of man to be risked on the uncertain combinations of the head. She laid their foundation therefore in sentiment, not science.

Although he otherwise wrote no more than was necessary because of his broken wrist, Thomas was not stinting in his letters to Maria. Most of her replies were brief and contained complaints that he did not write to her frequently enough. One letter, on a very small sheet of paper, was written after Thomas had made an Italian tour. In it she said:

Do you deserve a long letter, my friend? No. Certainly not, and to avoid temptation, I have a small sheet of paper. Conversing with you would break any resolution. I am determined to prevent it. How long do you like to keep your friends in anxiety! How many months was you without writing to me? And you felt no remorse?

I was glad to know you was well, sure of your being much engaged and diverted, and had only to lament I was not a castle hanging to cloud, a stream, a village, a stone on the pavement of Turin, Milan, and Genoa etc. . . . I am not sure if I had any share in the provoking part; oh! if I had been a shadow of this *Elysium* of yours! how you would have been tormented! I must excuse you a little, since you tell me you thought of me.

Maria's letters were sent to Jefferson through a French banker, Monsieur Grand. The correspondence was carried back and forth between the English and French capitals by Trumbull or by John Adams' new son-in-law, Colonel Smith. This did not necessarily mean that it was clandestine. In those times an American minister might as well have published his correspondence as entrust it to the French *poste*.

Maria had promised to come back to Paris. Jefferson wrote Trumbull, in London, "Tell Mrs. Cosway she is inconstant. She was to have been in Paris long ago, but she deceived us." And to Maria: "When are you coming here? If not at all, what did you ever come for? Only to make people miserable at losing you. Come, then, my dear Madam, and we will breakfast every day *à l'anglais,* hie away to the *Desert,* dine under the bowers of Marly, and forget that we are ever to part again."

It was almost a year before Maria returned to Paris, this time without her husband. Little is known of this second visit. Apparently, Jefferson saw her seldom, if his usually infallible account book can be relied on. She seemed to be determined to establish a position in Paris similar to the one she held in London and a contemporary said that her Paris residence "became the resort of all the English of talent, as well as many of the French of the same description. She held a court like the fair Aspasia of old, and Fiat stamped honor on every work she condescended to approve." Jefferson said that he saw her "only by scraps," whereas last time "we were half days and whole days together, and I found this too little." Despite his protestations, Thomas does not seem to have made much of an effort to be with Maria during this second Parisian interlude. Perhaps he feared that the absence of her husband would present too much temptation; but it seems more likely that he was, perhaps, a little "fed up" with the self-centered, complaining, somewhat temperamental artist who, before she left, again chided him with: "If my inclination had been your law, I should have had the pleasure of seeing you more than I have. I have felt the loss with displeasure."

Their correspondence, however, did not indicate a diminution of interest on his part. When his departure for home became imminent he exhorted her to come to America, whose beauties would make fine subjects for her ready pencil. He dreamed of entertaining her at Monticello. Shortly before he left Paris he wrote:

Fearing my dear Madam, that I might not be able to write to you by this occasion, I had charged my friend Trumbull to lay my homage at your feet. . . . We are so apt to believe what we wish that I almost believe I shall meet you in America, and that we shall make together the tour of the curiosities of that country. Be this as it may, let us be together in spirit. Preserve for me always a little corner in your affection in exchange for the spacious part you occupy in mine. *Adieu ma chère et très chère amie!*

To which Maria replied:

You are going to America, and you think I am going with you, I thank you for the flattering compliment. . . . And your return when is it to be? Why don't you announce me that, as well as your departure? T'is cruel not to do it.

The correspondence between Maria and Thomas continued until the end of his life, although often there were intervals of years between letters. In the early years after his return he still coaxed her to come to America, saying, "You know I always ranted about your bringing your pencil and harp here. They would go well with our groves, our birds, and our sun." Maria had a baby after Jefferson left Europe, and he added, "You may make children there but this is the country to transplant them to." Maria, her harp, her pencil, and her child would be most welcome at Monticello. Nothing was said about her husband.

Mrs. Cosway's life was not a happy one after Jefferson returned to America. She went to a convent in Italy for her health and the cynical Horace Walpole wrote "she is pleasing — but surely it is odd to drop a child and her husband and her country all in a breath." Many of her friends in Paris were victims of the Revolution. While she was away her husband went on a sketching trip with a female artist and kept a journal that his biographer could not publish because there were so many lascivious allusions to his traveling companion and invidious comparisons between her and his wife. Shortly after her return to London, her daughter died. Maria then started a girl's school in Lyons, which she ran until her husband became mentally deranged. She returned to London to nurse him and wrote Jefferson, in 1819:

To the length of silence I draw a curtain. Remembrance must be *ever green.* . . . Often have I read your name in the papers, therefore have been acquainted of your proceedings in that honorable way which was expected from you. . . . My humble situation could never bring to you any public information of me. . . .

Forgotten by the Arts, suspended from the direction of education (though it is going on vastly well in my absence), I am now exercising the occupations of a nurse. Happy in self-gratification of doing my duty, with no other consolation. In your dialogue your head would tell me, "that is enough," your heart perhaps will understand, I might wish *for more*. God's will be done.

Two years later she wrote, on paper edged in black:

The appearance of this letter will inform you that I have been left a widow. . . . He had neglected his affairs very much and when I was obliged to take them in my hands was astonished. . . . Everybody thought he was very rich and I was astonished when put to the *real* knowledge of his situation. . . . I shall retire from this bustling and *insignificant* world, to my favorite College at Lodi as I always intended, where I can employ myself so happily in doing good. . . . I wish *Monticello* was not *so far!*

Maria's college — which she had moved from Lyons to Lodi — prospered. It was later sponsored by an Austrian religious order and Francis I, Emperor of that country, made Maria a baroness in recognition of her labors in educating girls. Just at this time Jefferson was organizing the University of Virginia. In 1825 Maria wrote him a final letter.

I wish much to hear from you, how you go on with your fine seminary. I have had my great salon painted, with the representation of the four parts of the world, and the most distinguished objects in them. I have been at a loss for America, as I found very few small prints — however, Washington town is marked, and I have left a hill barren as I would place *Monticello* and the seminary: if you favor me with some description, that I might have it introduced, you would oblige me much.

Death intervened before Jefferson answered this letter. A later visitor to Maria's college described the painting in the salon and reported that the "little mountain" was still bare.

Thomas had many female friends in France, other than Maria, with whom he carried on mild flirtations, largely intellectual. He was, after all, a most eligible widower in his forties. Perhaps for this reason he selected for his principal female acquaintances women who had husbands in the background; Madame de Corny, Madame de Tesse, Madame de Brèhan, Madame de Tott, and Madame de Stael were frequent companions or correspondents — as well as two beautiful Americans, Anne Bingham and Angelica Church. Of the latter Abigail Adams mentioned her "softness, sweetness, and affability. Everything is delicate and agreeable, except her husband."

On the whole, Jefferson, like Adams, was critical of the morality of French women. Soon after his arrival he wrote:

Intrigues of love occupy the younger, and those of ambition the elder part of the great. Conjugal love having no existence among them, domestic happiness, of which that is the basis, is utterly unknown. . . . Much, very much inferior is this to the tranquil, permanent felicity with which domestic society in America blesses most of its inhabitants, leaving them to follow steadily those pursuits which health and reason approve, and rendering truly delicious the intervals of those pursuits.

When a young American queried him on the advantages of a European education he answered that a youth who came to France: "is led by the strongest of all the human passions into a spirit for female intrigue, destructive of his own and others' happiness . . . and . . . learns to consider fidelity to the marriage bed as an ungentlemanly practice and inconsistent with happiness."

In commenting on the order that might be produced by the French Revolution, Thomas averred:

In my opinion, a kind of influence, which none of their plans of reform take into account, will elude them all; I mean the influence of women in the government. The manners of the nation allow them to visit, alone, all persons in office, to solicit the affairs of the husband, family, or friends, and their solicitations bid defiance to laws and regulations. . . . Nor can . . . one, without the evidence of his own eyes, believe in the desperate state to which things are reduced in this country, from the omnipotence of an influence, which, fortunately for the happiness of the sex itself, does not endeavor to extend itself in our country, beyond the domestic line.

In passing it might be remarked that despite his interest in the intellectual, sophisticated, artistic, and cultured women of France, Thomas Jefferson firmly believed that woman's place — at least the American woman's place — was in the home.

In a letter to Anne Bingham, who had nought but reverence for the Parisian females of the *haute monde,* Jefferson drew this cynical picture:

At eleven o'clock it is day, *chez Madame.* The curtains are drawn. Propped on bolsters and pillows, and her head scratched into a little order, the bulletins of the sick are read, and the billets of the well. She writes to some of her acquaintances, and receives the visits of others. If the morning is not very thronged she is able to get out and hobble round the cage of the Palais Royal; but she must hobble quickly, for the coiffeur's turn is come and a tremendous turn it is! Happy if he does not make her arrive when dinner is half over! The torpitude of digestion a little past, she flutters half an hour through the streets by way of paying visits, and then to the spectacles. . . . After supper, cards; and after cards, bed; to rise at noon the next day and to tread, like a mill horse, the same trodden circle over again.

After almost five years in France, Jefferson applied for a leave of absence to take his daughters home. He wrote to Mrs. Eppes:

In my last of July 12, I told you that in my next I would enter into explanations about the time my daughters would have the happiness to see you. Their future welfare requires that this should be no longer postponed. It would have taken place a year sooner, but that I wished Polly to perfect herself in her French. I have asked leave of absence of Congress for five or six months of the next year, and if I obtain it in time, I shall endeavor to sail about the middle of April.

Jefferson's plans for a short furlough were foiled by the appointment as Washington's Secretary of State that he found waiting for him at Monticello.

For the final forty-six years there were no women in Jefferson's life except his two daughters — and the constantly increasing number of granddaughters with whom Patsy presented him. Six of her eleven children who grew to maturity were girls. In France, when she was sixteen, Patsy had fallen in love with a second cousin, Thomas Mann Randolph, who was studying in Europe. They were married at Monticello a week before her father left to take his place in Washington's cabinet. Polly, too, married a cousin, John Wayles Eppes, with whom she had played as a child before going to France.

It might be remarked in passing, that Jefferson's most virulent political critics did not agree that there were no other women in his life. Politics were even dirtier in the eighteenth century than in the twentieth, and sexual immorality was a favorite charge of the slandering pamphleteers. Franklin was accused of having a child by his serving wench Barbara and throwing her out in the cold. Adams was accused of sending his Secretary of War to England in a frigate to bring back four beautiful British women as mistresses — two for Adams and two for himself. Adams' comment on this was that, if it happened, he was cheated — he never got his two. Jefferson was a prime target for similar scurrilous innuendo.

In presenting the evils of slavery, the Northern abolitionists harped on the theme that southern planters bedded their female slaves. There were enough mulatto children on some southern plantations to provide a grain of truth for such allegations. Obviously Jefferson, a widower in his late forties living in a house with numerous female slaves, was suspect by such evil or irresponsible minds. It was the subject of some sermons preached by the northern clergy, who also insisted that he was an atheist. One poem of the time dwelt on him "dreaming of liberty in the arms of his slave."

A particular slave was mentioned by some gossip mongers as Jefferson's probable mistress. This was Sally Heming, the maid who had accompanied Polly to France. At that time Abigail Adams had assumed Sally to be about fifteen or sixteen years old. The Hemings were slaves whom Martha Jefferson had inherited from her father and, according to Isaac Jefferson, an old Monticello slave who dictated his memoirs in the mid-1800s, some of them were her half brothers and sisters. On the Hemings, Isaac wrote: "Sally Heming's mother Betty was a bright mulatto woman and Sally mighty near white; she was the youngest child. Folks said that these Hemingses was old Mr. Wayles' children. Sally was very handsome: long straight hair down her back."

There is nothing except the evil pens of the political character assassins to indicate an improper relationship between Sally and her master.

Patsy Jefferson took after her father in appearance and in temperament. She was not pretty, but she was a model daughter both as a child and in later life. A biographer described her by writing:

Never beautiful like the exquisite Maria, [Polly] she possessed rare traits of character. Poised, gifted in conversation and manners, she was her father's delight. It is not amiss to recall a distinguished occasion a few years later in Richmond, at which

Martha Randolph's health was offered as the toasts went round. Among those present was eccentric John Randolph of Roanoke, now bitterly estranged from Jefferson. To the astonishment of all, Randolph suddenly rose, glass in hand, to utter in his shrill voice: "Yes, gentlemen, let us drink — to the noblest woman in Virginia."

Despite Patsy's many fine qualities, Polly seems to have been Jefferson's favorite, probably because she reminded him of her mother. Every reference mentions her frail beauty. Unfortunately, she also resembled her mother in her constitution. She bore three children with great difficulty and died, as had her mother, as the result of her last confinement. She was but twenty-six years old.

During his five years as Secretary of State, and later, twelve years as Vice President and President, Jefferson usually got home only once a year to see his family, but he wrote some of his most interesting letters to his daughters and granddaughters at this time. He established a letter-writing schedule when he left for New York under which he would write every week and each daughter and his son-in-law were to write every third week. Patsy and her husband adhered faithfully to this but Polly was somewhat delinquent.

In his first letter to Patsy as Secretary of State her father seemed to be a little afraid that her new husband would supplant him in her affections. He wrote:

Your new condition will call for abundance of little sacrifices. But they will be greatly overpaid by the measure of affection they will secure to you. The happiness of your life depends now on the continuing to please a single person. To this all other objects must be secondary; even your love to me, were it possible that that could ever be an obstacle. But this it can never be. Neither of you can ever have a more faithful friend than myself, nor one on whom you can count for more sacrifices. My own is become a secondary object to the happiness of you both. Cherish then for me, my dear child, the affection of your husband, and continue to love me as you have done, and to render my life a blessing, by the prospect it may hold up to me of seeing you happy.

To twelve-year-old Polly he wrote from New York a list of questions in a vain effort to get a letter from her:

Write me a letter by the first post and answer me all these questions. Tell me whether you see the sun rise every day? How many pages a day you read in Don Quixote? How far you are advanced in him? Whether you repeat a grammar lesson every day? What else you read? How many hours a day you sew? Whether you have an opportunity of continuing your music? Whether you know how to make a pudding yet, to cut out a beefsteak, to sow spinach, or to set a hen? Be good, my dear, as I have always found you, never be angry with anybody, nor speak harm of them, try to let everybody's faults be forgotten, as you would wish yours to be; take more pleasure in giving what is best to another than in having it yourself, and then all the world will love you, and I more than all the world.

When Polly's first baby was born, and soon died, it became evident that, like her mother, she was too fragile for child bearing. After this her father was constantly concerned that she was ill when he did not hear from her. He repeatedly solicited her to write regularly and reiterated his love for her:

It is necessary for my tranquillity that I should hear from you often; for I feel inexpressibly whatever affects your health or happiness. My attachments to the world, and whatever it can offer, are daily wearing off, but you are one of the links which hold to my existence, and can only break off with that. You have never, by a word or deed, given me one moment's uneasiness; on the contrary, I have felt perpetual gratitude to Heaven for having given me in you a source of so much pure and unmixed happiness; go on then, my dear, as you have done, in deserving the love of everybody; you will reap the rich reward of their esteem, and will find that we are working for ourselves while we do good to others.

While Jefferson was President the wife of his Secretary of State, James Madison, acted as hostess in the White House when the President entertained, except for two winters when Patsy did the honors. The first visit of both daughters to the White House, in the winter of 1802, was a memorable occasion. Both of their husbands were in the House of Representatives. Jefferson's *maître d'hotel*, Petit, dreamed up culinary masterpieces for the reunited family and Dolley Madison, who surely knew her way around the Federal City, took the young wives shopping. Patsy delivered one of her numerous brood in the White House; the first baby to be born in the Executive Mansion.

A year after this happy occasion, Polly died. In reply to a letter of condolence from old friend John Page, now Governor of Virginia, Thomas wrote: "Others may lose of their abundance, but I, of my want, have lost even the half of all I have. My evening prospects now hang on the slender thread of a single life."

His granddaughters did not replace Polly in his affections but they did take her place as correspondents, particularly the second granddaughter, Ellen Wayles Randolph. When she was but six she received this exciting note from the President of the United States:

My very dear Ellen,
    I will catch you in bed Sunday or Monday morning.
                                        Yours affectionately
                                            Thomas Jefferson.

The child started to write her grandfather when she was five, with her mother holding the pen. Thomas answered her with serious courtesy, addressing the missive formally to "Miss Eleanor Randolph." He thanked her for the letter and added:

I inclose you two little books as a mark of satisfaction, and if you continue to learn as fast you will become a learned lady and publish books yourself. I hope you will at the same time continue to be a very good girl, never getting angry with your playmates nor the servants, but always trying to be more good-humored and more generous than they. If you find that one of them has been better tempered to you than you to them, you must blush, and be very much ashamed, and resolve not to let them excel you again. In this way you will make us all too fond of you, and I shall particularly think of nothing but what I can send you or carry you to show you how much I love you; . . . I have given this letter twenty kisses which it will deliver to you: half to yourself, and the other half you must give to Anne [Ellen's older sister]. Adieu my dear Ellen.

As a correspondent, Ellen apparently took after her aunt Polly, for when she was eight her grandfather sent her this facetious balance sheet:

Miss Eleanor W. Randolph to Th: Jefferson Dr.
1805 May 21   To a letter which ought to be written once
              in every three weeks while I am here, to wit
              from Jan. 1, 1805 to this day 15 weeks   5
                            Cr
      Feb 23 By one single letter of this day's date   1
              Balance due from E.W. Randolph to Th.J.   4
                                                            —
                                                             5

So stands the account for this year, my dear Ellen, between you and me. Unless it be soon paid off I shall send the sheriff after you.

After years of living in Paris, New York, Philadelphia, and Washington, Jefferson finally came home for good to Monticello in 1809, at the age of sixty-six. Patsy and her family moved to the parental home at the same time and she served as hostess for busy Monticello and took care of her father for the remaining seventeen years of his life. Patsy's role, in the final years when her father was in his eighties, was described by a student at the University of Virginia:

> Mr. Jefferson was always pleased to have us students at his table. Upon these occasions we were generally seated around the table, when Mr. Jefferson would enter and walk directly to an adjoining table specially prepared for him, and upon which were placed two lighted candles and a small vial by his plate. He would then say: "My daughter, I perceive there are several young gentlemen at the table, but I do not see well enough to distinguish who they are, so you must tell me their names." Whereupon his daughter would lead him up to each young gentleman, who would in turn rise, when Mr. Jefferson would shake hands and pass a pleasant word with him. At the close of the repast, as his own hand was too trembling, his daughter would pour from the vial into a tumbler a few drops of medicine to produce slumber in case he should be wakeful, and then he would take up the tumbler and a candle, make a stately bow to the assemblage, and retire to his bedroom.

Jefferson's last piece of writing was a poem that he addressed to Patsy, entitled:

A Death-bed Adieu from TH. J. to M.R.

Life's visions are vanished, its dreams are no more;
  Dear friends of my bosom, why bathed in tears?
I go to my fathers: I welcome the shore
  Which crowns all my hopes or which buries my cares.
Then farewell, my dear, my lov'd daughter, adieu!
The last pang of life is in parting from you!
Two seraphs await me long shrouded in death;
I will bear them your love on my last parting breath.

Tragedy seemed to stalk most of the women who were close

to Thomas Jefferson. The untimely deaths of his wife and younger daughter were the most significant instances, but there were others. Maria Cosway's life was far from happy after her interlude with Thomas. As a boy his favorite sister had been the oldest of the Jefferson children — Jane, three years older than himself. It was said that she, more than his mother, stimulated his boyish ambitions and encouraged him in his reading and cultivation of music. He taught his grandchildren psalms that she used to sing to him. Jane died, unmarried, at the age of twenty-five.

His sister Elizabeth, a year younger than himself, was mentally defective. On March 1, 1774, Jefferson noted in his account book: "My sister Elizabeth was found last Thursday, being February 24." On the seventh the same book credits Charles Clay forty shillings for "performing the funeral service this day on burying my sister, Elizabeth and 40/ more for preaching Mr. Carr's funeral service." Dabney Carr was the husband of a third sister. There had been an earthquake at Monticello on February 21 and it is assumed that Elizabeth, then aged thirty, had become terrified, wandered away from home, and died in the nearby wild country.

Tragedy even touched the life of the smooth-tempered Patsy. Her husband had shown great promise, and had performed well in Congress. But, by the time his family moved to Monticello, Thomas Randolph was broke. He was a fine farmer — his father-in-law said the best in Virginia — but he had a strange quirk of character which prevented him from following anything through. He would raise bountiful crops, and let them rot in the barns because it was too much trouble to send them to Richmond. Coupled with this he seemed to have a compulsion to give money away. Any distant relative — even some total strangers — with hard-luck stories found a ready ear and even more ready purse in Randolph. Soon, the purse was empty. After they moved to Monticello, Thomas Randolph seems to have had some kind of mental aberration that led him to believe that the family was conspiring against him. He shut himself up in a small house on the property and refused to have any intercourse with other members of the family.

Jefferson left Monticello to Patsy, but this was little more than a gesture of affection. Thomas died on the verge of bankruptcy. His liabilities overbalanced his assets by some forty thousand dollars. He, too, was generous to a fault. He endorsed a note for $21,000 for a distant relative, who defaulted. And he had a passion for architecture and hospitality. Even when there was no money he continued to improve Monticello and to offer generous entertainment to any and all who came there — twenty or thirty house guests were not uncommon. One European acquaintance arrived with a family of six and stayed ten months. Then, there were his "people" — as he called his slaves. There were some thirty-seven house servants in and around Monticello and the master could not bear to get rid of any of them. Field slaves had no incentive to work except fear of punishment; and Jefferson would not permit his overseers to drive the blacks. As a result, they produced little more than it cost to keep them. In one year he took in $3,500 from tobacco and his nailery and spent $7,000 running Monticello.

Jefferson was sustained in his final years by contributions from the cities of New York, Philadelphia, and Baltimore. He died thinking that his estate had been saved, but within six months Martha had to auction the furniture, china, and interior decorations of Monticello. At first there was no buyer for the mansion itself but it was finally acquired by a druggist in Charlottesville who planned to raise silk worms there. Patsy was nearing sixty when she came down the little mountain widowed, penniless, and homeless, except for the generosity of her children. She wrote in her notebook: "There is a time in human suffering when succeeding sufferings are but like snow falling on an iceberg."

CHAPTER VI

Two Women and Alexander Hamilton

ALEXANDER HAMILTON did not brood over his illegitimate birth. He *was* distressed — and very much distressed — at being a nobody. He wrote: "I *must* excel," and again, in *The Federalist:* "There are strong minds in every walk of life that will rise superior to the disadvantages of situation, and will command the tribute due to their merit, not only from the classes to which they particularly belong, but from the society in general." He was conscious of his superior talents and resolved to put himself in a position that would permit him to rise above his station in life.

The quickest and surest way to do this was to make a marital connection with a good family. When he was twenty-four he outlined his specifications for a wife to a fellow aide on Washington's staff, John Laurens, as follows:

She must be young, handsome (I lay most stress upon a good shape), sensible (a little learning will do), well bred (but she must have an aversion to the word *ton*), chaste and tender (I am an enthusiast in my notions of fidelity and fondness), of some good nature, a great deal of generosity (she must neither love money

nor scolding, for I dislike equally a termagant and an economist).
In politics, I am indifferent what side she may be of; I think I
have arguments that will easily convert her to mine. As to religion
a moderate stock will satisfy me. She must believe in God and
hate a saint. But as to fortune, the larger stock of that the
better. . . . Though I run no risk of going to purgatory for my
avarice, yet as money is an essential ingredient to happiness in
this world — as I have not much of my own and as I am very little
calculated to get more either by my address or industry — it must
needs be that my wife, if I get one, bring at least a sufficiency to
administer to her own extravagancies.

In justice to Hamilton it must be made clear that the above
was written in a facetious mood. He closed the letter by saying: "After reviewing what I have written, I am ready to ask
myself what could have put it into my head to hazard this
jeu de follie. Do I want a wife? No — I have plagues enough
without desiring to add to the number that *greatest of all. . . ."*
He added that his *jeu de follie* was merely an attempt to
frisk, but despite this avowal there was certainly a basis of
serious concern for a prospective wife's social and economic
standing. Hamilton's name was never associated with that of
any woman who did not rank high in this respect, except for
a later affair that was purely sexual.

If there were any women in Alexander's life during his
teens and early twenties, history knows them not. He lived in
the islands until he was seventeen and, as a clerk in Cruger's
store, it is possible that he had little opportunity to know the
daughters of white planters or professional men. The legend
that he had a child or children by one or more Negro girls
has no more foundation than that which attributes Negro
blood to Alexander. Although he may not have had anything
to do *with* girls, he certainly knew *about* them. This is evident from a poem that he sent to the *Royal Danish American*

Gazette, written when he was sixteen. The first three stanzas describe a love affair with a shepherdess. The final stanza read:

> Content we tend our flocks by day,
> Each rural pleasure amply taste;
> And at the sun's retiring ray
> Prepare for new delight:
> When from the field we haste away,
> And send our blithsome care to rest,
> We fondly sport and fondly play,
> And love away the night.

There is no record of an interest in girls during Alexander's stay at King's College in New York nor while he was a captain of artillery in the early days of the Revolution. This is somewhat strange because, from some accounts and later happenings, his was a rather passionate nature and except for his short stature — he was about five foot seven — he was the handsomest of the Founding Fathers. His portraits support this description by a contemporary: "His complexion was exceedingly fair, and varying from this only by the almost feminine rosiness of the cheeks. His might be considered, as to figure and color, an uncommonly handsome face. His hair . . . was of fine texture, brown, powdered and collected in a club behind." His eyes were dark blue and deep set and he was "remarkably erect and dignified in his deportment." Despite his attractiveness to women, if there were any casual relationships with the opposite sex during his early years Hamilton did not, like Franklin, report them.

So far as is known, the first female of whom Hamilton took notice was Kitty Livingston, one of the three daughters of New Jersey's Revolutionary Governor. Hamilton had undoubtedly met the Livingston girls when he first came to the

mainland in 1772 and briefly attended a school in Elizabeth-
town, N.J., near the Livingston mansion. He started to write
to Kitty in 1777 during the first year that Washington's
winter headquarters were at Morristown. It is probable that
Kitty and her younger sister visited headquarters when
Martha Washington or other of the generals' ladies were
there to chaperone. The oldest Livingston girl, Sarah, was
already married to John Jay.

From Alexander's letters to Kitty it is hard to tell whether
he was merely being gallant or had something more definite
in the back of his mind. He first wrote, he said, because her
sister Susanna — "Miss Suky" — told him that Kitty had "a
relish for politics, which she thinks my situation qualifies me
better for gratifying, than would be in her power." He made
a "cynical inquiry" as to whether her interest in politics
"proceed from sympathy in the concerns of the public, or
merely from female curiosity, yet I will not consent to be
limited to any particular subject. I challenge you to meet me
in whatever path you dare; and if you have no objection, for
variety and amusement, we will even sometimes make excur-
sions in the flowery walks and roseate bowers of Cupid." He
asked her to let him know her tastes in this regard. "After
knowing exactly your taste, and whether you are of a romantic or discreet temper as to love affairs, I will endeavor to
regulate myself by it."

When Kitty answered he showed her letter to "a gentleman
of our family" — that is, Washington's staff. This worthy, he
told her in a second epistle: "After attentively perusing your
letter, during which, the liveliest emotions of approbation
were pictured on his face, 'Hamilton!' cries he, 'when you
write to this divine girl again, it must be in the style of adoration: none but a goddess, I am sure, could have penned so

fine a letter!' " She had said that she hated war and he replied that he yearned for peace, not least because it would remove the obstacles "which now lie in the way of that most delectable thing, called matrimony — a state which, with a kind of magnetic force, attracts every breast to it in which susceptibility has a place, in spite of the resistance it encounters in the dull admonitions of prudence."

Unless subsequent correspondence has been lost, Alexander never made any more definite avowal to Kitty. His next known letter to her, two years later, is addressed jointly to "Catharine Livingston and Elizabeth Schuyler." The girls had apparently asked him to escort them to headquarters and he replied:

> Colonel Hamilton's compliments to Miss Livingston and Miss Schuyler. He is sorry to inform them that his zeal for their service make him forget that he is so bad a charioteer as hardly to dare to trust himself with so precious a charge; though if he were only to consult his own wishes, like Phaeton he would assemble the chariot of the sun, if he were sure of experiencing the same fate. Colonel Tilghman offers himself a volunteer.

This is the last letter (of this period) to Kitty and his first letter to his future wife.

But it seems that Alexander was not immune to the charms of the twittering females who visited headquarters, or the belles of the Morristown neighborhood. Colonel Webb of the Continental Line, who was visiting at headquarters, wrote a poem "To Lt. Col. Hamilton, on his being attentive to C. Lott, Jany, 1780."

The young lady was Cornelia Lott who lived near Morristown. The poem started:

> What, bend the Stubborn knee at last,
> Confess the days of wisdom past,

He that could bow to every shrine,
And swear the last the most divine: . . .
Now feels the inexorable dart
And yields Cornelia all his heart!

It was probably during that same month — January, 1780 — that Alexander's interest was deflected from Cornelia by Elizabeth Schuyler, one of four daughters of General Phillip Schuyler and Catherine Van Rensselaer Schuyler. This was a family that would meet any ambitious young man's qualifications in terms of social and financial standing. Catherine descended from one of the original Dutch Patroons who had parceled out the valley of the Hudson River among themselves. The General owned much land in upper New York state and maintained mansions at Albany and Saratoga. Early in 1780 Betsy Schuyler visited her uncle and aunt at Washington's headquarters and became part of the gay life at Morristown that winter. Alexander's courtship was a whirlwind one, for they were engaged by March of that year.

Betsey was neither as beautiful as her younger sister Margarita nor as intellectual as her older sister Angelica. She had little or no formal education and no reference is made to her accomplishments in music, art, or literature. Apparently when older sister Angelica went off to school it was left to the more amenable Betsey to help Mother run the house. One of Hamilton's fellow aides, Tench Tilghman, had met her earlier and described her by writing: "I was prepossessed in favor of this young lady the moment I saw her. A brunette with the most good-natured lively dark eyes that I ever saw, which threw a beam of good temper and benevolence over her whole countenance. Mr. Livingston informed me that I was not mistaken in my conjecture for that she was the finest tempered girl in the world." In her late teens Betsey seems to have been an outdoor type for Tilghman described how she disdained male assistance in climbing a hill and "made herself merry at the distress of the other ladies."

From Hamilton, in the early months of their engagement, we get two descriptions of his betrothed. To Laurens he gave this rather lukewarm and unromantic picture of his fiancée.

Have you not heard that I am on the point of becoming a benedict? I confess my sins. I am guilty. Next fall completes my doom. I give up my liberty to Miss Schuyler. She is a good-hearted girl who I am sure will never play the termagant; though not a genius she has good sense enough to be agreeable, and though not a beauty, she has fine black eyes — is rather handsome and has every other requisite of the exterior to make a lover happy. And believe me, I am lover in earnest, though I do not speak of the perfections of my mistress in the enthusiasm of chivalry.

To Betsey's sister Margarita, Hamilton described his loved one with somewhat more enthusiasm.

I have already confessed the influence your sister has gained over me; yet notwithstanding this, I have some things of a very serious and heinous nature to lay to her charge. She is most unmercifully handsome and so perverse that she has none of those pretty affectations which are the prerogatives of beauty. Her good sense is destitute of that happy mixture of vanity and ostentation which would make it conspicuous to the whole tribe of fools and foplings as well as to men of understanding so that as the matter now stands it is little known beyond the circle of these. She has good nature, affability, and vivacity unembellished with that charming frivolousness which is justly deemed one of the principal accomplishments of a *belle*. In short she is so strange a creature that she possesses all the beauties, virtues, and graces of her sex without any of those amiable defects, which from their general prevalence are esteemed by connoisseurs necessary shades in the character of a fine woman. The most determined adversaries of Hymen can find in her no pretext for their hostility, and there are several of my friends, philosophers who railed at love as a weakness, men of the world who laughed at it as a phantasie, whom she has presumptuously and daringly compelled to acknowledge its power and surrender at discretion. I can the better assert the truth of this, as I am myself of the number. She has had the address to overset all the wise resolutions I had been framing for more than four years past, and from a rational sort of being and a professed contemner of Cupid, has in a trice metamorphosed me into the veriest inamorato you perhaps ever saw.

It might be expected that the socially prominent Schuylers would frown on a West Indian of no position, and born under the bar sinister, as a match for one of their daughters. Instead, General Schuyler welcomed Alexander with great enthusiasm, writing:

You cannot my dear Sir, be more happy at the connection you have made with my family than I am. Until the child of a parent has made a judicious choice his heart is in continual anxiety; but this anxiety was removed the moment I discovered on whom she had placed her affections. I am pleased with every instance of delicacy in those who are dear to me, and I think I read your soul on that occasion you mention. I shall therefore only entreat you to consider me as one who wishes in every way to promote your happiness, and I shall.

It is assumed that the "instance of delicacy" was a confession by Hamilton of the irregularity of his birth.

The old General and the young Colonel had much in common. General Gates had replaced Schuyler in command of the army in New York and won a hero's stature by letting General Benedict Arnold win the battle of Saratoga for him. As a result there was no love lost between Schuyler and Gates. Nor was there between Hamilton and Gates. Alexander had had a dispute with Gates after Saratoga and had been one of his most vicious critics when Gates seemed to be involved in the "Conway Cabal" to unseat Washington. Hamilton and Schuyler also found that their political views were identical.

Some, particularly the French officers at headquarters, saw Hamilton's interest in Elizabeth as purely pecuniary. Colonel Fleury wrote: "You will get all that family's interest. . . . You will be in a very easy situation and happiness is not to be found without a large estate." Others saw an ulterior motive on the opposite side. Arthur Lee said upon his return from France: "If Schuyler is with us he may give his daughter to Hamilton to gain sway over Washington or be in the military plot with him to surrender America back to Great Britain." Actually, although Hamilton's immediate prospects did not extend beyond being a veteran at the end of the war, his great ability was already apparent and General Schuyler undoubtedly considered him as a worth while and honorable addition to the family.

In truth, although his connection with the Schuylers and, through them, the affluent Van Rensselaers, Livingstons, and others was of great benefit to Hamilton in his later legal practice, he never accepted direct financial aid from his father-in-law other than the sloop loads of hams, butter, and other provisions which the old General regularly sent down the Hudson to his daughter's family. And, three months before their marriage, Alexander made it quite clear to Betsey that she must expect to give up her life of affluence after their marriage. He started by asking her:

But now we are talking of times to come, tell me my pretty damsel, have you made up your mind upon the subject of housekeeping? Do you soberly relish the pleasure of being a poor man's wife? Have you learned to think a homespun preferable to a brocade and the rumbling of a wagon wheel to the musical rattling of a coach and six? Will you be able to see with perfect composure your old acquaintances flaunting it in gay life, tripping it along in elegance and splendor, while you hold an humble station and have no other enjoyments than the sober comforts of a good wife? Can you in short be an Aquileia and cheerfully plant turnips with me, if fortune should so order it? If you cannot, my dear, we are playing a comedy of all in the wrong, and you should correct the mistake before we begin to act the tragedy of the unhappy couple. . . .

Beloved by you, I can be happy in any situation, and can struggle with every embarrassment of fortune with patience and firmness. I cannot, however, forbear entreating you to realize our union on the dark side and satisfy, without deceiving yourself, how far your affection for me can make you happy in a privation of those elegancies to which you have been accustomed. . . . So far, my dear Betsey, as the tenderest affection can compensate for other inconveniences in making your estimate, you cannot give too large a credit for this article. My heart overflows with everything for you that admiration, esteem, and love can inspire; *I would this moment give the world to be near you only to kiss your sweet hand.*

This was but one of a stream of tender letters that poured from Alexander's pen during the nine months of his engagement and, in fact, during the twenty-four years of his marriage. From his courtship in Morristown until his last letter written a few hours before he dropped on the dueling ground at Weehawken, Hamilton's letters to his wife were models of tenderness, concern, and adoration. If he did not truly love his "Betsey" (and there is no reason to believe that he did not, despite a later fall from grace) none would ever guess it from the effusion of his pen. These are some expressions from his letters between their betrothal in March and their marriage in December, 1780.

I had written so far when the express arrived with your dear billet. . . . I cannot tell you what ecstasy I felt in casting my eyes over the sweet effusions of tenderness it contains. My Betsey's soul speaks in every line and bids me be the happiest of mortals. I am so and will be so. You give me too many proofs of your love to allow me to doubt it and in the conviction that I possess that, I possess every thing the world can give.

I love you more and more every hour. The sweet softness and delicacy of your mind and manners, the elevation of your sentiments, the real goodness of your heart, its tenderness to me, the beauties of your face and person, your unpretending good sense and that innocent simplicity and frankness which pervade your actions; all these appear to me with increasing amiableness and place you in my estimation above all the rest of your sex.

You are certainly a little sorceress and have bewitched me, for you have made me disrelish every thing that used to please me, and have rendered me as restless and unsatisfied with all about me, as if I was the inhabitant of another world, and had nothing in common with this. I must in spite of myself become an inconstant to detach myself from you, for as it now stands I love you more than I ought — more than is consistent with my peace. . . . But why do you not write to me oftener? It is again an age since I have heard from you. . . . When I come to Albany, I shall find means to take satisfaction for your neglect. You recollect the mode I threatened to punish you in for all your delinquencies.

Pardon me, my love, for talking politics to you. What have we to do with anything but love? Go the world as it will, in each other's arms we cannot but be happy. If America were lost we should be happy in some other clime more favorable to human rights. . . . I was once determined to let my existence and American liberty end together. My Betsey has given me a motive to outlive my pride, I had almost said my honor.

I would go on but the General summons me to ride. Adieu, my dear lovely amiable girl. Heaven preserve you and shower its choicest blessings upon you. Love me I conjure you. A. Hamilton.

In one of the letters above Alexander wrote: "The inclosed was sent to you at Morristown, but missed you; as it contains ideas that often occur to me, I send it now." While there is no assurance as to what the "inclosed" was, it is believed to be a sonnet that was found, written in Alexander's hand on torn and yellow paper, in a bag around Elizabeth's neck when she died — three quarters of a century after the letter was written. The poem reads:

Answer to the Inquiry Why I Sighed

Before no mortal ever knew
A love like mine so tender, true,
Completely wretched — you away.
And but half blessed e'en while you stay.

If present love [illegible] face
Deny you to my fond embrace
No joy unmixed my bosom warms
But when my angel's in my arms.

Another woman who touched Alexander's life briefly but not romantically during his engagement to Betsey was Peggy Arnold, wife of the traitorous General. Hamilton and Lafayette were breakfasting at Arnold's home near West Point when the General received word that Major André had been captured and his treachery discovered. Arnold told his wife privately and fled. Another courier arrived with dispatches for Washington which, when Hamilton read them, acquainted him with the affair. He galloped to West Point to give the information to Washington and then led a troop of dragoons in a futile pursuit of the traitor. Next day he wrote to Betsey:

Arnold, hearing of the plot being detected, immediately fled to the enemy. I went in pursuit of him, but was much too late; and could hardly regret the disappointment, when, on my re-

turn, I saw an amiable woman, frantic with distress for the loss
of a husband she tenderly loved; a traitor to his country and to
his fame; a disgrace to his connections: it was the most affecting
scene I ever was witness to. . . . All the sweetness of beauty, all the
loveliness of innocence, all the tenderness of a wife, and all the
fondness of a mother showed themselves in her appearance and
conduct. . . .

This morning she is more composed. I paid her a visit, and
endeavored to soothe her by every method in my power, though
you may imagine she is not easily to be consoled. . . . She received
us in bed, with every circumstance that would interest our sympathy; and her sufferings were so eloquent that I wished myself
her brother, to have a right to become her defender. As it is, I
have entreated her to enable me to give her proofs of my friendship. Could I forgive Arnold for sacrificing his honor, reputation,
and duty, I could not forgive him for acting a part that must
have forfeited the esteem of so fine a woman. At present she almost forgets his crime in his misfortunes; and her horror at the
guilt of the traitor is lost in her love of the man.

Here Hamilton's emotional reaction to beauty in distress
overruled his judgment. Peggy Arnold was no sweet, innocent, young bride, aghast at the treachery of the man she
loved. There are those who assert that Arnold's treachery was
a direct result of his May-December marriage to this beautiful
daughter of a Tory family. Certainly Peggy was a party to the
plot from the beginning. She exchanged letters with André
before her husband did, signed receipts for some of the money
that he received, and was later awarded £350 by the British
for "meritorious services." If she became hysterical at the disclosure it was either a fine piece of acting or based on the fear
that her involvement would be discovered.

Alexander and Betsey were married in the Schuyler mansion at Albany on December 14, 1780. Hamilton had wanted
to marry sooner, at headquarters, but graciously deferred to

General Schuyler in his wish that Betsey be married at home. Angelica had deprived her mother of a wedding by eloping; as did, later, Betsey's other two sisters. Hamilton left the staff soon after to command a regiment of artillery. During the last two years of the war he read law on the side and was admitted to the bar in 1782.

No complete picture can be formed of Elizabeth Hamilton, the wife and housekeeper. Few of her letters to her husband have been found and virtually none of his dealt with domestic matters. Unlike the other wives of the Founding Fathers, Betsey did not have a home of her own to take care of until near the end of her married life. For the first eighteen years of their marriage the Hamiltons lived in rented dwellings in New York City and Philadelphia. Elizabeth and the children spent much time at her parents' home in Albany during Alexander's frequent absences on legal and political business.

Betsey bore eight children, and had at least two miscarriages, over a period of more than twenty years. The first son, Philip, was born in 1782. He was killed in a duel, two years before his father met the same fate, while Elizabeth was carrying the last child; another Philip. The only glimpse that we have of Hamilton family life is this account from another son, James.

I distinctly recollect the scene at breakfast in the front room of the house in Broadway. My dear mother seated, as was her wont, at the head of the table with a napkin in her lap, cutting slices of bread and spreading them with butter, while the younger boys, standing at her side, read in turn a chapter in the Bible or a portion of Goldsmith's "Rome." When the lessons were finished the father and the elder children were called to breakfast, after which the boys were packed off to school.

It is unlikely that Betsey was a great housekeeper in the

tradition of Deborah, Martha, or even Abigail; she never had the opportunity. The real Hamilton home was, in a sense, the Schuyler mansion, although they never lived there regularly. When Alexander wed Betsey, he in effect married a family. He and his father-in-law were allies in politics and of like mind on government philosophy. Both believed that the country should be ruled by an upper class, which should have special privilege. The plan that Hamilton introduced at the Constitutional Convention for a very strong central government, at the expense of state sovereignty, was called the Schuyler-Hamilton plan. Betsey must have spent many evenings listening to her father and her husband planning the future of their country; its Constitution, its finances, and, later, the political maneuvering of the Federalist party.

In all of this Elizabeth was not a silent bystander. Unlike Abigail Adams she probably did not have the intellectual capacity to help mold her husband's ideas. But he did discuss affairs of moment with her and she helped with some of the drudgery, at least. As its initial secretary, Hamilton was the "father of the treasury" and formulated the country's first banking system. A contemporary left this record of a conversation with Elizabeth late in life.

Old Mrs. Hamilton, . . . active in body, clear in mind . . . talks familiarly of Washington, Jefferson, and the Fathers. I told her how greatly I was interested . . . on account of her husband's connection with the Government. "He made your Government," said she; "he made your bank. I sat up all night with him to help him to do it. Jefferson thought we ought not to have a bank, and President Washington thought so. But my husband said, "We must have a bank." I sat up all night, copied out his writing, and the next morning he carried it to President Washington and we had a bank."

And if she did not contribute to Washington's Farewell Address, Betsey at least held her husband's hand while he wrote much of it.

For most of his life after the war Alexander Hamilton made a good income from his law practice — and spent every penny of it. The nobody from the West Indies had large ideas in private as well as public finance. He speculated in real estate — not always shrewdly — and, in his final years, built a country home that was far beyond his means. It is probable that Betsey was sometimes grateful for the sloop-loads of food that her father sent down river from Albany and that, had she not kept a check on the family finances, the Hamiltons might have had greater difficulties in this direction. McHenry once told Hamilton that: "She has as much merit as your Treasurer as you have as Treasurer of the wealth of the United States." Certainly Alexander trusted her in financial matters. Five years after their marriage he wrote her:

Colonel Burr just tells me, that the house we live in is offered for sale at £2100. I am to request you to agree for the purchase for me, if at that price. If you cannot do better, you may engage that the whole shall be paid in three months; but I could wish to pay half in a short time and the other half in a year. Adieu, my Angel."

This transaction was not then completed.

For twenty-four years of their married life Elizabeth was a tender, helpful, comforting, and consoling wife to a somewhat difficult man of genius. Except for one "debunking" biographer who intimates, without evidence, that she was somewhat dull, there is naught but praise for her from all who knew her. Another biographer says, simply, that she was "a blessing to her husband." It is certain that she was the soul of fidelity; which cannot be said for her husband, in whose

life there was at least one other woman. Alexander described
the beginning of his affair with a female named Maria Reynolds in this wise:

> Some time in the summer of the year of 1791, a woman called
> at my house in the city of Philadelphia, and asked to speak with
> me in private. I attended her into a room apart from my family.
> With a seeming air of affliction she informed me that she was a
> daughter of Mr. Lewis, sister to a Mr. G. Livingston of the State
> of New York, and wife to a Mr. Reynolds, whose father was in
> the Commissary Department during the war with Great Britain;
> that her husband, who for a long time had treated her very
> cruelly, had lately left her to live with another woman, and in so
> destitute a condition that, though desirous of returning to her
> friends, she had not the means; that knowing I was a citizen of
> New York, she had taken the liberty to apply to my humanity for
> assistance.
>
> I replied that her situation was a very interesting one — that I
> was disposed to afford her assistance to convey her to her friends,
> but this at the moment not being convenient to me (which was
> the fact), I must request the place of her residence, to which I
> should bring or send a small supply of money. She told me the
> street and the number of the house where she lodged. In the
> evening I put a bank-bill in my pocket and went to the house. I
> enquired for Mrs. Reynolds and was shown upstairs, at the head
> of which she met me and conducted me into a bedroom. I took
> the bill out of my pocket and gave it to her. Some conversation
> ensued, from which it was quickly apparent that other than
> pecuniary consolation would [also] be acceptable.
>
> After this I had frequent meetings with her, most of them at
> my own house; Mrs. Hamilton with her children being absent on
> a visit to her father.

These frequent meetings continued until mid-December.
While they were going on Alexander wrote Betsey, in Albany,
expressing solicitude for her health: "Consider how much our
happiness depends upon it. . . . I have been to see your new

house. . . . Twill soon be ready and I shall obey your orders about papering etc. Adieu, my precious wife. Blessings without number on you and my little ones."

During this time Mrs. Reynolds told him that her husband was seeking a reconciliation. Alexander advised her to agree. She then said that Reynolds could give Hamilton information about connivance on the part of someone on the Treasury staff in speculation. Hamilton sent for Reynolds, who said that a clerk who had since resigned had given him classified information. Reynolds wanted a job in the Treasury. Hamilton recorded: "The situation of the wife would naturally incline me to conciliate this man. It is possible I may have used vague expressions which raised expectation; but the more I learned of the person, the more inadmissible his employment in a public office became."

Somewhere along the line Hamilton must had had a dawning suspicion that he might be the victim of what is now crudely called the "badger game." He wrote:

The intercourse with Mrs. Reynolds in the meantime continued; and though various reflections (in which a further knowledge of Reynolds' character and the suspicion of some concert between the husband and wife bore a part) induced me to wish a cessation of it; yet, her conduct made it extremely difficult to disentangle myself. All the appearances of violent attachment, and of agonizing distress at the idea of relinquishment, were played with a most imposing art. This, though it did not make me entirely the dupe of the plot, yet kept me in a state of irresolution. My sensibility, perhaps my vanity, admitted the possibility of a real fondness; and led me to adopt the plan of a gradual discontinuance rather than of a sudden interruption, as least calculated to give pain, if a real partiality existed. Mrs. Reynolds, on the other hand, employed every effort to keep up my attention and visits. Her pen was freely employed, and her letters were filled with those tender and pathetic effusions which would have been natural to a woman truly fond and neglected.

Any doubts that Hamilton had as to the connivance of husband and wife were dispelled when, late in December, he received two letters. Maria wrote him:

Dear Sir: — I have not tim to tell you the cause of my present troubles only that Mr. has rote you this morning and I know not whether you have got the letter or not and he has swore that If you do not answer It or If he dose not se or hear from you to day he will write Mrs. Hamilton he has just Gone oute and I am a Lone I think you had better come here one moment that you May know the Cause then you will the better know how to act Oh my God I feel more for you than myself and wish I had never been born to give you so mutch unhappiness do not rite to him no not a Line but come here soon do not send or leave any thing in his power. Maria.

The husband's letter was a longer one, telling how he had discovered a letter that his wife had written to Hamilton, made a copy, put the original back, and followed "a Black man" who delivered it to Hamilton's home. He had then confronted his wife with the evidence and "she fell upon her knees and asked forgiveness and discovered every thing to me Respecting the matter and ses that she was unhappy." He charged that Hamilton "took the advantage of a poor Broken harted woman. instead of being a Friend. you have acted the part of the most Cruelist man in existence. you have made a whole family miserable. She ses there is no other man that she Care for in this world. now Sir you have bin the Cause of Cooling her affections for me. She was a woman. . . . and I would Sacrefise almost my life to make her Happy, but now I am determined to heve satisfaction. it shant be onely one family thats miserable. . . . now Sir if I Cant see you at your house call and see me. for there is no person that Knowes any thing as yet."

Reynolds' first idea of "satisfaction" was a job in the Treasury. When Alexander definitely refused this the husband made an alternate demand: "now Sir I have Considered on the matter Serously. I have this preposial to make to you. give me the Sum of Thousand dollars and I will leve the town and take my daughter with me and go where my Friend Shant here from me and leve her to Yourself to do for her as you think proper."

Hamilton paid the $1,000, but if he thought he was rid of the precious pair this easily he soon learned his error. Two weeks after he paid Reynolds off he received another letter from the compliant husband inviting him to renew his visits to Maria; "I have not the Least Objections to your Calling. as a friend to Boath of us." He closed: "I Rely on your be-friending me if there should any thing Offer that would be to my advantage."

When Hamilton did not rush to Maria she bombarded him with letters calculated to arouse his pity and passion. She had, she said,

Ben Sick moast Ever since I saw you . . . I solicit a favor . . . for the last Time. Yes Sir Rest assured I will never ask you to call on me again. I have kept my Bed those tow dayes and now rise from my pillow wich your Neglect has filled with the sharpest thorns. . . . I only do it to Ease a heart wich is ready Burst with Greef. I can neither Eat or sleep. I have Been on the point of doing the moast horrid acts. . . . I feel as If I should not Contennue long and all the wish I have is to se you once more . . . for God Sake be not so voed of all humanity as to deni me this Last request but if you will not Call some this night I no its late but any between this and twelve a Clock I shall be up Let me Intreat you If you wont Come to send me a Line oh my head I can rite no more do something to Ease my Heart. . . . if my dear freend has the Lest Esteeme for the unhappy Maria whos greatest fault is Loveing him he will come as soon as he shall get this. . . .

P.S. If you cannot come this Evening to stay just come only for one moment as I shal be Lone Mr. is going to sup with a friend.

Maria calculated well. Hamilton did call again, and again, and again through the spring and into the summer of 1792. And while Alexander called on the wife, the husband called on Alexander, in person and by letter, for "loans": "it hurts me to let you Know my Setivation. I should take it as a protickeler if you would Oblige me with the lone of about thirty Dollars." And again, "I am sorry to inform you my setivation is as such. I am indebted to a man in this town about 45 dollars which he will wate no longer on me. now sir I am sorrey to be troubleing you So Offen." And again; "I must Sir ask the loan of thirty dollars more from you, which I shall esteem as a particular favour."

In May, 1792, Reynolds had a twinge of conscience — or he decided that his feelings were hurt because Hamilton always sneaked in the back door of his house. In any event he wrote:

I must now forever forbid you of visiting Mrs. R any more I was in hopes that it would in time ware off, but I find there is no hopes. So I determined to put a finell end to it. if its in my power. for I find by your Seeing her onely Renews the Friendship, and likewise when you Call you are fearful any person Should see you. am I a person of Such a bad Carector that you would not wish to be seen Coming in my house in the front way, all any Person Can say of me is that I am poore and I don't know if that is any Crime.

This was followed, a month later, by another piteous plea from Maria: "what have I done that you should thus Neglect me. . . . I am now A lone and shall be for a few days I believe till Wensday. . . . oh my deer freend how shal I plede Enough what shal I say Let me beg of you to Come." And Hamilton's next visit was followed by another letter from Reynolds. This time he wanted three hundred dollars. He settled for fifty.

The affair finally ended in August when Reynolds and an associate, Jacob Clingman, were jailed as a result of a confidence racket that they had perpetrated on veterans who had claims against the government. When Hamilton refused to raise a finger to help Reynolds, that worthy sent for Frederick A. Muhlenberg, Democratic Speaker of the House, saying that he could "make disclosures injurious to the character of some head of a department." Muhlenberg got Reynolds released and then called at his home with two other Democrats, Abraham Venable of the House and James Monroe of the Senate. Reynolds was not there, but Maria told them enough to convince these political foes of Hamilton's that he was involved in some dishonest deal with Reynolds and gave them some letters that showed that Reynolds was receiving money from the Secretary.

The Congressmen first proposed to take the story directly to President Washington, but then decided to hear Hamilton's side first. When they called on the Secretary of the Treasury he vigorously denied any financial wrong doing and explained his relations with Reynolds by laying bare his affair with Mrs. Reynolds. Since his sexual pecadillos were not within the province of the Congressmen, Venable tried to stop Alexander when he was half through, but the distrait Secretary insisted on completing his confession to fully prove his innocence of malfeasance. The Congressmen assured him that his sordid story was safe with them — after all they were all gentlemen. When they left, said Hamilton, "Mr. Muhlenberg and Mr. Venable, in particular, manifested a degree of sensibility on the occasion. Mr. Monroe was more cold but entirely explicit."

Five years passed. Hamilton thought that the knowledge of his affair with Maria was safe with the three Congressmen; but it was not confined to these. Jefferson knew of it, from Monroe. And John Beckley, clerk of the House of Representatives, had a copy of the Congressmen's private report, together with the correspondence. When the Federalists secured the removal of Beckley the disgruntled ex-clerk sought revenge on their leader by taking this material to a Democratic publisher, James T. Callander. This was the same Callander whose release from jail seven years later by Jefferson would so enrage Abigail Adams.

Callander promptly published an account of the affair in his *Memoirs of the United States, for the Year 1796.* He was not primarily interested in disclosing Hamilton's adultery. He wanted to ruin Alexander politically by proving that he had been in league with Reynolds to defraud the government. Hamilton's disclosure of the affair with Maria, he claimed, was merely a smoke screen to becloud the graver crime. "So much correspondence," wrote Callander, "could not refer exclusively to wenching."

Considering his public honor of more importance than an admission of misconduct in his private life, Alexander wrote and published in pamphlet form a complete history of his relations with the Reynoldses, including all of Maria's impassioned letters and her husband's blackmailing notes. The quotations above, in which Hamilton describes the affair, are from this pamphlet, which must have been hard reading for his wife. He realized this when he composed it, for he wrote:

This confession is not made without a blush. I cannot be the apologist of any vice because the ardor of passion may have made it mine. I can never cease to condemn myself for the pang which it may inflict in a bosom eminently entitled to all my gratitude,

fidelity, and love. But that bosom will approve, that, even at so
great an expense, I should effectually wipe away a more serious
stain from a name which it cherishes with no less elevation than
tenderness. The public, too, will, I trust, excuse the confession.
The necessity of it to my defence against a more heinous charge
could alone have extorted from me so painful an indecorum.

The pamphlet must have caused Elizabeth private grief,
but she never disclosed it nor, apparently, did her faith in
her husband lessen. His brother-in-law wrote to Alexander
of the perfect confidence of his wife: "I am this instant returned from your house. Eliza is well, she put into my hand
the newspaper with James Thomson Callander's letter to you,
but it makes not the least impression on her, only that she
considers the whole knot of those opposed to you to be
scoundrels."

The Democratic press was not so lenient as the wronged
wife. They were annoyed that Hamilton had successfully re-
futed the charge of malfeasance and made the most of his
admission of infidelity. One paper described his pamphlet as
"not a vindication of the ex-Secretary, but . . . of adultery."
Another said that Hamilton "holds himself out as trotting
from one lodging in Philadelphia to another after . . . a
prostitute!" A third said that his ambition was "to bring a . . .
strumpet to the level of his own personal infamy." One
Democratic editor thundered at Alexander: "Even the frosts
of America are incapable of cooling your blood and the
eternal snow of Nova Zembla would hardly reduce you to
the standard of common propriety." Hamilton, he added, had
made his home "the rendezvous of his whoredom; taking
advantage of the absence of his wife and children to introduce
a prostitute to those sacred abodes of conjugal and filial retirement to gratify his wicked purposes." Somewhat later,

after Hamilton and Adams had become deadly enemies, the old Puritan would attribute all of what he called Hamilton's "grandiose schemes" to "a super-abundance of secretions which he could not find whores enough to draw off."

Alexander did not know that John Beckley had a copy of the report of the investigation by the three Congressmen at the time of the Reynolds affair and assumed that Callander must have secured his information from James Monroe, who was more rancorous in his political opposition to Hamilton than the others. The two men had a meeting and some correspondence which Hamilton construed as a challenge to a duel from Monroe. Monroe said that he had not challenged Hamilton, but was willing to fight if Hamilton wanted to. An uneasy peace was negotiated between the two statesmen by, ironically, Aaron Burr, who would be Alexander's Nemesis in a later duel.

Even before the Reynolds affair — and increasingly after it — gossip connected Alexander's name with other women; but this was true of many men in a like position. John Adams described Hamilton's "audacious and unblushing attempts upon ladies of the highest rank and purest virtue" in Philadelphia, but there is no reason to believe that the ex-President was not drawing wholly upon his imagination, heightened by resentment toward the man who he believed had wrecked his political career. When the Government was in Philadelphia, Alexander was something of a "man about town" when Betsey was at Albany. His attentions to the ladies were marked, but there is no evidence that they were improper.

One woman with whom scandalmongers have tried to link Alexander is his sister-in-law Angelica Church, or Angelica Carter — her husband used the latter alias during the Revolution. Angelica was fashionable, gay, witty, more intellectual than her younger sister, and probably bored with her dull husband. John Church had little interest in anything except making money and, when the couple went to England after the Revolution, in getting into Parliament. He was successful in both endeavors, but not in holding the interest of his wife. Angelica, who spent several postwar years in Europe, became an intimate of Maria Cosway's and was one of the charming American women with whom Jefferson carried on an intellectual flirtation.

It is possible that Angelica had more than a sisterly interest in her sister's husband, but this seems to have embarrassed rather than encouraged Alexander. There was some byplay in their frequent letters to each other. For instance, in one letter Alexander wrote: "You ladies despise the pedantry of punctuation. There was a most critical *comma* in your last letter. It is in my interest that it should have been designed, but I presume it was accidental. Unriddle this if you can. The proof that you do it rightly may be given by the omission or repetition of the same mistake in your next." But all of this could properly be interpreted in terms of personal pleasantries. Angelica admitted to Betsey that she "loved" her husband, but "love" was used loosely. In one letter she wrote: "I sincerely congratulate you, my dear Eliza, on the resignation of our dear Hamilton [as Secretary of Treasury] and on your return to New York where I hope to pass with you the remainder of my days, that is if you will be so obliging as to permit my *Brother* to give me his society, for you know how much I love and admire him."

In another letter Angelica told her sister: "By my *Amiable* you know that I mean your Husband, for I love him very much and if you were as generous as the old Romans, you would lend him to me for a little while. . . . Ah! Bess! you were a lucky girl to get so clever and so good a companion."

A member of a dinner party described an incident involving Alexander and Angelica and his younger sister-in-law, Margarita, who seems to have been a little bit "catty" and whom the commentator described as "a young wild flirt from Albany." Angelica lost a bow from her shoe and Margarita "picked it up and put it in Hamilton's buttonhole, saying, 'there, Brother, I have made you a Knight.' 'But of what order,' asked Angelica, 'he can't be a Knight of the Garter in this country.' 'True, Sister,' replied Miss Schuyler, 'but *he would be if you would let him.*'" Perhaps Margarita was jealous. Elizabeth surely was not.

It was in a letter to Angelica that Hamilton last mentioned his first love — if she was such — and in a rather malicious manner, although he described it as levity. He wrote:

> You ask if your friend Kitty Livingston is married? You recollect the proverb. She was ready, with as much eagerness as can be ascribed to the chaste wishes of a virgin heart, to sip the blissful cup, when alas! it slipped through her fingers — at least for a time, if not for ever. Her lover, a buxom widower of five and forty braving summer heats and wintry [blasts] exerted himself with so much zeal in the service of his Dulcinea that there is every appearance it will cost him his lungs. He is gone to the South of France, if possible to preserve them.

Alexander was poorly informed in this instance. Kitty had married a few months before.

Tragedy started to strike at the Hamiltons in 1801. Twenty-year-old Philip, the oldest and most promising of the Hamilton children, took exception to remarks about his father that a Captain George Eaker made in a speech. Philip and a friend insulted Eaker at the theater. Eaker challenged both of the young men. The friend came off unscathed, but Philip received a mortal wound. A Columbia classmate described the scene shortly before his death.

Never did I see a man so completely overwhelmed with grief as Hamilton has been. The scene I was present at when Mrs. Hamilton came to see her son on his deathbed (he died about a mile out of the city) and when she met her husband and son in one room, beggars . . . description. Young Hamilton was . . . promising in genius and acquirements and Hamilton formed high expectations of his future greatness. . . . At present Hamilton is more composed and is able again to attend to business; but his countenance is strongly stamped with grief.

At the time of Philip's death his father was building a country home in upper Manhattan. Harking back to his noble Scotch forebears, he called it the Grange. He knew that he could not afford this mansion, in addition to their house downtown but, he wrote: "To men who have been so much harassed in the base world as myself, it is natural to look forward to a comfortable retirement. . . . A garden is a very useful refuge for a disappointed politician. . . . Experience more and more convinces me that true happiness is only to be found in the bosom of one's own family."

Betsey apparently supervised much of the building of the Grange. From his frequent trips her husband sent back letters of instruction. "Don't forget to visit the Grange. From what I saw there, it is very important the drains should be better regulated." And again: "Wife, children, and hobby are the only things upon which I have permitted my thoughts to run. As often as I write, you may expect to hear something of the latter. Don't lose any opportunity which may offer of ploughing up the new garden spot, and let the wagon make a tour of the ground lately purchased. When it is too cold to go on with grubbing, our men may be employed in cutting and clearing away the underbrush in the grove and the other woods; only let the center of the principal wood in the line of the different rocks remain rough and wild." Betsey was also advised to have a ditch run around the ground on which the orchard stood, and to see that the ice house was ventilated with two chimneys.

After they moved into the Grange, for the last two years of his life, Alexander apparently commuted there for weekends, living downtown during the week with some of the older children. A few weeks after her husband's death Elizabeth retracted a plan for her eighteen-year-old son Alexander to enter a counting house in Boston, saying: "Do I not owe it to the memory of my beloved husband to keep his children together? It was a plan he made in his last arrangement of his family that they should not be without a parent's care at all times, a plan to [execute?] I made the greatest sacrifice of my life. It was that of being one half the week absent from him to take care of the younger while he took care of the elder."

In connection with Alexander's commuting it might be noted that the distance from the Grange, at 142 Street and Convent Avenue, to his office was about eight miles and is now less than a twenty-five-minute subway ride. The mansion was recently moved a few hundred feet to make room for a housing project and there are now plans to place it permanently on the campus of the nearby College of the City of New York.

As the election of 1804 loomed, Hamilton, as the Federalist leader, was the ardent political foe of Democrat Aaron Burr. His fellow New Yorker had aspirations towards the Presidency or, as a consolation prize, the Governorship of New York. When he failed in both endeavors Burr chose to take as personal some of the political aspersions that Hamilton had cast and challenged him to a duel. Hamilton could not have been criticized for refusing the challenge; his comments on Burr were mild in terms of the rough politics of the day, but, although Alexander disapproved of dueling, he was so touchy of his honor that he could not decline the challenge. He explained this in a last letter to his wife, written the evening before the duel:

This letter, my dear Eliza, will not be delivered to you, unless I shall first have terminated my earthly career, to begin, as I humbly hope, from redeeming grace and divine mercy, a happy immortality. If it had been possible for me to have avoided the interview, my love for you and my precious children would have been alone a decisive motive. But it was not possible without sacrifices which would have rendered me unworthy of your esteem. I need not tell you of the pangs I feel from the idea of quitting you, and exposing you to the anguish I know you would feel. Nor could I dwell on the topic, lest it should unman me. The consolations of religion, my beloved, can alone support you; and these you have a right to enjoy. Fly to the bosom of your God, and be comforted. With my last idea I shall cherish the sweet hope of meeting you in a better world. Adieu, best of wives — best of women. Embrace all my darling children for me.

Hamilton had determined that he would not fire at Burr; would accept the latter's fire and then discharge his pistol into the ground. He referred to this in a second "last letter" to his wife, written a few hours after the first because he recalled an obligation to another woman in his life whom he had not seen in thirty-two years:

Mrs. Mitchell is the person in the world to whom, as a friend, I am under the greatest obligation. I have not hitherto done my duty to her. But resolved to repair my omission to her as much as possible, I have encouraged her to come to this country, and intend, if it shall be in my power, to render the evening of her days comfortable. But if it shall please God to put this out of my power, and to enable you hereafter to be of service to her, I entreat you to do it, and to treat her with the tenderness of a sister. This is my second letter. The scruples of a Christian have determined me to expose my own life to any extent rather than subject myself to the guilt of taking the life of another. This much increases my hazards, and redoubles my pangs for you. But you had rather I should die innocent than live guilty. Heaven can preserve me, and I humbly hope will; but, in the contrary event, I charge you to remember that you are a Christian. God's will be be done! The will of a merciful God must be good. Once more, adieu, my darling wife.

The Mrs. Mitchell to whom Alexander was under the "greatest obligation" was a cousin, a daughter of his mother's sister who had stayed on the islands. It is presumed that she had provided the funds, at least in part, for Hamilton to come to the mainland and go to college.

Alexander fell, mortally wounded, on the dueling field in Weehawken, N.J. on July 11, 1804. He was rowed across the river to the home of a friend. Betsey knew nothing of what had happened. When she was summoned from the Grange they let her think "the cause of his illness . . . to be spasms — no one dare tell her the truth — it is feared she would become frantic." She was with her husband until he died. Angelica wrote: "My sister bears with saintlike fortitude this affliction."

Elizabeth lived for fifty years after her husband's death. She was a widow more than twice as long as she was a wife, but she never entirely put off her mourning. To protect the non-income producing real estate from foreclosure, friends of Hamilton raised a subscription that saved the Grange for Elizabeth. Her father gave her land in upper New York State and she sold off parcels from time to time to support her family and the charities that she made a special care. Principal among these was the Orphan Society of the City of New York, of which Betsey Hamilton was one of the original organizors in 1806, and a director for almost forty-five years. This, said to be the oldest non-sectarian child care organization in the country, is still going strong, under the name Graham School, as a private institution serving underprivileged children at Hastings-on-the-Hudson.

But Betsey's greatest project, for half a century after her husband's death, was to make sure that he received the recognition that she considered his due. During the several Democratic administrations that followed the death of the Federalist leader — with whom the party also died — there were few to sing his praise. Elizabeth sought in vain for a competent biographer. It was not until 1840 that her son, John Church Hamilton, published an incomplete biography of his father.

Meanwhile, Betsey had been doing some writing herself, although she did not want it published until after her death. Her husband, she believed, should at least get the credit for writing the most famous document attributed to Washington. When she was eighty-three she prepared a signed, witnessed, statement which said in part:

Desirous that my children should be full acquainted with the service rendered by their Father to our country, and the assistance given by him to General Washington during his administration, for the one great object, the Independence and Stability of the Government of the United States, there is one thing in addition to the numerous proofs which I leave them and which I feel myself in duty bound to State; which is: that a short time previous to General Washington's retiring from the Presidency in the year of 1796 General Hamilton suggested to him the idea of delivering a farewell address to the people on his withdrawal from public life, with which idea General Washington was well pleased, and in his answer to General Hamilton's suggestion gave him the heads of subjects on which he would wish to remark, with a request that Mr. Hamilton would prepare an address for him; Mr. Hamilton did so, and the address was written, principally at such times as his office was seldom frequented by his clients and visitors, and during the absence of his students to avoid interruption; at which times he was in the habit of calling me to sit with him, that he might read to me as he wrote, in order as he said, to discover how it sounded upon the ear, and making the remark, "My dear Eliza, you must be to me what Molière's old nurse was to him."

The whole or nearly all the "Address" was read to me by him as he wrote it and a greater part if not all was written by him in my presence. The original was forwarded to General Washington who approved of it with the exception of one paragraph, of, I think, about four or five lines, which if I mistake not was on the Subject of public schools, which was stricken out. It was . . . afterwards delivered by General Washington, and published in that form, and has ever since been Known as "General Washington's Farewell Address." Shortly after the publication of the address, my husband and myself were walking in Broadway, when an old soldier accosted him, with a request of him to purchase General Washington's Farewell Address, which he did and turning to me Said "That man does not know he has asked me to purchase my own work."

For the record, Washington had planned to issue a farewell address at the end of his first term, in 1792. He requested James Madison to write a draft, which he did. By the end of the second term Madison was politically *persona non grata* with the President and Washington sent his own draft of an address, containing four paragraphs from Madison's, to Hamilton, asking him to revise it, but to retain Madison's material so that the document could not be criticized as a one-sided political pronouncement. The final Farewell Address was a combination of Madison's, Washington's, and Hamilton's prose. Hamilton deserves most, but not all, of the credit.

Elizabeth never forgave James Monroe who, she seemed to feel, was more at fault than her husband in connection with the Reynolds affair. When she was in her nineties ex-President Monroe called upon her. She was in the garden when he was announced and a fifteen-year-old nephew left this account of the interview:

The maid went back to the house, my aunt followed, walking rapidly, I after her. As she entered the parlor Monroe rose. She stood in the middle of the room facing him. She did not ask him to sit down. He bowed, and addressing her formally, made her rather a set speech — that it was many years since they had met, that the lapse of time brought its softening influences, that they both were nearing the grave when past differences could be forgiven and forgotten — in short, from his point of view, a very nice, conciliatory, well-turned little speech. She answered, still standing, and looking at him, "Mr. Monroe, if you have come to tell me that you repent, that you are sorry, *very* sorry, for the misrepresentations and the slanders, and the stories you circulated against my dear husband, if you have come to say this, I understand it. But, otherwise, no lapse of time, no nearness to the grave, makes any difference." She stopped speaking, Monroe turned, took up his hat and left the room.

During the last years of her long life Elizabeth lived with a daughter, another Elizabeth, in Washington D.C. She almost reached the century mark; she was ninety-seven when she died in 1854. To the end she was active, alert, interested in affairs — and interesting. The last description of her says:

The widow of Alexander Hamilton has reached the great age of ninety-five and retains in an astonishing degree her faculties and converses with much of that ease and brilliancy which lent so peculiar a charm to her younger days. And then, after passing the compliments and congratulations of the day, insists upon her visitors' taking a merry glass from General Washington's punch bowl, which with other portions of his table set remains in her possession.

CHAPTER VII

The Late Love of James Madison

IN HIS LATE TEENS or early twenties Benjamin Franklin con-
sorted with "low women." At like age George Washington
dreamed of his "lowland beauty"; Thomas Jefferson mooned
for his "Belinda"; John Adams was almost caught by the
husband-seeking Hannah Quincy; and Alexander Hamilton
toyed with thoughts of Kitty Livingston. James Madison, the
last of the Founding Fathers, differed from his predecessors
in that he showed no interest in the fair sex until he was past
thirty.

Much later the character-wrecking political scandalmongers, who were a mark of the times, would darkly hint that
Madison was impotent; an innuendo for which there was
absolutely no basis except that he fathered no children. A
much more reasonable, if less titillating, explanation for
James' lack of interest in the opposite sex is that he liked
books better than girls. Combined with this he had an over-
whelming shyness in the presence of attractive women, a frail
physique that did not impress the girls as that of a virile lover,
and was recurrently ill throughout most of his youth. In any

event, he went through Princeton, served as a delegate to the Virginia Convention, the state legislature, the state council, and arrived in Philadelphia as a member of the Continental Congress at the age of twenty-eight, all without digressing from his work and his studies long enough to notice that such delightful things as females existed.

In Philadelphia there was a boardinghouse owned by a Mrs. Mary House and managed by her daughter, Mrs. Eliza Trist. Several of the Congressmen stayed there, including Madison and others of the Virginians. Jefferson was a boarder for a few months in 1782 and asked Madison to get Mrs. Trist's advice on a boarding school for Patsy. Mrs. Trist was apparently a motherly woman who took not only Patsy but the older James under her wing. (Incidentally, one of her grandsons later married one of Patsy's daughters and Mrs. Trist lived at Monticello in her old age.) When Jefferson told her that Madison could be elected Governor of Virginia, she replied:

He deserves everything that can be done for him, but . . . I think it rather too great a sacrifice for a man to make when he accepts the office of governor under the present forms of government in America. . . . He has a soul replete with gentleness, humanity, and every social virtue and yet I am certain that some wretch or other will write against him. You I am sure would not advise him to it. I have no idea that men are to live only for the public; they owe something to themselves. Mr. Madison is too amiable in his disposition to bear up against a torrent of abuse. It will hurt his feelings and injure his health, take my word.

Another Congressman who was part of the House-Trist "family" was William Floyd, a signer of the Declaration of Independence. With him were his three children, the youngest thirteen-year-old Kitty. Madison was at ease with Mrs. Trist, and with Kitty; he was not at his best, socially, with women of his own age. He remained at ease with Kitty while she became, progressively, fourteen, fifteen, and sixteen. Then, he decided that he was in love with her. He was within a few months of being twice her age.

Father Floyd approved the romance, as did others in the House-Trist family, including Thomas Jefferson, who undertook to intervene as a matchmaker for his younger friend. Jefferson and Madison carried on their correspondence in a mathematical cipher, and after Thomas went back to Virginia he wrote James this message in code:

Be pleased to make my compliments affectionately to the ladies and gentlemen. I desire them to Miss Kitty particularly. Do you know that the raillery sometime experienced from our family, strengthened by my own observation, gave me hopes there was some foundation for it. I wished it to be so as it would give me a neighbor whose worth I rate high, and as I know it will render you happier than you can possibly be in a single state, I often made it the subject of conversation, more exhortation, with her and was able to convince myself that she possessed every sentiment in your favor which you could wish. But of this no more without your leave.

Madison replied to this letter, partly in cipher. After Jefferson's death the epistle came back into his hands and he carefully crossed out the ciphered passage and wrote beside it "Undecipherable." He apparently did not realize that, not only was their code childishly simple to "crack," but inks with different chemical compositions have varied fading characteristics. During one hundred and fifty years the numbers that he had crossed out turned brown and were readable through the overmarking. The message that he had twice sought to keep secret was simply this:

I did not fail to present as you desired your particular compliments to Miss K. Your inference on that subject was not groundless. Before you left us I had sufficiently ascertained her sentiments. Since your departure the affair has been pursued. Most preliminary arrangements, although definitive, will be postponed until the end of the year in Congress.

Kitty and her family left the boardinghouse shortly after, and James rode with them as far as New Brunswick, New Jersey. Here he said good-by to his youthful fiancée; and that was the last he ever saw of her. There were letters, presumably, but they have never been found. We know that Kitty wrote him enclosing a letter to be forwarded to Patsy Jefferson and that Jefferson sent him a letter from Patsy to be forwarded to Kitty. The most significant act of Madison's romance seems to have been conducting a post office for his sixteen-year-old fiancée and her eleven-year-old girl friend. Finally came a "Dear John" letter from Kitty dismissing the man who, to her, must have been an ancient suitor. It seems that there was a nineteen-year-old medical student named William Clarkson in Philadelphia. Back in Long Island she decided that this was the man whom she really loved. She married him three years later. If she ever regretted not becoming the fourth First Lady there is no record of it.

Madison advised Jefferson of the blow to his matrimonial hopes in a letter of which the writer later so mutilated the copy that little can be deciphered. He mentioned that the delay in his return to Virginia "proceeded from several dilatory circumstances on which I had not calculated. . . . One of them was the uncertain state into which the object I was then pursuing has been brought by one of those incidents to which such affairs are liable. This has rendered the time of my return to Virginia less material as the necessity of my visiting the State of New York no longer exists." Jefferson replied:

I sincerely lament the misadventure which has happened. Should it be final, however, the world presents the same and many other resources of happiness, and you possess many within yourself. Firmness of mind and unremitting occupations will not long leave you in pain. No event has been more contrary to my expectations, and these were founded on what I thought a good knowledge of the ground. But of all machines ours is the most complicated and inexplicable.

This was apparently the end of romance in James' life for eleven years, although during his thirties he became more at ease with women. While spending four months in New York he at least became well enough acquainted with one female to inspire this letter: "While Congress sat in New York it was reported that he [Madison] was fascinated by the celebrated Mrs. Colden, of our city, she who was so noted for her masculine understanding and activity, as well as for feminine graces and accomplishments."

He was also on friendly terms with the mistress of a French minister, Madame de Brèhan. The marchioness had arrived in the United States with the Count de Moustier and was introduced as his sister-in-law; which she was, but the couple made no effort to disguise that theirs was more than a brother-sister relationship. Jefferson, who was then in Paris, gave de Moustier a letter of introduction to Madison which said, of Madame de Brèhan: "She is goodness itself. You must be well acquainted with her. You will find her well disposed to meet your acquaintance, and well worthy of it. . . . The husband of Madame de Brèhan is an officer, and obliged by the times to remain with the army."

After the illicit relationship of the French couple became a subject of scandal in government circles, Madison remained friendly with the marchioness, although, as he wrote: "The

ladies of New York (a few within the official circle excepted)
have for some time withdrawn their attentions from her. She
knows the cause, is deeply stung by it, views everything
through the medium of rancor and conveys her impressions
to her paramour over whom she exercises despotic sway."
When he returned to Montpelier, James received several in-
direct messages from Madame de Brèhan, including this
unusual one: "The marchioness received your compliments
with great pleasure. She and the Count most cordially return
them. The lady has procured a Negro girl, and only wants a
boy *in order that they may breed,* to use her own language."
When he returned to New York James apparently discussed
this breeding project with Madame, for he wrote his father:
"Tell my brother Ambrose if you please he must draw on
Mr. Shepherd for the price of the Negro boy for the French
marchioness."

While James was paying very mild attention to Mrs. Colden
and Madame de Brèhan, a young Quaker maid in Philadelphia was paying more serious attention to the wooing of
a lawyer named John Todd. Her name was Dolley Payne —
Dolley with an "e." Early biographers, perhaps seeking a
more dignified cognomen for a First Lady, called her Dorothy
or Dorothea, using Dolly as a nickname. But the church official who recorded her birth wrote "Dolley," probably because
that is what her parents told him to write. And, more significant, she said that her name was Dolley — with an "e."

The church register also recorded the date of her birth:
May 20, 1768. Here Dolley did not agree. As she got older
she took advantage of the feminine prerogative of controlling
her age. First she knocked three years off, then four, and
finally five. In 1839 she wrote to a friend: "Being anxious to
disavow the affectation of curtailing some precious years I

will give you a true copy of the notice of m
Bible. Dolley Payne, born May 20, 1773."

Dolley's parents had started as small Virginia
moved to the New Garden Quaker settlement in 1
lina where Dolley was born, and then returned t
with the infant girl. She spent her childhood in a house that
had been Patrick Henry's home. When she was fifteen her
father followed Quaker principals and freed his slaves, without whom he could not continue as a planter. He moved to
Philadelphia and went into the starch business.

Because she was a Quaker, Dolley's education embraced
somewhat more than the skimpy learning to which most girls
of the period were exposed, although she is not famed for her
erudition. On the surface Dolley was a prim, well-disciplined
Quaker miss, but in spirit she was no Friend. Her wit, vivacity, and love of life did not accord with Quaker austerity.
She was pretty, though not beautiful, but it was her manner
rather than her physique that attracted attention — particularly male attention. By the time she was sixteen it was evident that young men liked her. Elizabeth Drinker, a Quaker
matron, kept a diary in which this entry is found:

1784 July 10. Sally Drinker and Walter Payne, Billy Sansom and
Polly Wells, Jacob Downing and Dolly Payne, went to our place
at Frankford. Sally and Josey Sansom and Nancy Drinker (from
Par la Ville) met them there. A squabble. Nancy returned home
in the evening with her sister. . . . etc.

The squabble was not explained, but all of the other young
people mentioned were four or five years older than Dolley,
and Jacob Downing had been courting Nancy Drinker. It
may be assumed that Nancy was somewhat put out to find
herself as the odd girl in the group when her boy friend

showed up with an attractive sixteen-year-old. Dolley was never again mentioned in the chronicles of the Drinkers.

During her late teens Dolley's father's business failed and he was expelled from the Quaker Meeting for failure to pay his debts. Her mother converted their home into a boarding-house and Dolley, when she was twenty-one, married twenty-six-year-old lawyer John Todd, who had been courting her for some time. The marriage lasted three years and Dolley bore two sons before one of the yellow fever epidemics that periodically swept Philadelphia carried off her husband and one infant son. In the meanwhile her fifteen-year-old sister Lucy eloped with George Steptoe Washington, an event that distressed her Quaker mother but delighted the President of the United States. Young George was a favorite nephew and ward of the principal George.

Dolley did not long remain a widow. Six months after Todd's death she penned this excited little note to her friend, Eliza Collins: "Thou must come to me. Aaron Burr says that the great little Madison has asked to be brought to see me this evening."

Nothing is known as to where or how Madison met his future wife. This call with Burr was probably not the initial meeting. James and Dolley lived less than three blocks apart in Philadelphia and she was a cousin of a Congressman who was one of Madison's firm supporters. Both Dolley and her first husband were acquainted in official circles. She was related by marriage to the President, and the wife of the Vice-President, Abigail Adams, had consulted John Todd about getting a job for an educated Negro. With all of this Madison must have known her.

Dolley's acquaintance with Aaron Burr is more of a mystery. At about the time that Burr brought Madison to Dolley she made a will naming the New Yorker as sole guardian of her young son, John Payne Todd. Considering Burr's later reputation as a lady killer, confirmed by the profligate pages of his diary, he seems like an incredible choice as the guide and mentor for a growing boy. However, at the time, Burr's wife was still alive in New York, and as one biographer wrote, "he had a veritable passion for adopting and rearing children."

Because of the manner in which he formally asked Burr to present him on a spring evening in 1794 it is likely that Madison had something in mind other than a casual call. What followed is obscure, except that six months later they were married. A tradition in the Madison family, of questionable veracity, has it that Martha Washington had a hand in the courtship. Dolley's grandniece, editor of her letters, reported that the first lady summoned Dolley to the executive mansion, where this conversation took place:

Mrs. Washington: Dolley, is it true that you are engaged to James Madison?

Dolley: No; I think not.

Mrs. W.: If it is so, do not be ashamed to confess it; rather be proud; he will make thee a good husband, and all the better for being so much older. We both approve of it; the esteem and friendship existing between Mr. Madison and my husband is very great, and we would wish thee to be happy.

That Dolley was undecided for some time as to whether to accept the shy little suitor, almost twenty years her senior, is evident by a letter from her lawyer, William Wilkens. The older lawyer was probably in love with Dolley himself, but had adopted the role of brother to the girl he called Julia.

She had obviously asked his opinion on the match, and he replied:

> Mr. M—on is a man whom I admire. I knew his attachment to you and did not therefore content myself with taking his character from the breath of popular applause — but consulted those who knew him intimately in private life. His private character therefore I have every reason to believe is good and amiable. He unites to the great talents which have secured him public approbation those engaging qualities that contribute so highly to domestic felicity. To such a man therefore I do most freely consent that my beloved sister be united and happy . . . and am satisfied that an honorable asylum is offered to my gentle friend who has been so undeservedly and vindictively persecuted and over whose safety I have long anxiously watched. . . .
>
> Heaven is my witness that nothing is less selfish than my attachment to you. That I have not been insensible to your charms ought not, I think, to be regarded as a fault — few persons in similar situations would not have felt their irresistible influence; but none I will venture to say could have mingled in their emotions more true respect and more fraternal affection than I have.

Dolley had another question for her lawyer. What should she do about a property settlement for her young son by John Todd? Unlike the widow Dandridge, who placed all of her children's affairs in the hands of their stepfather Washington, the widow Todd sought to make independent provision for her son by a former marriage. Wilkens advised her that "Mr. M—n is as I am informed a man of genteel though not of large property. He has a right to expect some part but does not want the whole of your Estate." He added that she should put her real property in trust for John Payne before her marriage, and commented: "You are placed in a critical situation in this affair — the eyes of the world are upon you and your enemies have already opened their mouths to censure and condemn you." On her wedding day Dolley wrote to her friend Eliza that her real property and a considerable sum of money had been settled on her son "with Mr. M—'s full approbation. . . . You also are acquainted with the unmerited censure of my enemies on the subject."

No explanation has ever been offered for the comment by both Dolley and Wilkens on her "enemies" nor for the lawyer's reference to the manner in which his "gentle friend" had been "vindictively persecuted." Apparently there were some in Philadelphia who were rather violently opposed to some aspect of Dolley's life or character.

It is probable that at the time of her union with her mature suitor Dolley viewed her marriage as a practical rather than a passionate union. There is little of romance in the letter that she wrote to Eliza on her wedding day:

And as proof, my dearest Eliza, of that confidence and friendship which has never been interrupted between us I have stolen from the family to commune with you — to tell you in short that in the course of this day I give my hand to the man of all others I most admire. You will not be at a loss to know who this is as I have been long ago gratified in having your approbation. In this union I have everything that is soothing and graceful in prospect — and my little Payne will have a generous and tender protector.

This was signed Dolley Payne Todd. Below the signature was the cryptic statement: "Evening — Dolley Madison! Alass! Alass!"

Regardless of what Dolley felt on her wedding day there is no question that "the great little Madison" was deeply and sincerely in love with his youthful wife. Nor can it be questioned that the respect and admiration which seemed to be the limit of Dolley's early feeling for her spouse soon blossomed into a love to match his own. Official circles were pleased with the match. Thomas Jefferson, of course, was delighted, as was Madison's other Virginia neighbor, James Monroe. But even politically opposed John Adams blessed the union in this letter to his Abigail:

My dearest Friend,

I dined yesterday with Mr. Madison. Mrs. Madison is a fine woman, and his two sisters [i.e. sisters-in-law] are equally so. One of them is married to George Washington, one of the nephews of the President who were sometimes at our house. Mr. Washington came and civilly inquired after your health. These ladies, whose name was Payne, are of a Quaker family, once of North Carolina.

Jefferson had one reservation. Madison was the wheel-horse of the Democrats in the lower house, and he had talked of retiring from Congress. Thomas feared that a bride might distract him from his political responsibilities and make retirement to Montpelier more alluring. In his congratulations on the marriage he dangled the prospect of the presidency before both of the newlyweds by writing:

Hold on then, my dear friend, that we may not shipwreck in the meanwhile. I do not see in the minds of those with whom I converse a greater affliction than the fear of your retirement; but this must not be, unless to a more splendid and a more efficacious post. There I should rejoice to see you; I hope I may say, I shall rejoice to see you. . . . Present me respectfully to Mrs. Madison, and pray her to keep you where you are for her own satisfaction and the public good, and accept the cordial affections of us all.

For the moment, Jefferson's fears were unfounded. Madison did not even take time for a proper honeymoon, or to take his bride to Montpelier, before throwing himself back into his work in Congress; which he did not leave until the triumph of the Federalists when Adams was elected in 1796. The newlyweds took James Monroe's house in Philadelphia;

that Virginian had conveniently been sent to France. Hoping for some good bargains as a result of the turmoil of the French Revolution, Madison commissioned Monroe to buy from distressed French aristocrats draperies, rugs, china and what else might be useful in setting up housekeeping.

As with Betsey Hamilton, there is no record of Dolley's skill or interest as a housekeeper. Her role as the national capital's first official hostess so far overshadows her daily domestic duties that the latter are never mentioned. Although he was not a wealthy man, as compared to Washington or Franklin, Madison could well afford to maintain a competent staff in his Philadelphia domicile. Later, when she first stayed at Montpelier, James Madison Sr. was still alive and Dolley's mother-in-law was the distaff head of the establishment.

An immediate result of Dolley's marriage was a resolution passed by the Monthly Friends' Meeting that Dolley Madison, the former Dolley Todd, "having disregarded the wholesome order of our discipline, in the accomplishment of her marriage with a person not in membership with us, before a hireling priest" was declared to be no longer a member of the Society of Friends. During the first three years of her marriage Dolley made the transition from a young Quaker matron to a young woman of fashion, who would ultimately be the social arbiter for Washington.

Part of Dolley's fame seems to be based on her taste in clothes. The neat Quaker garb had never been to her liking, and she now blossomed as a peacock, albeit a tastefully plumed peacock. She quietly launched her younger sister Anna, who had lived with her since Todd's death, in Philadelphia society and became known for the quiet but rather distinguished entertainment at her home on Spruce Street. James was increasingly involved in the rabid partisan politics that marked the end of Washington's second term but Dolley had the happy faculty of remaining aloof from partisanship. Federalists as well as Democrats were welcome in her drawing room, a situation which would be of much help to her husband on several critical occasions.

Dolley Madison probably had some influence on her husband's opinions but, unlike Abigail Adams, she never talked or wrote about politics. Little things in the few letters that passed between husband and wife indicate that she was well informed, but she was so discreet that she never mentioned any political subject, even in letters to her adored sister Anna. Yet on one occasion when tempers ran so high that a duel was imminent between Democratic Congressman John Eppes and Federalists John Randolph it was, wrote French Minister Securier "converted into an accommodation by Mrs. Madison. The Federalist apologized to the Republican. Everybody is astonished at an issue so contrary to custom, and all the honor of the affair remains with Mrs. Madison."

James and Dolley made their last public appearance in Philadelphia at the inauguration of John Adams in 1797. Then they quietly left for Montpelier and let the Federalists take over, not to return until four years later when Madison became Secretary of State in Jefferson's cabinet. When she came back it was to start the second phase of her career as Washington's social mentor by serving frequently as Jefferson's hostess. When they first came to Washington the Madisons stayed for a few weeks at the White House with Jefferson, which caused the Federalists to quip that the President was taking in boarders.

Dolley had much to do with creating the social atmosphere of the new Federal City. Washington had established a certain grandeur in New York and Philadelphia. The Adamses entertained with less elegance but with much formality. Abigail had reigned but for a few weeks in Washington as a "lame duck" First Lady and had made little effort to see anybody whom she did not like. Jefferson, as the "people's choice," was resolved that things would be much simpler and less regal; but some standards had to be maintained in relation to the diplomatic corps. Here Dolley's tact and genius for hospitality were invaluable. Although Jefferson said that the ladies of his cabinet served as hostesses when necessary, this almost invariably meant the lady of the Secretary of State. Hers was not a simple job. Jefferson cared little for protocol and touchy foreigners resented being treated casually by the President of the United States.

One of the best pictures of early days in Washington was drawn by Margaret Bayard Smith, wife of the publisher of the *National Intelligencer,* in her correspondence and a book *The First Forty Years of Washington Society.* Of the beginning of Jefferson's administration she wrote: "Mr. Smith and I dined at the President's; he has company every day, but his table is seldom laid for more than twelve. . . . This prevents all form and makes the conversation general and unreserved. . . . Before and after dinner, Mrs. Cranch and myself sat in the drawing room with Mrs. Madison and her sister, whose social dispositions soon made us well acquainted with each other." And two days later: "Mrs. Madison is at the President's at present, I have become acquainted with and am highly pleased with her; she has good humor and sprightliness, united to the most affable and agreeable manners." Any visitor of consequence to the city was soon seeking an introduction to Mrs. Madison. One painter, with a letter of introduction, recorded in his diary that Dolley was the "leader of everything fashionable in Washington."

Because she had been raised as a Quaker, Dolley had never learned to dance, but she graced every ballroom. And some female in the crowd always wrote a description of her costume to out-of-town relatives. One of the earliest reads: "She had on her head a turban of white satin, with three large white ostrich feathers hanging over her face, very becoming indeed! Her dress, too, of white satin, made high in the neck, with long sleeves, and large capes trimmed with swan's down was rich and beautiful. . . . She looked remarkably well, and as much like a bride as a queen, for she wore no colors."

The turban with ostrich or egret plumes was a trade mark of Dolley's, as was the jeweled snuff box that she always carried. Men were starting to smoke cigars by the early years of the nineteenth century, but many smart ladies took snuff. Aaron Burr wrote of Dolley: "Mrs. Madison is still pretty, but oh, that unfortunate propensity to snuff-taking!" Burr may have considered snuffing unbecoming a lady — or he may have been looking for something to criticize in Dolley. During Jefferson's first term he was Vice-President and, like the President, a widower. Dolley saw him at official functions, but she never mentioned him and there is no record that the man who had introduced them, and who had been the guardian of Dolley's son, was ever a guest at the Madisons'.

Few letters passed between Dolley and her husband because they were seldom separated. An exception was a four-month period that Dolley spent in Philadelphia while being treated for an infection on her leg. Washington doctors had tried without success to cure this and Dolley, bedridden, had written to Anna — who was now Mrs. Cutts and lived in Maine:

Still, my dear Anna, must your sister write to you from the bed. . . . I had a long friendly note from the President yesterday, begging me to get Virginia's [his eldest granddaughter] wedding

garments, also trinkets and dresses for all the family. I shall drive
to the shops, but am not able to alight; and so little variety in
Georgetown; but I must do my best for them, and have promised
to be at the wedding, if possible, the last of this month. . . . The
Fourth of July I spent at the President's, sitting quite still, and
amusing myself with the mob.

And again to Anna, after her husband had taken her to
Philadelphia:

And here I am on my bed, with my dear husband sitting
anxiously by me, who is my most willing nurse. But you know
how delicate he is. I tremble for him; one night on the way he
was taken very ill with his old complaint, and I could not fly to
aid him as I used to do. Heaven in its mercy restored him next
morning.

Dolley was convinced that her husband was in precarious
health. Actually, after recurrent illness during his college
days, the frail James seems to have had considerable stamina.
During the long, hot summer of the Constitutional Convention he was the only delegate who never missed a session,
and he had the best record of attendance in Congress. There
is no record of unusual illness during his later life, but his
wife was constantly concerned for his health and fussed over
every headache, fever, and cold. There was surely a great deal
of mother instinct in Dolley's love for her little spouse. This
feeling ran through the only love letters that she ever wrote
him, from Philadelphia, starting the day he left:

A few hours only have passed since you left me, my beloved,
and I find nothing can relieve the oppression of my mind but
speaking to you, in this, the only way. . . . Betsey Pemberton and
Amy are sitting by me, and seem to respect the grief they know
I feel at even so short a separation from one who is all to me. I
shall be better when Peter returns with news, not that any length
of time could lessen my first regret, but an assurance that you are

well and easy will contribute to make me so. . . . Betsey puts on
your hat to divert me, but I cannot look at her.

October 24 — What a sad day! The watchman announced a
cloudy morning at one o'clock, and from that moment I found
myself unable to sleep, from anxiety for thee, my dearest husband.
Detention, cold, and accident seem to menace thee. . . .

October 25 — This clear, cold morning will favor your journey,
and enliven the feelings of my darling. I have nothing new to
tell you. The knee is mending, and I sit just as you left me. The
doctor, during his short visits, talks of you. He regards you more
than any man he knows, and nothing could please him so much
as a prospect of passing his life near you; sentiments so congenial
to my own, and in such cases, like dewdrops on flowers, exhilarate
as they fall.

The next day a servant returned with a letter from James,
and Dolley again wrote:

My dearest Husband, — Peter returned safe with your dear
letter, and cheered me with a favorable account of the prospects
of your getting home in the stage. . . . In my dreams of last night,
I saw you in your chamber, unable to move, from riding so far
and so fast, I pray that an early letter from you may chase away
the painful impression of this vision. I am still improving, and
shall observe strictly what you say on the subject of the doctor's
precepts.

As Jefferson's second term drew toward a close it was apparent that Madison was favored as his successor. The eccentric James Randolph of Roanoke had turned violently
against him and sought to push James Monroe forward. Monroe listened to his siren song and this brought on a temporary
coolness between him and Jefferson and Madison. John
Quincy Adams is authority for the statement that on this
occasion Dolley forsook her usual position of impartiality in
politics. He noted in his diary: "Mr. Bayard told me he had
last evening some conversation with Mrs. Madison upon the

presidential electioneering now so warmly carried on, in which she spoke very slightingly of Mr. Monroe."

In writing to Monroe, Randolph made an unexplained allusion to Dolley: "There is another consideration which I know not how to touch. You, my dear sir, cannot be ignorant — although of all mankind you, perhaps, have the least cause to know it — how deeply the respectability of any character may be impaired by an unfortunate matrimonial connection — I can pursue this subject no further." This may have had some connection with the whispering campaign that the foulest of the Federalists were conducting against Dolley, which ultimately moved from the barrooms to the press. An unsigned pamphlet contained a chapter titled *"L'Amour et la fumée ne peuvent se cacher"* which contained much innuendo about the sexual infidelities of the wife of a prominent impotent husband. In justice, only the lunatic fringe of the Federalists were guilty of such libel. Staunch Federalist Charles Carroll wrote: "The attack on Mrs. Madison is very reprehensible and the calumny unfounded."

Madison's inauguration ceremonies set the standard which has become a tradition. Jefferson and his successor did not go to the Capital together, but Madison did start the inaugural parades by proceeding in state down Pennsylvania Avenue with a military escort. After his speech the new President and his wife went to their home — Jefferson was still collecting his many possessions in the White House. At home James and Dolley held open house which Mrs. Smith described by writing: "The street was full of carriages and people, and we had to wait near half an hour before we could get in — the house was completely filled, parlors, entry, drawing room, and bedroom. Near the door of the drawing room Mr. and Mrs. Madison stood to receive their company. She looked extremely beautiful, was dressed in a plain cambric dress with a very long train, plain round the neck without any handkerchief, and beautiful bonnet of purple velvet and white satin, with white plumes. She was all dignity, grace, and affability." Dolley's simple costume was worn in deference to her husband's plain brown garb: "A full suit of the wool of Merinos raised in this country."

But Dolley blossomed that night at the Federal City's first formal public Inaugural Ball. This had been announced in the *National Intelligencer:* "Inauguration Ball, A Dancing Assembly will be held on the 4th inst, at Mr. Long's Hotel. Tickets to be obtained at the bar, on application to a Manager." The price of admission was four dollars. The ball was planned by Dolley with the help of a social arbiter whom she had by this time picked up. Naval Captain Thomas Tingy was a sort of early-nineteenth-century Ward McAllister who was described as having impeccable manners and little brains. The *National Intelligencer* called the affair "the most brilliant and crowded ever known in Washington," and Mrs. Smith wrote:

It was scarcely possible to elbow your way from one side to another, and poor Mrs. Madison was almost pressed to death, for everyone crowded round her, those behind pressing on those before, and peeping over their shoulders to have a peep of her, and those who were so fortunate as to get near enough to speak to her were happy indeed. . . .

She looked a queen. She had on a pale buff-colored velvet, made plain, with a very long train, but not the least trimming, and beautiful pearl necklace, earrings, and bracelets. Her headdress was a turban of the same colored velvet and white satin (from Paris) with two superb plumes, the bird-of-paradise feathers. It would be *absolutely impossible* for any one to behave with more perfect propriety than she did. Unassuming dignity, sweetness, and grace. It seems to me that such manners would disarm envy itself, and conciliate even enemies.

Dolley also set the standard for the gracious hostess to which subsequent first ladies have been expected to conform. During the first administration it had been George, rather than Martha, who set the social standards; the host, rather than the hostess, was important and Martha was largely confined to her decorous levees. Abigail Adams had been more interested in saving what she could of John's salary than in formal entertaining.

Dolley's evenings at the White House soon became famous. Washington Irving left this brief description of his attendance at one.

I arrived at the Inn about dusk and understanding that Mrs. Madison was to have her levee or drawing room that very evening, I swore by all my gods I should be there. . . . In a few minutes I emerged from dirt and darkness into the blazing splendor of Mrs. Madison's drawing room. Here I was most graciously received; found a crowded collection of great and little men, of ugly old women and beautiful young ones, and in ten minutes was hand and glove with half the people in the assemblage. Mrs. Madison is a fine, portly, buxom dame, who has a smile and a pleasant word for everybody. Her sisters, Mrs. Cutts and Mrs. Washington, are like the two merry wives of Windsor; but as to Jemmy Madison — ah poor Jemmy! — he is but a withered apple-john.

Dolley Madison was the first First Lady to concern herself with the interior decoration of the White House. In this she was assisted by Benjamin Latrobe, an architect who was on the Congressional payroll. There is some evidence that there were minor disputes between Dolley and the professional. One had to do with the placing of George Washington's portrait. Latrobe wrote her:

I am sorry to have counteracted any wish of yours as to General Washington's picture. The dining room is properly the picture room, and in speaking to the President as to the furniture of the room, I understood it to be arranged that not only the General but the succeeding Presidents should have a place there. I therefore intended him to occupy either the place at the west end of the room between the windows, or the fireplace at the east end. . . . But if you have the slightest wish to the contrary remember that the motto of my family, of my art, of my duty, is *tutto se fa — tout se fait*. . . . The curtains! Oh the terrible velvet curtains! Their effect will ruin me entirely, so brilliant will they be.

Dolley wanted the picture hung in the drawing room, but this time Latrobe apparently departed from his family's motto. The picture was placed in the dining room.

Dolley's entire life was not devoted to the social demands of the First Lady. In fact, she had two sets of work clothes. In the morning she invariably wore the garb in which she had grown up, the gray dress, white apron, and white kerchief of the Quakers. In this costume she supervised the domestic arrangements of the Executive Mansion. Later she changed to her evening work clothes, characterized by the plume topped turban and her jewels. Little "Jemmy" delighted in buying jewelry for his wife. A man named William Preston was a guest at the White House for several weeks in his youth and later left this description of the Madisons:

She was always prompt in making her appearance in the drawing room, and when out of it was very assiduous in household offices. She told me that Mr. Madison slept very little, going to bed late and getting up frequently during the night to write or read; for which purpose a candle was always kept burning in the chamber. . . .

His labors were incessant; his countenance was pallid and hard, his social intercourse was entirely committed to Mrs. Madison, and was arranged with infinite tact and elegance. He appeared in society daily, with an unmoved and abstracted air, not relaxing, except towards the end of a protracted dinner, with confidential friends. Then he became anecdotal, facetious, a little broad in his discourse, after the manner of the old school. . . .

Mrs. Madison told me the necessities of society made sad inroads on his time, and that she was wearied of it to exhaustion. As she always entered the drawing room with a book in her hand, I said: "Still you have time to read." "Oh, no," she said, "not a word: I have this book in my hand — a very fine copy of Don Quixote — to have something not ungraceful to say, and, if need be, to supply a word of talk."

This description had a curious aftermath. Of the full figures of the Presidents' wives displayed in the Smithsonian Institution, Dolley Madison's is the only one in which the First Lady carries a book. Detractors have sought to interpret her comment that she carried it as a conversation piece to mean that she did not read. Actually, Dolley did read for relaxation; not profoundly like Abigail. She wrote to a niece:

Do you ever get hold of a clever novel, new or old, that you could lend me? I bought Cooper's last, but did not care for it, because the story was so full of horrors. . . . If you can send me the *Romance of History,* I will be very glad and will make proper dispatch in the perusal of it.

The climactic occurrence of Madison's administration was the War of 1812. During the second year of the conflict British Admiral Sir George Cockburn sailed up Chesapeake Bay with a naval force and fear for the safety of Washington became widespread. At this time Dolley wrote:

And now if I could I would describe to you the fears and alarms that circulate around me. For the week all the city and Georgetown (except the Cabinet) have expected a visit from the enemy, and were not lacking in their expressions of terror and reproach. . . . We are making considerable efforts for defence. The fort is being repaired, and five hundred militia, with perhaps as many regulars, are to be stationed on the Green, near the windmill, or rather Major Taylor's. The twenty tents already look well in my eyes, who have always been an advocate for fighting when assailed, though a Quaker. I therefore keep the old Tunisian sabre within reach.

One of our generals has discovered a plan of the British; it is to land as many chosen rogues as they can about fourteen miles below Alexandria, in the night, so that they may be on hand to burn the President's house and offices. I do not tremble at this, but feel hurt that the admiral (of Havre de Grace memory) should send me word that he would make his bow at my drawing room very soon.

The last sentence referred to a jocular brag of Cockburn's that he "would soon dine in Washington and make his bow in Mrs. Madison's drawing room."

The British did not come that year, although the fears continued and James was unfairly reviled by many for the dangers of what some called "Mr. Madison's war." After months of anxiety Dolley wrote:

We have been in a state of perturbation here for a long time. The depredations of the enemy approaching within twenty miles of the city, and the disaffected making incessant difficulties for the government. Such a place as this has become! I can not describe it. I wish for my own part we were in Philadelphia. The people here do not deserve that I should prefer it. Among other exclamations and threats, they say, if Mr. M. attempts to move from this house, in case of an attack, they will stop him; and that he shall *fall with it*. I am determined to stay with him. Our preparation for defence, by some means or other, is constantly retarded; but the small force the British have on the Bay will never venture nearer than at present, twenty-three miles.

Dolley, and supposedly wiser military heads, did not seem to realize that Cockburn could be reinforced; as he was in the summer of 1814 when Wellington's veterans were released from service in Europe by Napoleon's defeat. In August the British landed and started their march toward the capital. In the ensuing battle at Bladensburg and the subsequent partial burning of the Capital only an old privateersman named Joshua Barney and Dolley Madison won praise from history.

No real effort had been made to defend the city. Brigadier General William Winder was supposed to be in command of the militia that was rapidly assembled, but Secretary of War Armstrong took to the field and issued conflicting orders and Secretary of State Monroe, perhaps feeling that his service as a lieutenant in the Revolution gave him military stature, galloped around moving troops at his own discretion. Madison strapped on a pair of dueling pistols — probably the first weapons he had ever carried — and conducted the government from the saddle. After a brief conflict the American troops fled in all directions, except for old Barney and 500 sailors, who stood firm.

Dolley went about her business with calm confidence. The officers of the government would be hungry when the fighting was over, so she ordered the table set with forty places. After capturing the city, and before firing the White House, the British drank the wine and ate the food that she had prepared. During two days of waiting for the outcome of the engagement, Dolley wrote a long, calm letter to her sister Lucy:

Dear Sister;
My husband left me yesterday morning to join General Winder. He inquired anxiously whether I had courage, or firmness, to remain in the President's house until his return, on the morrow, or succeeding day; and on my assurance that I had no fear but for him and the success of our army, he left me, beseeching me

to take care of myself, and of the Cabinet Papers, public and private. I have since received two dispatches from him, written with a pencil; the last is alarming, because he desires I should be ready at a moment's warning to enter my carriage and leave the city; that the enemy seemed stronger than had been reported, and that it might happen that they would reach the city with intention to destroy it. . . .

I am accordingly ready; I have pressed as many Cabinet Papers into trunks as will fill one carriage; our private property must be sacrificed, as it is impossible to procure wagons for its transportation. I am determined not to go myself until I see Mr. Madison safe, and he can accompany me, as I hear of much hostility towards him. . . .

Disaffection stalks around us. . . . My friends and acquaintances are all gone — even Colonel Carroll with his hundred men, who were stationed as a guard in this enclosure. . . . French John [the White House doorman] with his usual activity and resolution, offers to spike the cannon at the gates, and to lay a train of powder which would blow up the British should they enter the house. To the last proposition I positively object, without being able, however, to make him understand why all advantages in war may not be taken.

Wednesday morning, twelve o'clock
Since sunrise I have been turning my spyglass in every direction and watching with unwearied anxiety, hoping to discern the approach of my dear husband and his friends; but, alas, I can descry only groups of military wandering in all directions, as if there was a lack of arms or of spirit to fight for their own firesides!

Three o'clock
Will you believe it, my sister? We have had a battle or skirmish near Bladensburg, and I am still here, within sound of the cannon! Mr. Madison comes not; may God protect him! Two messengers covered with dust come to bid me fly; but I wait for him. . . . At this late hour a wagon has been procured; I have had it filled with the plate and most valuable portable articles belong-

ing to the house; whether it will reach its destination, the Bank of Maryland, or fall into the hands of British soldiery, events must determine. Our kind friend, Mr. Carroll, has come to hasten my departure, and is in a very bad humor with me because I insist on waiting until the large picture of General Washington is secured, and it requires to be unscrewed from the wall. This process was found too tedious for these perilous moments, I have ordered the frame to be broken, and the canvas taken out; it is done — and the precious portrait placed in the hands of two gentlemen from New York, for safe keeping.

And now my dear sister, I must leave this house, or the re-treating army will make me a prisoner in it, by filling up the road I am directed to take. When I shall see or write to you, or where I shall be tomorrow, I cannot tell!

The stories of the next three days are conflicting and con-fusing. Political opponents left accounts of Madison fleeing in terror into Maryland or cowering in a hut in Virginia. Actually, he spent most of the time, in both nearby Virginia and Maryland, looking for his wife and trying to find an army to rejoin. Dolley is variously portrayed as sleeping in a soldier's tent and traveling from house to house seeking shel-ter. One anecdote has her entering a house where she was reviled by the mistress who said: "Your husband has got mine out fighting and, damn you, you shan't stay in my house." Dolley seems to have stayed with some friends named Love, a short distance from Washington, and then gone to Wiley's tavern, where James caught up with her. He then left to continue his search for the army and sent back a note:

I have just received a line from Colonel Monroe saying that the enemy were out of Washington and on the retreat to their ships and advising our immediate return to Washington. We shall accordingly set out thither immediately, you will all of course take the same resolution. I know not where we are in the first instance to hide our heads; but shall look for a place on my arrival. Mr. Rush offers his house in the six buildings and the offer claims attention.

Shortly after Madison arrived in the Capital the British fleet attacked a fort on the Potomac and he sent his wife a second message.

I cannot yet learn what has been the result. Should the port have been taken, the British ships with their barges will be able to throw the city again into alarm, and you may be again compelled to retire from it, which I find would have a disagreeable effect. Should the ships have failed in their attack, you cannot return too soon. . . . In the meantime it will be best for you to remain in your present quarters.

Dolley never received this last communication. She was already in Washington at the home of her sister, Anna Cutts. A neighbor noted in her diary; "Mrs. M. came to Mrs. Cutts' in a parrotty carriage." The only explanation for "parrotty" that has ever been advanced is that Dolley had stopped to rescue a pet macaw which "French John" had deposited with the French Ambassador. Mrs. Smith dropped in after dinner and quoted Dolley as saying that she "wished we had 10,000 such men as were passing [a few troopers] to sink our enemy to the bottomless pit."

The only reference that Dolley made to her three-day adventure was in a letter to Mrs. Latrobe in which she said:

Two hours before the enemy entered the city, I left the house where Mr. Latrobe's elegant taste had been justly admired, and where you and I had so often wandered together; . . . I confess that I was so unfeminine as to be free from fear, and willing to remain in the *Castle!* if I could have had a cannon through every window; but alas! those who should have placed them there fled before me, and my whole heart mourned for my country!

I remained nearly three days out of town, but I cannot tell you what I felt on re-entering it — such destruction — such confusion. The fleet full in view and in the act of robbing Alexandria! The citizens expecting *another visit* — and at night the rockets were seen flying near us.

The year and a half that remained of Madison's second term after the close of the war was the only pleasant part of his administration. For over six years he had been a very unpopular President who, but for his wife, would have faced an almost unbearable situation. Suddenly, with the peace, he became a hero to the fickle public. But he was certainly content to leave Washington in the spring of 1817. If Dolley was reluctant to depart from the scenes of her social triumphs and rusticate at Montpelier, she made no complaint. Although she was brilliant as the First Lady, her duty, and her happiness, were with her husband. A niece, Anna Payne, described their relationship: "Mr. Madison dearly loved and was proud of his wife, the ornament of his house — she was his solace and comfort. . . . No matter how agreeably employed, he was her first thought, and instinct seemed to tell her when she was wanted; if engaged in conversation she would quickly rise and say 'I must go to Madison.' "

Except for a trip to Richmond to attend a state convention with James, Dolley did not leave Montpelier for twenty years. She was forty-nine when her sixty-six-year-old husband left the Presidency. After his father died James had enlarged Montpelier, converting it to its present form. As with Mount Vernon, a seventy foot portico is its principal feature. Here, in earlier days, James and Dolley used to run foot races. According to Mrs. Smith, Dolley really could run.

It was well that Montpelier had been enlarged before Madison retired because, like Mount Vernon and Monticello, it was a mecca for swarms of visitors during the remaining twenty years of the ex-President's life. For the first ten years,

when Jefferson was alive, it became the custom for guests to
spend a few days with him at Monticello and then pay a visit
to Madison at Montpelier. In one letter Dolley wrote: "Yesterday we had ninety persons to dine with us at one table,
fixed on the lawn under a large arbor." On another occasion
she told Mrs. Smith: "At this moment we have only three and
twenty guests in the house — but we have house room in
plenty." Mrs. Smith commented: "She certainly has always
been, and still is, one of the happiest of human beings. . . .
She seems to have no place about her which could afford a
lodgment for care or trouble. Time seems to favor her as
much as fortune. She looks young and she says she feels so. I
can believe her, nor do I think she will ever look or feel like
an old woman."

James continued to spoil his adored wife. In the White
House he had given her jewelry. Now he imported a French
gardener to lay out a beautiful brick-walled enclosure —
which still survives — for Dolley's pleasure. As she had with
Latrobe in decorating the White House, Dolley worked with
the Frenchman in creating the garden. Lafayette sent her
tiger lilies from France and Nicholas Trist forwarded Cape
jasmine from New Orleans. In the later years of their retirement, Dolley worked as her husband's secretary in organizing
his papers for publication and in guiding the fledgling University of Virginia, a duty which he inherited from Thomas
Jefferson. Letters concerning the university's affairs, written
by Dolley and signed by James, are still in that institution's
archives.

A female editor from Washington left this description of
Dolley toward the end of her retirement at Montpelier, when
she was in her late sixties:

I listened for her step, and never was I more astonished. I expected to have seen a little old dried-up woman; instead of this, a tall, young, active, elegant woman stood before me. "This Mrs. Madison? Impossible!" She was the selfsame lady of whom I had heard more anecdotes than any family in Europe or America. No wonder she was the idol at Washington — at once in possession of everything that could ennoble woman. But chiefly she captivated by her artless though warm affability — affectation and her [sic] are farther asunder than the poles; and her fine full eye and countenance display a majestic brilliancy found in no other face. She is a stout, tall, straight woman, muscular but not fat, and as active on her feet as a girl. Her face is large, full, and oval, rather dark than fair; her eye is dark, large, and expressive; her face is not handsome, nor does it ever appear to have been so. It is diffused with a slight tinge of red, and rather wide in the middle — but her power to please, the irresistible grace of her every movement shed such a charm over all she says and does that it is impossible not to admire her.

She was dressed in a plain black silk dress, and wore a silk turban on her head, and black glossy curls, but to witness how active she would run out — bring a glass of water, wipe the mud off my shoes and tie them. Seeing I was fatigued she pressed me with much earnestness to await dinner. I was greatly disappointed in her size and height, but much more in her youthful appearance. She appears young enough for Mr. Madison's daughter; there is more indulgence in her eye than any mortal's.

During all of her later life Dolley had one burdensome cross to bear — her son, John Payne Todd. To put it bluntly, Todd was a loafer, a compulsive gambler, and a drunkard. His worthlessness may have been partly Dolley's fault. From birth he was thoroughly spoiled, but did not receive the maternal attention that she lavished on her husband. James, who would do nothing to distress his wife, never interfered. At the age of thirteen John Todd had been sent to a boarding school in Baltimore — surprisingly, a Catholic school. Here he stayed for seven years, supposedly preparing for Princeton, but he never went to college. When he was twenty-one his stepfather sent him to St. Petersburg, Russia, with the peace commission, under the wing of Albert Gallatin, his Secretary of the Treasury. If he had any duties he did not take them seriously. Henry Clay, one of the peace commissioners, later reminded him: "Do you remember when we were in Russia together, how John Quincy Adams and all the rest of us sat in a gallery and watched you dance with the Czar's sister, we being debarred because we were not of the royal blood?"

After his return from Europe, during the last years that his mother was in the White House and the first years in Mont-pelier, John Todd took to wandering. He spent long periods in the taverns of Baltimore, Philadelphia, and New York. Usually his mother did not know where he was until she received a letter asking for money. She told others that he was away on business, and wrote him many pitiful letters:

> Your Papa and myself entreat you to come to us — arrange your business with those concerned to return to them when necessary and let us see you here as soon as possible with your interest and convenience. Your Papa thinks as I do that it would be best for your reputation and happiness, as well as ours, that you should have the appearance of consulting your parents on subjects of deep account to you. . . .
>
> I enclose you $30 instead of $20 which you mentioned, and though I am sure 'tis insufficient for the journey, I am unable to add to the sum today. I recently paid Holloway $200 on your note; with interest for two years.

James, too, added his entreaties:

> What shall I say to you? It is painful to utter reproaches; yet how can they be avoided? Your last letter to your mother made us confident that we should see you in a few days. Weeks have passed without even a line explaining the disappointment, or

soothing the anxieties of the tenderest of mothers, wound up to the highest pitch by this addition to your long and mysterious absence. As ample remittances were furnished for all known purposes, your continuance where you are under such strange appearances, necessarily produced distressing apprehensions.

His parents finally learned of the young man's whereabouts from Anna Cutts — he was in jail in Philadelphia for debt. Madison sold some property and bailed him out. Shortly before his death James gave a package to Dolley's brother, John C. Payne, asking him to examine it, seal it, and give it to Dolley after he died "as an evidence of the sacrifice he had made to insure her tranquillity by concealing from her the ruinous extravagance of her son." The package, according to the brother, contained vouchers for payments by James to John Todd of about $20,000. Wrote Payne: "Mr. Madison assured me these payments were exclusive of those he made with her knowledge and of the remittances he had made and furnished her the means of making. The sum thus appropriated probably equaled the same amount."

Before Madison died in 1836 he was in serious financial difficulties similar to those that had plagued Jefferson, though not as acute. The extravagance of the wastrel stepson was only one factor. Tobacco crops had been poor and Virginia land was a drug on the market. James had sold some land to keep going, but kept the slaves — whom he did not need — because they were part of the "family." He hoped that Dolley would be able to keep Montpelier and their house in Washington by publishing his papers after his death. Before he died, Anna Payne, daughter of Dolley's brother John, had come to live with them and, for the remainder of Dolley's life, the girl was like a daughter to her. Anna left this description of Dolley, two weeks after her husband's death:

She no longer gives way to the grief and dejected spirit which could not at first be restrained. . . . She is even now striving to be composed, if not cheerful, as Uncle Madison begged and entreated her to be. . . . She has at present and will have for some months so much important business to give her attention to that I hope when she has time to reflect on the past her distress will be so softened as in a measure to pass away, though I know it can never be forgotten. Cousin Mary is here; Mrs. Randolph, three Miss R's, with other persons, as well as three clerks finishing copies of Uncle's manuscripts.

The Mrs. Randolph referred to is, of course, Jefferson's Patsy. The three Miss R's are some of her numerous progeny.

For a year after James' death Dolley stayed at Montpelier, working on the first volume of her husband's papers. This was his *Debates in the Federal Convention*. The delegates at the Constitutional Convention had pledged themselves to fifty years of secrecy as to what had transpired in Philadelphia. That period had now expired, and the only accurate record of how the United States Constitution had come into being was in the meticulous and complete record that James Madison had made of every word uttered at the convention. This document, and *The Federalist* from the pens of Hamilton, Madison, and Jay, are the two most important sources of information on the birth and political philosophy of the United States Government. After Dolley's son had made an abortive deal with a New York publisher, under which Dolley was to pay half the cost of publication, she took better advice and offered the material to President Andrew Jackson. Congress paid her $30,000 for this section of Madison's papers. When she finished paying her immediate debts — and John Todd's — she had $9,000 left.

With this she moved back to the small house in Washington, with young Anna. Her son remained to manage Montpelier, where he did less gambling but much more drinking. His mother later returned for two years to try to save the place, but she finally had to sell it to a considerate neighbor, at a lower price than it might have commanded in return for an agreement that he would not sell the slaves.

When Dolley returned to Washington she stepped back into her old position as social mentor by popular acclaim, although she had been gone for a generation and most Washingtonians knew her only by reputation. She came back at a good time. During her absence the Capital had been rather dull while James Monroe and John Quincy Adams held office. Then it had become raucous and somewhat hysterical during the two terms of Andrew Jackson. Now the urbane New Yorker Martin Van Buren was in the White House; by coincidence, like Jefferson, a widower. Dolley never served as Van Buren's hostess, but on the first New Year's Day after her return a new custom was started. After they left the White House the President's guests trooped across Lafayette Square and paid their respects to Mrs. Madison. As long as Dolley lived she maintained open house on New Year's and July Fourth, and her little house was the accepted stop after the White House. At one of these levees a very young grandniece clung to her mother's hand and observed her fabulous aunt. Later she wrote still another of the many descriptions of Dolley's costume:

Aunt Madison wore a purple velvet dress, with plain straight skirt amply gathered to a tight waist, cut low and filled in with soft tulle. Her pretty white throat was encircled by a lace cravatte, such as the old-fashioned gentlemen used to wear, tied twice around and fastened with an amethyst pin. . . . Thrown lightly over the shoulders was a little lace shawl or cape, as in her portrait. . . . I thought her turban very wonderful, as I had never seen anyone else wear such a headdress. It was made of some soft silky material and became her rarely. . . . There were little bunches of curls on either side of the smooth white brow; her eyes were blue and laughed when she smiled and greeted her friends who seemed so glad to see her. I wondered at her smooth soft skin, as I was told that she was over seventy, which at that time seemed a great age to me. . . . I have a distinct consciousness in connection with this levee that she disliked nothing so much as loud talking and laughing.

Dolley's clothes and her ever present turban were by this time long out of style; but neither Dolley nor the style, when she wore it, seemed to age.

Van Buren was followed in the White House by William Henry Harrison who lived but a month after his inauguration. His successor, John Tyler, was again without an active First Lady — Mrs. Tyler was a paralytic. The duty fell to the President's daughter-in-law and that young lady promptly came to Dolley for guidance. She said: "The greatest difficulty I anticipate is paying visits. There was a doubt at first whether I must visit in person or send cards; but I asked Mrs. Madison and she says return all my visits by all means."

During the next administration, that of James Polk, Dolley played a somewhat different role. Mrs. Polk was the first bona fide mistress of the White House since the second Mrs. Adams and she was a close friend of Dolley's. The new First Lady served as her husband's secretary and was the first official female secretary in the White House, although Dolley had unofficially filled a similar role for her husband. The two women had much in common, but Mrs. Polk had one quirk as a White House hostess. She was a staunch Tennessee Presbyterian who walked in the shadow of John Knox; a shade in which cards, dancing, and alcoholic beverages were sinful. While she ruled, lemonade was served at White House functions. Some of the guests grumbled, but not too much. They knew that after they had paid their respects to the President they could go across to Dolley's house where they would be offered what they considered a more palatable beverage.

There are innumerable anecdotes of Dolley's last years in Washington, when she was in her late seventies. She was aboard the *Princeton* when the gun exploded that killed the Secretaries of State and Treasury and several other prominent guests. She was present when Samuel F. B. Morse opened the telegraph line from Washington to Baltimore. When the query "What hath God wrought?" was received from Baltimore, Morse asked Dolley for a return message. She dictated: "Message from Mrs. Madison. She sends her love to Mrs. Wethered." This was the first personal telegram. When Congress would not appropriate money to build the Washington Monument, Dolley served on a committee with Mrs. John Quincy Adams and Betsey Hamilton to raise funds. All three of the ex-first ladies were present when the cornerstone was laid.

An amusing story in which Dolley played but an incidental part has to do with the Russian Ambassador, Bodisco. This fabulously wealthy diplomat, in his mid-fifties, was a bachelor who happily hosted all night poker sessions with Webster, Clay, and Benton. Suddenly tongues wagged when he was seen walking the seventeen-year-old daughter of a minor government clerk, Miss Hattie Williams, to and from school, carrying her books. But Bodisco's intentions were honorable. He proposed to the teen-ager and planned a wedding that would do credit to his Czar. The bridesmaids were Hattie's schoolmates — Bodisco's old housekeeper made the youngsters take a nap between the afternoon wedding and the evening reception. The British Ambassador was best man and Henry Clay gave the bride away. The cabinet, the diplomatic corps,

and the Congress were represented among the ushers. But
the high point of the ceremony came when President Martin
Van Buren escorted Dolley Madison down the aisle on his
arm. The child bride, Madame Bodisco, was one of Dolley's
most frequent visitors during her last years. Presumably the
eminent Dolley advised her on how to behave as mistress of
the Russian Embassy.

When Daniel Webster became Secretary of State in Tyler's
cabinet he took a large house near Dolley's and entertained
lavishly. It was here that he settled the Maine boundary question with the British envoy, Lord Ashburton. Dolley played
a prominent role in Webster's salon. A participant described
a whist game in which he played with Lord Ashburton
against Dolley and John Quincy Adams. All three were over
seventy. When Webster left the cabinet he sent her a little
note: "My dear Mrs. Madison: I am going to drive this morning at ½ twelve for the first time and I feel a desire to see
you *once more*. Will you allow me to ask you to accompany
me if you have no other engagement."

Webster knew that Dolley's financial circumstances were
getting desperate. He quietly proposed that he and a few of
his "tightfisted, dividend-loving, Yankee friends" buy her a
small annuity. It was supposed to be a secret, but Dolley
heard of it and gracefully refused. She never took part in
politics, but she knew that for her to accept such largesse
from Webster and his friends would be political dynamite.
The New Englanders were Whigs, who had inherited the
Federalist mantle. Dolley's mere presence in Washington held
much prestige for the Democrats. William Seward, a Whig
boss and later Lincoln's Secretary of State sensed this when
he wrote: "All the world paid homage to her, saying that she
was dignified and attractive. It is the fashion to say so. But, I

confess, I thought more true dignity would have been displayed by her remaining, in her widowhood, in the ancient country mansion of her illustrious husband."

Dolley's final days were made secure financially when Congress at long last purchased the remainder of her husband's papers for $25,000. Well knowing that her worthless son would soon get the money if it were paid in cash, the legislature provided that $5,000 was to be used to pay the mortgage on her house and redeem some of her silver from pawn, and the balance invested to provide her an income.

The provision was well taken. John Todd promptly came to Washington and threatened the Congressionally appointed trustees with legal action. This brought from Dolley, in her eightieth year, the only bitter letter that she ever wrote her son. Symbolic of motherhood, Dolley forgave and forgave John Todd and hoped to the end that he would reform. But now she wrote him:

At this moment I am much distressed at the *conversations* you held, and the *determinations* you expressed, on the subject of bringing suit against my Trustees, and request the favor of you to make them easy and content with you, by the assurance that you abandon the idea, or that you never had any such intention.

I say all this *for you* because I do not believe even *yourself* if you *declared* such an intention, which would at once ruin your fair fame. Your mother would have no wish to live after her son issued such threats which would deprive her of her friends, who had no other view in taking charge than pure friendship. This I do wish you to put at rest, on the receipt of this, without losing a moment.

Of course John Todd never answered the letter.

No showman could have staged a better final public appearance for Dolley than the actual one that took place in the spring of 1849. Polk had been defeated for re-election by

Whig Zachary Taylor. Before he left office he gave one last reception, which he described in his diary as follows:

General notice had been given in the city papers that the President's mansion would be open for the reception of visitors this evening. All the parlors, including the East Room, were lighted up. The Marine Band of musicians occupied the outer hall. Many hundreds of persons, ladies and gentlemen, attended. It was what would be called in the society of Washington a very fashionable levee. Foreign ministers, their families and suites, judges, members of both Houses of Congress, and many citizens and strangers were of the company present. I stood and shook hands with them for over three hours. Towards the close of the evening I passed through the crowded rooms with the venerable Mrs. Madison on my arm.

As Mrs. Polk stood smilingly aside, Mrs. Madison, aged eighty-one, again performed the function which she had initiated for Thomas Jefferson almost half a century earlier: she gracefully greeted the President's guests in the White House.

Dolley Madison died on July 12, 1849. Perhaps the best summary of her life is that printed in the *National Intelligencer* at the time:

Beloved by all who personally knew her, and universally respected, this venerable lady closed her long and well-spent life with the calm resignation which goodness of heart combined with piety only can impart. It would seem an abuse of terms to say that we regret the departure of one so ripe and so fitted for a better world. But, in the case of this excellent Lady, she continued until within a few weeks to grace society with her presence, and to lend to it those charms with which she adorned the circle of the highest, the wisest, and best during the bright career of her illustrious husband. Wherever she appeared, everyone became conscious of the presence of the spirit of benignity and gentleness, united to all the attributes of feminine loveliness.

For ourselves, whose privilege it was to know and admire her through the last forty years of her life, it would not be easy to speak in terms of exaggeration of the virtues and winning manners of this eminent lady. All in her own country and thousands in other lands will need no language of eulogy to inspire a deep and sincere regret when they learn the demise of one who touched all hearts by her goodness and won the admiration of all by the charms of dignity and grace.

James Madison was buried at Montpelier. Dolley was interred in the Congressional Cemetery in Washington. Nobody seemed to see anything amiss in this. Dolley belonged to Washington. It took her nephew Richard Cutts, who was in California when she died, nine years to carry the point that her primary loyalty in life was not to Washington nor the White House but to the man who lay buried at Montpelier. In 1858 her body was moved to rest beside that of her husband.

Of all the women in the lives of the Founding Fathers, Dolley Madison served her country, if not her husband, longest. She knew at least a dozen Presidents and was more or less involved with all of the first eleven except John Adams. Martha Washington is supposed to have helped as matchmaker for Dolley and James. She was Jefferson's hostess before her husband's. Monroe was their firm friend, except for a temporary coolness. John Quincy Adams was a frequent visitor to the house on Lafayette Square. Andrew Jackson engineered the first purchase of her husband's papers. Martin Van Buren took her to a wedding. She advised John Tyler's daughter-in-law on her duties as the President's hostess. She made her final public appearance on the arm of James Polk. And she reached into the future. James Buchanan, who occupied the White House before Lincoln, was one of the trustees of her Congressional trust fund.

Epilogue

DESPITE THE cliché to the effect that behind every successful man stands a good and loving woman, biographers and historians have made little capital of the women who stood behind the Founding Fathers. True, Martha Washington, like her husband, has been idolized as a saintly paragon devoid of human faults; and the colorful Dolley Madison has sparked the imagination of a few writers. For the rest, the women who helped and supported the noble and heroic men who supervised the birth of this nation have been largely unsung or relegated to a dim and shadowy background. In recent years the contribution of Abigail Adams to the success and welfare of her husband has gained some recognition, but history has virtually ignored the hard-working Deborah Franklin and the faithful Betsey Hamilton; and Martha Jefferson is, and must always remain, a shade who dwelt briefly atop the little mountain.

The six principal women who shared the lives of the Founding Fathers, although they ranged from the peasant to the patrician, had surprisingly much in common. Or perhaps it is not surprising. They all had what it takes to make a good wife for any man, then or now. Principally, they were sterling examples of that old-fashioned word "helpmate." All were virtuous, all were industrious, all possessed a high degree of integrity, all had deep love for and faith in their husbands. And none felt that fulfillment as a woman must be based on personal accomplishment in some area independent of a man. They were all content to be the other halves of the six most important pairs of scissors that shaped their nation.

For four of the wives—all but Betsey and Abigail—the unions with their outstanding spouses were second marriages; perhaps there is something to be said for experience. And all of the partners in the six marriages took seriously their vows; "till death do us part." The Jefferson marriage was cut short by Martha's untimely death after little more than ten years. The Hamilton marriage lasted almost a quarter of a century before Alexander was killed. All of the other unions passed the forty year mark—the Adams' lasted fifty-four years.

Only two of the six wives could be called outstanding women in their own right; Abigail Adams, intellectually, and Dolley Madison, socially and diplomatically. The others were basically housewives, each of whom helped her husband with his work. Deborah ran the house and minded the store. Martha ran the plantation and helped at the general's head-quarters. Betsey raised a family in a series of rented houses, often with less than enough money to do so comfortably, and provided a necessary sounding-board for her husband's ideas. Of the shadowy Martha Jefferson we know little more than that he adored her and that she shared his love for music.

Four of these men who loomed so large in America's his-tory were not the easiest consorts to get along with in the home. In the early years Franklin's passion for frugality must have been something of a trial to Deborah, and his widespread interests in things that did not concern his wife must have been frustrating. One can imagine Deborah wanting to talk about domestic concerns or personal matters while Benjamin was poring through the "wit and wisdom of the ages," organizing a philosophical society, or making electrical sparks jump with his cronies from the Junto. Deborah had frequent cause for her outbursts of temper.

Martha had to put up with quite a bit of rather dictatorial management from George, particularly in later years when he was a national idol and became a little pompous. She might have wanted to express her opinion about the decorating of the President's mansion in Philadelphia, and she did mildly rebel at being told whom she could see and where she could go in New York. But on the whole she seems to have been dutifully acquiescent when George was difficult, except where her adored and well spoiled Jacky was concerned.

To put it bluntly, John Adams at home was a bigoted hypochondriac with a persecution complex, who, to a lesser extent than Washington, was sometimes prone to make family decisions on his own—witness the six cows that he imposed on his wife when they returned from Europe. Fortunately, Abigail was bigoted in the same direction as her husband and quite willing to nurse his hypochondria and bolster his persecution complex. Only once, late in life, after they had been married for fifty years, did she complain that the old man was sometimes a little difficult to get along with.

Betsey Hamilton's only known cross was the Reynolds affair, and this must have been a heavy burden, not only because of the infidelity involved but because of Alexander's insistence on defending his honor by publicizing it. Betsey was not only a wronged wife, but she had to accept the humiliation of having her husband's unfaithfulness proclaimed from the housetops. Yet she found it possible not only to forgive him, but to support him.

If Martha Jefferson and Dolley Madison had any complaints—and there are no records of such—they would have been indeed hard to please. Little "Jemmy" Madison, particularly, thoroughly spoiled his maternal spouse. In fact, it might be said that they spoiled each other.

In terms of fidelity, it is virtually certain that three of the Founding Fathers can be justly described with the trite phrase; "he never looked at another woman." This is surely true of Adams and Madison, and of Jefferson while his wife lived. It is just as surely not true for Hamilton, at least so far as the Reynolds woman is concerned. In the cases of Franklin and Washington there is a possible justification for gossip if only because both of them were virile men who liked and sought the company of women and both were away from home for extended periods.

The Founding Fathers were fortunate in their wives. They were also lucky in the character of the other women in their lives of whom history has record—always excepting the iniquitous Mrs. Reynolds. Sally Fairfax may have been something of a flirt and it is probable that she was a tease, but her integrity would permit her to go no farther. With a woman who was less virtuous on the receiving end of his "great passion" Washington might not have come through the affair unscathed.

So far as is known the other women in Franklin's life after he married Deborah were social or intellectual contacts, but he too was fortunate that no designing woman involved him in irrefutable scandal, particularly during his lengthy stay in England while Deborah lived. The widowed Mrs. Stevenson,

with whom he lived for the greater part of fifteen years, deserves praise either for virtue or circumspection.

Maria Cosway's reputation was less than saintly and it is
possible that if this relationship was platonic it was the
Virginian rather than the pretty blond Italian who kept it
that way. But on the whole the lady seems to have so conducted herself that no scandal was attached to America's
ambassador to France.

For the rest—the teen-aged flames of Washington and Jefferson, the "low women" of Franklin's youth and the designing Hannah Quincy who briefly beguiled Adams—they left
no marks and would be unknown to history but for casual
letters and other references by the men who loved them—or
thought that they did at the time.

The women who stand out in the lives of the Founding
Fathers are their six wives, each of whom deserves, for her
faith, fidelity and affection, a more prominent niche than
has been attributed to her in America's history.

Index

335

338 *Index*

Madison, Dolley (nee Payne), 30, 248, 294-329, 330, 331
Madison, James, 27-30, 223, 286, 289-329
Madison, James, Sr., 27-29
Madison, Nelly (nee Conway), 27-30
Madison, Reuben, 29
Marbois, Marquis de, 225
Marchesi (singer), 231
Marshall, John, 209
Martin, Mrs., 217-18
Mazzei, Phillip, 217
Medea (Euripides), 210
Meredith (printer), 38-39
Mitchell, Mrs., 283-84
Monroe, James, 203, 275, 278, 287, 306-7, 313, 329
Monticello, 212, 217, 218, 252-53
Morell, Madame, 85
Morris, Roger, 104
Morse, Samuel F. B., 325
Motherhood in the eighteenth century, 1-2
Mount Vernon, 100, 135-36
Moustier, Count de, 293
Muhlenberg, Frederick A., 275
Murray, Robert, 130
Murray, Mrs. Robert, 130

Orphan Society of the City of New York, 285
Osgood, Judith, 71
Ottway, Thomas, 209

Page, John, Thomas Jefferson's letters to, 205-9, 212, 248
Paradise Lost, 210
Parke, Frances, 109
Payne, Anna (niece of Dolley Madison), 317, 321
Payne, Anna (sister of Dolley Madison), *see* Cutts, Anna
Payne, Dolley, *see* Madison, Dolley
Payne, John C., 321
Payne, Lucy, Dolley Madison's letter to, 313-15
Pennsylvania Gazette, The, 39, 51-55
Philipse, Mary (Polly), 103-4, 108, 131
Philipse, Susanna, 103
Polignac, Comtesse de, 84

Polk, James, 324, 327-28, 329
Poor Richard's Almanac, 54
Preston, William, 310-11

Quincy, Hannah, 151-52, 153, 181, 204
Quincy, Josiah, 204

Ralph, James, 36-37
Randall, Henry, 19
  on Martha Jefferson, 214-15
Randolph, Ellen Wayles, 248-49
Randolph, Isham, 18, 20
Randolph, James, 306-7
Randolph, Jane, *see* Jefferson, Jane
Randolph, Martha, *see* Jefferson, Martha (Patsy)
Randolph, Thomas Mann, 244, 251-52
Randolph, William (cousin of Jane), 20, 21
Randolph, William (grandfather of Jane), 20
Ray, Catherine, 60-64
Read, Deborah, *see* Franklin, Deborah
Reynolds, Maria, 270-78, 333
Riedesel, General von, 218
Robins, Sally Nelson, on Sally Fairfax, 101-2
Robinson, Beverly, 103
Robinson, Perdita, 232
Rogers (potter), 37-38, 41-42
Roosevelt, Sara Delano, 31
Royal Danish American Gazette, 255-56
Rush, Benjamin, 200

Schuyler, Angelica, *see* Church, Angelica
Schuyler, Catherine Van Rensselaer, 259
Schuyler, Elizabeth, *see* Hamilton, Elizabeth
Schuyler, Margarita, 259, 260, 280
Schuyler, Phillip, 259, 261-62, 268
Schuyler-Hamilton plan, 268
Seward, William, 326
Shadwell (estate), 20-21
Shakespeare, William, quoted, 55-56
Shipley, Georgina, 78-80

Shipley, Jonathan, 77
Shipley, Kitty, 77-78
Short, William, 233
Skelton, Martha, *see* Jefferson, Martha
Smith, Abigail, *see* Adams, Abigail
Smith, Margaret Bayard, 303, 307, 308-9, 318
Smith, Mary, 152, 201
Smith, Page, 187
Smith, William (husband of Abigail "Nabby" Adams), 176-77
Smith, William (father of Abigail Smith), 152, 154
Stamp Act, 75
Sterne, Laurence, 164, 220
Stevenson, Margaret, 68-69
Stevenson, Mary (Polly), 68-74, 333-34
Storer, Ebenezer, 181
Strahan, William, 65-66

Tilghman, Tench, 259-60
Tingy, Thomas, 308
Todd, John, 294, 296, 322
Todd, John Payne, 297, 298-99, 319-29, 327
Townley, Charles, 230, 231
Trist, Eliza, 290
Trist, Nicholas, 318
Tristram Shandy (Sterne), 164, 220-21
Trumbull, John, 232-33, 238
Tyler, John, 324, 329
Tyler, Royall, 176-77

Valley Forge, Martha Washington at, 131-32
Van Buren, Martin, 323, 329
Van Doren, Carl, on Benjamin Franklin, 3-4

Venable, Abraham, 275
Vernon, Edward, 100
Villars, Madame de, 85
Von Riedesel, General, 218

Walpole, Horace, 240
War of 1812, 311-17
  Abigail Adams on, 203-17
Warren, Mercy, 188
  Abigail Adams' letters to, 174, 178-79, 196, 203
  Martha Washington's letters to, 136, 141
Washington, Augustine, 5, 7
Washington, Betty, *see* Lewis, Betty
Washington, George, 1, 4-11, 23, 94-149, 191
Washington, George Steptoe, 296
Washington, John Augustine, 7-8
Washington, Lawrence, 5-6, 100-1
Washington, Lund, 128
Washington, Martha (nee Dandridge), 4, 7, 94, 105-10, 115-29, 131-49, 192, 297, 329, 330-32
Washington, Mary (nee Ball), 4-11
Washington, Robin, 97
Washington, Sarah, 101
Washington Monument, 325
Wayles, John, 212
Wayles, Martha, *see* Jefferson, Martha
Webb, Colonel, 258
Webster, Daniel, 326
Wilkens, William, 297-99
William and Mary Quarterly, The, 28
Williams, Hattie, 325-26
Wilson, Woodrow, 31
  biography of Washington by, 108-9